Cultural
Psychotherapy

To my wife, Stephanie Schechter
To my children, Alexander and Jessica La Roche
To my mother, Carmen Adela Lopez, and in memory of my father, Humberto La Roche

Cultural
Psychotherapy
Theory, Methods, and Practice

Martin J. La Roche
Harvard Medical School

Los Angeles | London | New Delhi
Singapore | Washington DC

Los Angeles | London | New Delhi
Singapore | Washington DC

FOR INFORMATION:

SAGE Publications, Inc.
2455 Teller Road
Thousand Oaks, California 91320
E-mail: order@sagepub.com

SAGE Publications Ltd.
1 Oliver's Yard
55 City Road
London, EC1Y 1SP
United Kingdom

SAGE Publications India Pvt. Ltd.
B 1/I 1 Mohan Cooperative Industrial Area
Mathura Road, New Delhi 110 044
India

SAGE Publications Asia-Pacific Pte. Ltd.
3 Church Street
#10-04 Samsung Hub
Singapore 049483

Acquisitions Editor: Kassie Graves
Editorial Assistant: Elizabeth Luizzi
Production Editor: Astrid Virding
Copy Editor: Taryn Bigelow
Typesetter: Hurix Systems Pvt. Ltd.
Proofreader: Scott Oney
Indexer: Will Ragsdale
Cover Designer: Anupama Krishnan
Marketing Manager: Lisa Sheldon Brown
Permissions Editor: Adele Hutchinson

Printed in the United States of America

Library of Congress Cataloging-in-Publication Data

La Roche, Martin.
Cultural psychotherapy : theory, methods, and practice / Martin La Roche.

p. cm.
Includes bibliographical references and index.

ISBN 978-1-4522-2515-9 (pbk.)

1. Cultural psychiatry. 2. Psychotherapy—Cross-cultural studies. I. Title.

RC455.4.E8L36 2013

616.89'14—dc23

2012025639

This book is printed on acid-free paper.

12 13 14 15 16 10 9 8 7 6 5 4 3 2 1

Contents

Preface

It is a daunting task to write a book in an area of psychology about which much has already been written. And yet I have become increasingly convinced throughout the writing of this book that this is a crucial time for those of us involved in the mental health field to be casting our gaze toward our own cultural contexts and those of our clients. Not only are culturally diverse individuals visiting our offices in growing numbers but socioeconomic and political forces are influencing, whether we know it or not, what happens within our sessions. A growing understanding of how our psychotherapeutic interventions are embedded within cultural contexts is necessary if we are to effectively practice psychotherapy. There are two main questions guiding the ideas developed in this book. First, how is culture influencing our psychotherapeutic treatment, and second, how can our psychotherapeutic interventions use culture more effectively? The main goal of this book is to provide a systematic and concrete set of psychotherapeutic strategies that will help clinicians benefit from taking into account cultural influences. I am calling this emerging set of ideas cultural psychotherapy.

Perhaps not surprisingly, my motivation for teaching and writing about cultural psychotherapy comes from my years as a psychologist working with clients of culturally diverse backgrounds, as well as my personal experiences as an immigrant. When I was 11, my family moved from Venezuela to Westchester, New York, for a year. I spoke some English, but very little. I was the only Latino in the sixth grade. In order to place me in classes, the public school tested me with a standardized verbal test and I scored several standard deviations below the mean, placing me far below average in intelligence and academic ability. I was placed in a special education classroom. The school psychologist informed my mother of my placement, and she immediately knew that the testing had been an inaccurate assessment of my true ability. She began a vigorous battle with the school to have my real abilities recognized and to have me properly placed. Fortunately for me, she was successful.

Granted, this is a dramatic example. Often the ways in which we base our perceptions and assumptions about others on culture are far more subtle; but for this reason, they are also insidious. My mother immediately recognized the mistake that had been made by the school and advocated strongly on my behalf. But biases and assumptions often go underground when they are not consciously recognized by the parties involved, and so often there is no chance for a battle to be waged. The defining feature of cultural psychotherapy is that, as humans, our understandings of one another are deeply embedded within our relationships and culture. Culture gives meaning to what unfolds in the therapeutic session, and without it, our understandings are incomplete. Cultural psychotherapy explains that if we do not attempt to be aware, as much as possible, of the multiple, ongoing cultural forces influencing the psychotherapeutic process, the treatment will necessarily suffer, because we will be operating while observing only a small piece of the therapeutic field. An enhanced awareness of the cultural forces at play leads us to have a greater degree of freedom, flexibility, and empowerment. And although culture shapes our behaviors, we can also influence it.

In addition to culture, cultural psychotherapy also underscores the importance of individualistic and relational variables and the contribution of numerous and diverse psychotherapeutic approaches. However, cultural psychotherapy emerged as a response to the limitations of individualistic and relational paradigms. Cultural psychotherapy asserts that the individualistic and relational models that are currently the dominant and prevalent types of psychotherapy are insufficient to fully grasp the complexity of the psychotherapeutic process. A third level of understanding, that of the contextual/ecological, is required to more thoroughly understand what happens in therapy and in research. Because this is a cultural psychotherapy book, a thorough review of this level is often underscored throughout all the pages of the book.

This book was written with several goals and audiences in mind. First, it attempts to make a contribution to the literature and offers alternatives and new possibilities for the application of cultural thought. It aims to introduce students of psychotherapy to an important body of new developments and new ideas and to clearly spell out how these new ways of looking at the psychotherapeutic process can be applied in their clinical work. This book also aims to enrich the work of seasoned clinicians by suggesting specific strategies that can broaden their understanding and refine their interventions. This book aims, as does much of my work, to provide a bridge between different theoretical approaches and to enable therapists, clinical researchers, and teachers of psychotherapy of varying orientations to see commonalities that may be obscured by different vocabularies as well as socioeconomic and political emphases.

The cultural psychotherapeutic ideas are systematized through a clinical model, the *three-phased cultural psychotherapeutic model,* which constitutes the core of this book. The introduction describes this model and some of its basic assumptions. The first three chapters of the book describe the three phases of the cultural psychotherapeutic model. Each phase is specified by concrete clinical recommendations that can increase the clinical sophistication of any clinician or student. These clinical recommendations are illustrated through multiple clinical examples that bring these ideas to life. It is herein important to note that as a means to protect the confidentiality of my clients, any identifying information has been altered, and in some cases these clinical discussions are composites of several clinical vignettes. Some of these are cases that I have treated indirectly through supervision.

The fourth chapter, "Addressing Cultural Differences in the Psychotherapeutic Process," is an extension of the three phases of cultural psychotherapy. In this chapter, 10 specific clinical recommendations to address cultural differences in psychological treatment are discussed. These recommendations are again illustrated through several clinical examples. This chapter spells out clear ideas and strategies of when and how to address cultural differences. An important conceptual innovation of this chapter and this book is that cultural differences are defined as more than ethnicity and race. Cultural differences include socioeconomic background, religion, and gender orientation, among many other variables. The basic idea running throughout all the chapters of this book is that we all (irrespective of ethnicity or race) live in cultural contexts that give meaning to our lives, and if we address these meanings appropriately, we can increase the effectiveness of our psychotherapeutic interventions. Failure to effectively use the cultural context can be detrimental to the well-being of our clients.

The fifth chapter, "The Cultural Formulation and Conceptual Foundations of Cultural Psychotherapy," describes the ongoing process of formulating clients' issues within different cultural contexts and including clients' individual characteristics and the psychotherapeutic relationship. This chapter also describes more thoroughly some of the conceptual foundations of cultural psychotherapy through a clinical case.

The chapter on "Developing Culturally Competent Interventions" identifies some of the cultural assumptions guiding dominant research paradigms and illustrates through a clinical case and my ongoing research on the culturally competent relaxation intervention (CCRI) empirical strategies to validate psychotherapeutic interventions with culturally diverse individuals. This chapter suggests additional empirical strategies to develop culturally competent interventions.

The seventh chapter, "A Clinical Illustration of the Three-Phased Cultural Psychotherapeutic Model," integrates through one clinical case not only the three phases of cultural psychotherapy but also examples of when and how to address cultural differences, formulate cases, and develop culturally competent strategies. The aim of this chapter is to present a vivid case that illustrates in a comprehensive manner many of the clinical recommendations presented in previous chapters.

To conclude, "Beyond Cultural Psychotherapy: Cultural Thinking" identifies the conceptual model used to develop the different psychotherapeutic ideas presented here and adds some of its applications in different realms such as law, peace work, and education. Cultural thinking is not limited to the practice of psychotherapy; it extends to many activities. This chapter gives a brief glimpse of these possibilities and applications. Finally, it is important to understand that the psychotherapeutic model described here is a result of a specific time and context and as such it should evolve as our context changes. While culture has been written about before, the degree to which it has been the missing link to our deepest understanding of the psychotherapeutic process has yet to be fully explicated.

Martin J. La Roche, PhD
Cambridge, Massachusetts

Acknowledgments

This book owes its existence to the cultural movement that has been instrumental in spreading the notion that what we think, feel, and know is highly influenced by our cultural contexts. We are embedded in contexts that give meaning to our identity and interactions; without an understanding of our culture, we are unknowable. This book translates this general assumption into specific psychotherapeutic interventions that are not only applicable to ethnic minorities but may also be useful with each and all of us.

Many of the basic assumptions of this book have grown from the cultural, multicultural, and cross-cultural literature and from my many intellectual mentors: Janet Helms, Harry Triandis, Derald Sue, Philip Cushman, and Allen Ivey, just to name a few. However, I am even more indebted to the many clients who have shared their stories and struggles with me. I have been honored to learn from and with them. What they have shared with me has taught me different strategies to cope with adverse and at times inhumane situations. I have often been impressed by their skills and resilience. This book builds upon their experience, efforts, and accomplishments. The energy running through this book is enhanced by their pain, love, tears, and wisdom. Nevertheless, as means to protect their confidentiality all names and identifiable information is changed. Furthermore, at times some cases have been merged with other cases as a means to better illustrate the ideas being conveyed in this book.

Many of the current advances and challenges of the psychotherapeutic literature are poured into these pages, particularly many of the ideas of my current and former colleagues at the Harvard Medical School such as Judith Herman, Margarita Alegria, Ed Tronick, Arthur Kleinman, William Pollack, and Devon Hinton or former Harvard instructors Drew Westen and Judith Jordan, who have highly influenced the development of the ideas in this book. Nevertheless, the psychological wisdom of many are included, such as Paul Wachtel, Marsha Linehan, and Phil Zimbardo.

This book has also benefited from many friends and colleagues who read and provided me with feedback and encouragement that enriched many of the chapters of this book. I will just name a few: Jill Bloom, Allen Ivey, Devon Hinton, Maryam Jernigan, Mari Janikian, Roslyn Murov and Esteban Cardemil. Similarly, I have been honored to work with many of my former students, such as Leyla Gualdron-Perez, Cynthia Batista, Aprile Maxie, John Tawa, and Kara Lustig, whose work has made this book possible. I am particularly, thankful to Erin Brahms, who repeatedly read all the chapters of this book and provided me with invaluable feedback that grounded the text in experience rather than abstract ideas.

English is my second language, and I am thankful to Taryn Bigelow, who patiently and thoroughly copy edited this book. Her work has allowed many of the ideas being conveyed to be articulated more effectively. I am also indebted to the staff of SAGE Publications, particularly Kassie Graves and Astrid Virding, whose support and guidance made this book a reality.

This book is the fruit of many good people. I could not have written it without the advice of my mentor in graduate school, Cass Turner, who was one of the few who seemed to have faith in my academic skills, particularly when I was a struggling immigrant stumbling to make it through graduate school. Even at this challenging time in my life, Cass provided me with the best piece of advice on how to write this book. He suggested that I write an outline and publish articles in different journals from which I could develop chapters for a book. Following his advice, many of the chapters in this book are more elaborate versions of articles published over the last decade. For example, Chapter 4, "Addressing Cultural Differences," is highly influenced by an article Aprile Maxie and I published over 10 years ago. Similarly, Chapter 3, "Fostering Empowerment," is a significant refinement of an article that John Tawa and I wrote several years ago. However, the main ideas of these articles are now interconnected and they build upon each other. Often I have feared that my articles give a fragmented view of my ideas. This book is an opportunity to address this issue.

During the last 16 years of my life, I have worked as director of training at the Martha Eliot Health Center, which is the second oldest community health center in the country, part of Children's Hospital Boston and affiliated with Harvard Medical School. It is located in a very diverse and poor area of urban Boston. In this health center, I have worked primarily with an underserved Latino and African American population. When I think of this book, I often identify it with my work at the Martha Eliot Health Center, which is still my intellectual home. Many of the ideas written in this book germinated and grew in this context. Some of the ideas expressed in this book are indebted to my colleagues of the Human Service team at the Martha Eliot Health Center, including David Green, Yvonne Nieves, Roslyn Murov, Cynthia Batista, and Andrew Richards. Furthermore, the ups and downs of this health center have taught me invaluable political, intellectual, and psychotherapeutic lessons. They have reminded me that psychotherapy occurs in a context that has a powerful influence on what we do or chose not do.

At the Children's Hospital Boston I would like to acknowledge Dr. Eugene D'Angelo, without whose support I would not have been able to write this book. Gene repeatedly and consistently trusted and encouraged me to write my ideas. He has been an incomparable mentor reminding me that we can learn much in times of crises and that these are opportunities for growth. Similarly, at the Children's Hospital Boston, Jessica Daniels' commitment to diversity and social justice has been a model and inspiration to strive for.

In addition to my work at the Martha Eliot Health Center, I have a private practice in which I have had the opportunity to treat people from different ethnic backgrounds (e.g., Asian, Native American, Middle Eastern, and White) as well as from different socioeconomic backgrounds. The contrasts between my Martha Eliot Health Center clients and my private practice clients have often allowed me to hypothesize about which issues are more contextual and cultural.

I did not write this book during a sabbatical, or because of a lessened clinical load. Instead, it was written in the trenches of a more-than-full caseload, meetings, and multiple and simultaneous deadlines. It was mostly written during early mornings (often starting at 4:00 a.m.) and driven by the hope of acknowledging those who seemed forgotten from the psychotherapeutic literature—the culturally diverse, the poor, and those suffering from cultural marginalization. My hope is that this book serves as a testimony to the plight of so many people, groups and communities that have often been left out of mainstream psychotherapy.

Finally, I am indebted to my family, who supported me with their love and humor: my parents, who inspired me with their commitment to social justice; my children, who at the early ages of six and eight were carrying banners publicly protesting the Iraq War or reminding me on a Saturday morning that it was time to go to work at our town's food pantry; and mostly my wife, who has stood with me through it all.

The following reviewers are gratefully acknowledged:

Ricardo Bianco, Massachusetts School of Professional Psychology, Boston

Jill Betz Bloom, Massachusetts School of Professional Psychology, Boston

Michael Goh, University of Minnesota—Twin Cities, Minneapolis

Usha Tummala-Narra, Boston College, Chestnut Hill

Allen Ivey, University of Massachusetts, Amherst

Maryam M. Jernigan, Yale University School of Medicine, New Haven

Maxine L. Rawlins, Bridgewater State College, Bridgewater

Van Vaughn, Missouri Baptist University, Saint Louis

Introduction

What Is Cultural Psychotherapy?

It would hardly be fish who discovered the existence of water.
—Clyde Kluckhohn, *Mirror for Man,* 1959

Psychotherapists often ignore culture until it is too late. When our interventions backfire or fail to work, we find ourselves like fish out of water; only then do we recognize the unspeakable importance of our surroundings, context, and culture. Culture, however, is ever present in complex and multifold ways both in the psychotherapeutic session and in people's lives. Cultural psychotherapy underscores cultural influences and explains that our understandings are embedded within cultures, which gives significance to what unfolds in the therapeutic session. Without a cultural understanding that includes clients' and therapists' contexts, underlying meanings are likely to be misinterpreted. Cultural psychotherapy explains that if we are not aware of the multiple, ongoing cultural forces influencing the psychotherapeutic process, then we will unknowingly reproduce them. We will blindly follow cultural norms and assume that they are rigid, unquestionable, or universal. An enhanced awareness of these cultural forces can lead us and our clients to have a greater degree of freedom, flexibility, and empowerment.

In this book, I describe an emerging field of study and type of psychotherapy that is transforming the psychotherapy literature. Labels such as cross-cultural psychotherapy and counseling (Marsella & Pedersen, 1980), ethnic family therapy (McGoldrick & Giordano, 1996), multicultural counseling (Sue, Ivey, & Pedersen, 2007), medical anthropology/cultural psychiatry (Kleinman, 1988), and diverse culturally sensitive or cultural competent psychotherapies are often used to describe similar ideas. I, however, believe that the term *cultural psychotherapy* is more accurate because it is broader and more inclusive than other prominent terms.

In addition to the fast growth of cultural approaches, an increasing number of culturally adapted interventions for specific disorders (e.g., depression, conduct disorder, and anxiety) are being developed and tested (see Griner & Smith, 2006; Huey & Polo, 2008, for reviews). As a result of these investigations, many ethnic minorities who would not have otherwise received treatment (or would have received inappropriate care) are benefiting from culturally competent psychotherapeutic strategies. However, what in fact differentiates most culturally competent psychotherapies from others is that they are designed for specific racial and/or ethnic groups.

In contrast, cultural psychotherapy emphasizes the need to understand that race and/ or ethnicity alone is insufficient to design a psychotherapeutic intervention. Race and ethnicity do not predict psychological attributes (Helms, Jernigan, & Mascher, 2005); thus, it is necessary to measure, rather than to assume, psychological characteristics to design psychotherapeutic interventions (see Chapter 6). Cultural psychotherapy defines cultural variables not only through ethnicity and race, but also through sexual orientation, gender,[1] disability status (e.g., deaf, blind), socioeconomic status (SES), religious background, ethnic identity, and discrimination experiences, among other variables. The large number of differences within ethnic or racial groups raises questions about the standard use of culturally adapted interventions for specific ethnic/racial clients, as well as their viability (Lau, 2006).

Unfortunately, cultural differences are often construed as deficits that lead to segregation, over-pathologization, substandard treatment, and discrimination. For example, at times some characteristics of ethnic minorities (e.g., intellectual quotients) are considered inferior to those of Whites[2] (e.g., Herrnstein & Murray, 1994). Cultural psychotherapy attempts to move beyond these shortsighted views by emphasizing the need to understand these differences within their cultural context. Furthermore, we all live in contexts that give meaning to our lives; thus, these recommendations are applicable not only to ethnic minorities, but to each and every one of us. A thorough and more complex consideration of cultural variables rather than the use of more broad terms such as race and ethnicity enhances the efficacy and effectiveness of psychotherapy. Cultural variables are herein defined as meanings that are overall more frequent in one cultural group (e.g., ethnic, religious, gender orientation) than others. Nevertheless, there is much variability amongst individuals within each cultural group.

In addition to this conceptual and methodological approach, cultural psychotherapy operationalizes and systematizes a model to intervene that I call the three-phased cultural psychotherapeutic model, which is a coherent and specific set of interventions derived from these conceptual ideas. An overview of this psychotherapeutic model is presented in this introduction with significantly more detail in later chapters (1–3, 7).

The purpose of this book is not to review the fast-growing number of cultural psychotherapeutic models or to summarize important and new research or to develop a thorough conceptual definition of culture; instead, the goal of this book is to propose a coherent type of psychological treatment that considers individual, relational, and contextual factors. This model is illustrated through numerous clinical cases and some research studies. The bulk of this book is a description of this psychotherapuetic model. However, it is important to acknowledge that many important ideas have influenced the development of this model. For this reason, some of cultural psychotherapy's historical antecedents are summarized here first.

SOME HISTORICAL ANTECEDENTS OF CULTURAL PSYCHOTHERAPY

Cultural psychotherapy is not a new movement. Its origins can be traced back to 1879 and the official birth of psychology as a scientific discipline. Wilhelm Wundt is traditionally considered the father of psychology and was the first to introduce the scientific method into the study of mental processes (Boring, 1957). The mind, Wundt argued, could be measured and explained according to the cannons of experimental science. In addition, Wundt conceived psychology as consisting of two parts, where each part is based on a distinctive layer of human conscience and each follows its own laws and methodology. The first part Wundt talked about was physiological psychology, which is assessed through the experimental method (e.g., laboratory studies) and investigates the fundamental mental processes that underlie all human beings. The second part that Wundt (as quoted by Cole, 1998) spoke about was the *Volkerpsychologie,* or elements of folk psychology, which is the study of human behavior in different cultural contexts.

Although Wundt wrote 10 volumes on the *Volkerpsychologie,* these ideas were neglected for almost a century before experiencing a recent revival. A growing number of researchers (e.g., Cole, 1998; Heine, 2008; Markus & Kitayama, 1991; Triandis, 1994) have rediscovered and expanded his ideas. These fruitful efforts are producing a vast and fast-growing cross-cultural and cultural psychology, much of which is the conceptual foundation of cultural psychotherapy. Researchers have noted that the basic psychological processes such as attention, memory, perception, and motivation and even the wiring of the brain are dependent upon cultural processes (e.g., Heine, 2008; Markus & Kitayama, 1991; Park & Huang, 2010). Cultural psychotherapy, like cultural psychology, argues that it is impossible to understand any psychological processes without understanding the context in which these processes are embedded. Cultural psychotherapy, however, emphasizes the need to use these findings to develop effective psychotherapeutic interventions, whereas the tenets of cultural psychology focus more on the understanding of basic psychological processes.

Cultural psychotherapy is highly indebted to medical anthropology (e.g., Hinton & Good, 2009; Kleinman, 1988) and multicultural counseling and therapy (Sue et al., 2007). Both have advanced important ideas on how to assess and treat people in culturally sensitive manners. Medical anthropology explains that psychological disorders are unlike viruses or bacteria. Bacteria, for example, present similarly wherever they appear, whereas the presentation of psychological disorders may vary by context (Kleinman, 1988). Multicultural counseling and therapy starts with the premise that culture always permeates how we assess and treat others. Research, assessment, psychotherapy, consultation, and supervision are culture bound. Similarly, cultural psychotherapy underscores the need to consider the cultural context in all aspects of a theory—research, assessment, treatment, and supervision. Psychological concepts, research methodologies, and even data are embedded in the social systems that influence their meanings (Kleinman, 1988). If the cultural context is not taken into account in these practices, they will inevitably end up being restricted by this absence. Although cultural psychotherapy aligns with most of the basic tenets of medical anthropology and multicultural counseling and therapy, practitioners of cultural psychotherapy attempt to further specify into concrete psychotherapeutic interventions their theoretical assumptions. The three-phased cultural psychotherapeutic model is a result of these efforts. Additionally, cultural psychotherapy underscores the need to bridge findings from different psychotherapies and disciplines.

As such, cultural psychotherapy is also influenced by diverse disciplines that range from anthropology to physics. I will briefly highlight three major and very distinct influences from the realms of cultural anthropology, hermeneutic theory, and the theory of relativity. Cultural anthropology (e.g., Geertz, 1973; Shweder, 1990) emphasizes the impact of culture in understanding psychological processes. It underscores the influence of the context on all human behaviors and meanings. Hermeneutic theory (e.g., Gadamer, 1975) construes the meanings of texts (e.g., the Bible, the American Constitution), actions, or behaviors as inseparable from the historical times from which they are derived. Hermeneutic approaches warn us about the dangers of analyzing texts without the contexts in which they are embedded. If a text is analyzed in a historical vacuum, we will very likely misinterpret its meanings. Finally, Albert Einstein's relativity theory dethroned the dominant Newtonian conception of a universal and inert space and time. Einstein explained space and time as active, dynamic change agents that shape reality. Furthermore, Einstein specified the mechanisms (e.g., the warping and curving of space) by which space/time shapes events. Similarly, cultural psychotherapy aims to identify cultural processes that affect the psychotherapeutic process and systematically use these—through the development of the three-phased cultural psychotherapeutic model—to enhance the effectiveness of our psychological interventions. Below is a description of a couple I treated in my Cambridge private practice. It is a case that will help to introduce the three-phased cultural psychotherapeutic model and clarify some of the basic assumptions of cultural psychotherapy.

Case Illustration: Sophie and Omar

A young professional couple came to psychotherapy because they were increasingly arguing for no apparent reason. Omar, a 26-year-old, soft-spoken Palestinian software engineer had been dating Sophie, a 25-year-old, assertive, Jewish clinical social worker for 2 years. They both felt it was time to define their relationship, that is, to move in together, or end it. Their therapeutic goal was to clarify the future of their relationship and if they were to stay together to reduce their frequent arguments. Omar and Sophie reported "loving each other very deeply" and agreed that their arguments were "absurd" and "seemed to come out of the blue." Neither could identify triggers for these arguments, which would escalate and lead to prolonged and tense periods of silence. During these periods, Omar retreated emotionally and Sophie demanded his attention. Furthermore, Omar and Sophie's frustration would lead them to get angry at each other for long periods of time. As a result, Omar felt bombarded by her demands and Sophie felt abandoned by him. In discussing these interpersonal dynamics, they decided to call this the "retreat-demand pattern." As we started psychotherapy, much of the clinical effort was directed toward exploring, identifying, and then having them express their feelings of being "bombarded" or "abandoned." In treatment, Omar realized that his tendency to be quiet was a result of his father's belief that Muslim men should solve problems in silence. In contrast, Sophie described how she would have been criticized if she had remained silent. In treatment, they agreed that if either one started noting the emergence of the retreat-demand pattern, they would bring it into the open and explore strategies to prevent it from building up.

In therapy, we further explored how Omar and Sophie's relational and cultural histories contributed to the retreat-demand pattern. Omar explained that as a Muslim it was his duty and part of his upbringing to unquestionably listen and follow his father's prescriptions even though he would at times feel enraged by his father's traditional views. In fact, Omar reminded Sophie that the word *Islam* meant surrendering, an act of love, which is what he attempted to do during his silences. In contrast, Sophie described how she was repeatedly encouraged to voice her opinions as she was growing up. Although her parents divorced when she was a child, both consistently supported her efforts to assert herself. As she came to disagree with them on certain issues, however, they seemed to distance themselves from her, just as she feared Omar would do. With tears in her eyes, Sophie explained that she now often kept her views to herself, as she feared that Omar would retreat emotionally just as her parents had. With new understanding of how their past relational histories contributed to their retreat-demand pattern and through the use of different behavioral techniques (e.g., they would identify when they were sinking into the retreat-demand pattern), the intensity of their problems was assuaged but they both felt there was still much yet to be addressed.

As we continued to explore possible triggers for their conflicts, we discovered that Omar's preparations for Ramadan irritated Sophie, while Sophie's activities for Passover and Rosh Hashanah annoyed Omar. Soon, we also noticed how their "silences" intensified as religious holidays approached as well as when the Israel-Palestine[3] conflict escalated. In the early stages of their relationship, Sophie and Omar learned to avoid political discussions given that these inevitably led to endless arguments and painful silences. However, with my encouragement they hesitantly discussed their views on religion and the Palestine-Israel conflict. At that time, the latest news had Hamas gaining strength in Gaza and threatening to violently separate from Israel. Although Omar did not believe in war, he sympathized with this movement and repeatedly expressed his anger toward the state of Israel for appropriating his family's home (one that had been in the family for generations) in the West Bank. Omar voiced his belief that the only way to deal with Israel was through force, a statement that offended Sophie. Sophie firmly supported Israel's right to protect itself, particularly given the history of genocide involving Jewish people. During the Second World War, many of her family members were executed in Nazi concentration camps.

Their clashing views intensified, making the relationship unbearable for both. Many times it seemed inevitable that they would break up, just as Israel and Palestine seemed headed inevitably toward bloodshed. The conflict in the Middle East seemed too large and beyond the reach of psychotherapy. It seemed futile to discuss a conflict that had been raging for generations, just as it seemed hopeless that Omar and Sophie would be able resolve their differences. It was almost as if a heavy shadow of hopelessness had enveloped the sessions that clouded their ability to see each other and their willingness to work things out. In exploring this hopelessness, Sophie and Omar noted how increased tension in their relationship seemed to occur in tandem with the growing intensity of the Palestine-Israel conflict. They shared their fears that the Israel-Palestine conflict would never be resolved. Similarly, they discussed the possibility that their relationship would end.

Just as they were disappointed in the international community's lack of support in the Palestine-Israel conflict, they blamed me for not saving their relationship. Although the goal of treatment was to define their relationship, not save it, I too felt disappointed in my inability to "rescue" their relationship. In exploring the intensity of my feelings, I realized that my desire to "rescue" them was not just a result of sociopolitical interpersonal and forces; it was also heightened by my identification with them. My wife and I are also from different ethnic and religious backgrounds, and I wondered if my failure to help them would undermine my belief that differences can enrich relationships, including my own. An important premise of cultural

(Continued)

(Continued)

psychotherapy is that multiple forces (e.g., individual, relational, societal) constantly affect our behavior, and it is important to identify what forces are in play to more effectively respond to them. In this case, my sensitivity to their situation was greater because of the similarity between their issues and mine. This self-awareness increased my effectiveness. Thus, I was able to contrast their initial treatment goal with our current hope of "rescuing" their relationship. This allowed them to explore why they now wanted their relationship to be rescued, while at the beginning of treatment they did not feel that way.

Despite Omar and Sophie's significant political differences, they kept talking and coming to therapy, and slowly they found common ground. They agreed on the need to establish a sovereign Palestine state that worked in conjunction with a strong Israel, as they agreed on the need to listen to each other even when "bombarding" or "retreating." As they identified, explored, and at times reconciled their differences, their relationship grew stronger. They also started to understand the impact of political forces on their relationship: When the turmoil in Israel-Palestine increased, Sophie construed Omar as a threat to the foundation of her faith and identity. In turn, Omar viewed Sophie as part of a group that had robbed his family of its land, wealth, and security. Throughout their sessions, I was left feeling as if I represented the international community that led and fueled the conflict. Our views of each other and our feelings (e.g., hopelessness) were affected by historical and political events that transcended our experiences and relationships.

Powerful sociocultural and political forces that had been shaping lives and countries even before we were born were in play both inside and outside the psychotherapeutic session. For example, Sophie and Omar would often hear their friends exclaim, "It is unbelievable that you guys are together!" As Omar and Sophie's awareness of these contextual forces expanded, they realized they did not have to respond to them in the same ways they had in the past. Instead of automatically reacting to them (e.g., getting defensive or hopeless) or following cultural expectations (including the expectation of being rescued), they had a choice in how they responded and they could do so "head on." They realized they could discuss events in the Middle East rather than avoiding them until they escalated and "exploded." They educated themselves about the Palestine-Israel conflict and started to participate and support organizations that promoted both the State of Palestine and the existence of Israel by frequenting rallies, particularly those in support of Palestinian refugees. They wrote to their legislators and attended fund-raisers for Palestinian refugees. As they became more politically active, they met other Muslim-Jewish couples that were dealing with similar issues. This helped them realize they were not alone and that others felt the same way. After a few more months of psychotherapy, they moved in together.

THE CONCEPTUAL FOUNDATIONS OF CULTURAL PSYCHOTHERAPY

Cultural psychotherapy starts by assuming that we can understand the psychotherapeutic process in multiple and simultaneous ways. Although there are countless theories that make sense of our clients' issues, in this book I emphasize only three of the most relevant sets of psychotherapeutic theories, or paradigms, namely (1) individualistic, (2) relational, and (3) contextual/ecological. Underlying cultural psychotherapy's integrative approach is the assumption that clinicians are more effective as they are able to conceptualize the psychotherapeutic relationship through different conceptual lenses (Gold & Wachtel, 2006; Ivey, 1999). Below, each of these three approaches is briefly explained.

For individualistic approaches, the basic unit of analysis is the client. The object of treatment is to understand and heal individuals. Concepts such as ego-strength, self-actualization, self-esteem, self-coherence, self-efficacy, and insight have grown in individualistic treatments. In the case illustration, I noted how understanding Sophie and Omar's individual characteristics and history benefited treatment of the retreat-demand pattern. For example, it was clear that Omar's father's belief that Muslim men should solve their problems in silence influenced the way he expressed (or did not express) himself with Sophie.

In contrast to individualistic approaches, relational psychotherapies underscore the exchange between clients and therapists as central for the understanding and treatment of individuals. For these approaches, the relationship is the unit of analysis. The emergence of relational psychotherapies has created a revolution within the psychotherapeutic literature that has not only expanded our ability to understand and treat our clients but also developed research methods that emphasize the influence of the observer on the observed. Clients cannot be understood without therapists, just as Omar and Sophie's relationship in the session could not be understood without consideration of my influence (e.g., my feelings of hopelessness, or my identification with them).

An integral component of cultural psychotherapy is the assertion that individualistic and relational approaches are insufficient to fully grasp the complexity of the psychotherapeutic process. This leads to a third level of understanding, the contextual/ecological level, which is required to more thoroughly understand what happens in assessment, treatment, supervision, and research. In cultural psychotherapy, the context is an important and complex element that influences the psychotherapeutic process. Not taking the context into account is missing an important set of variables within the psychotherapeutic process. Omar and Sophie were highly influenced by events outside the four walls of psychotherapy (the Israel-Palestine conflict). The underlying issues affecting their relationship could not have been appropriately explained solely by using relational or individual variables. Only as these forces are understood can people develop strategies to respond differently to contextual forces. Furthermore, an acknowledgment that individuals and relationships are embedded in cultural contexts also motivates people to change unjust social situations. Often, it is not enough to transform oneself (as individualistic psychotherapies aim for) or our relationships (as relational psychotherapies aim for). Sometimes, it is also necessary to change our contexts.

For the most part, relational psychotherapies highlight the importance of the cultural context (e.g., Ballou, Matsumoto, & Wagner, 2002; Brown, 1994) to the point where some talk about relational cultural therapy (Jordan, 2010); however, more frequently relational therapists seem to lump relationships and culture into one broad category (e.g., Slife & Wiggins, 2009). Systematic recommendations to address contextual issues are often lacking. Throughout this book, I argue that the influence of the context (e.g., influence of the Palestine-Israel conflict) is distinct and irreducible to that of relationships and individual characteristics. Not distinguishing these different influences limits our ability to understand and intervene. As clients and therapists recognize the impact of contextual influences on the psychotherapeutic process, they become more effective in dealing with these social forces (see Chapter 3).

The context is a multilayered construct that includes systems, situations, and people (Zimbardo, 2008). The context is more than the time and place (socioeconomic conditions, history, and geography) of a person. The context influences the interaction between client and therapist as well as the prevalent cultural meanings (e.g., cultural values, beliefs, gender roles) and language (verbal and nonverbal) of a specific group. Some of these contextual influences may be interiorized; nevertheless, this does not mean that the contextual attributes parallel those of an individual. Furthermore, some of these contextual meanings are expressed relationally, but this does not mean they are equivalent. Contextual forces are not reducible (although they can overlap) to individual or relational variables (Na et al., 2010; Shweder, 1973), and there is much individual variability within cultural groups. For example, most Muslims may adhere to the precepts of the Qur'an; however, the meanings people make of it vary from group to group and from person to person. Not all Muslims and perhaps only a very reduced number would agree with Omar's interpretation that to submit or to surrender is the ultimate act of love. Omar did not understand why Sophie kept "attacking" him by repeatedly inquiring about why he did not express his feelings. Omar explained that he experienced these remarks as accusations, or "what is wrong with you?" In fact, in psychotherapy we may often convey this stigmatizing feeling when our clients do not conform to our specific cultural norms.

"Expressing feelings," "being assertive," or "connecting," as Sophie assumed was appropriate, is not always a culturally appropriate way to address clients' issues. Each culture reinforces specific relational styles from which healing strategies are derived (Cushman, 1995; Kleinman, 1988; Sue et al., 2007). The question of what is normal or abnormal arises at this point. Was Omar's "surrender" or Sophie's "assertive" approach correct? Who defines what is normal or abnormal? Much of the American psychotherapeutic literature is highly influenced by Judeo-Christian values that clearly side with Sophie's approach and probably stigmatize or even pathologize Omar's "surrender," which could be misconstrued as a "passive-aggressive pattern" or as "learned helplessness." Cultural psychotherapy attempts to avoid pathologizing clients' problems by exploring and including their context and cultural understandings. In exploring Omar and Sophie's context, it was revealed that Omar was attempting to show love and strength by his restraint, which was perceived by Sophie as neglect. Understanding Omar's silences in context permitted both Sophie and myself to avoid stigmatizing his behavior and allowed us to develop strategies to effectively work with it.

Noting the ways in which cultural meanings vary highlights how culture is present in not just one, but multiple and complex ways (e.g., the influence of the Israel-Palestine conflict in Sophie and Omar's arguments). Cultural psychotherapy recognizes that the cultural context affects the nosology and etiology of mental disorders—their presentation, course, and outcomes, and the development of interventions required to treat them. Cultural psychotherapy attempts to expand our understanding of the psychotherapeutic process by contextualizing the psychotherapeutic relationship and the client's individual history. To accomplish this goal, however, clinicians need to actively and constantly explore how our actions, beliefs, comments, or lack thereof are informed by cultural assumptions (Sue & Sue, 2008), as these will have a powerful impact on the therapeutic relationship. In working with Omar, I reread the Qur'an and literature about psychotherapy with Muslims. I am also aware of the strong negative biases toward Muslims in the United States, particularly heightened after the attacks on the World Trade Center and the Pentagon on 9/11 and the growing tensions in Iran, Iraq, and Syria. In psychotherapy, we explored how these events were affecting Sophie and Omar.

One of the main assumptions of cultural psychotherapy is that the psychotherapeutic process is embedded within a context that gives significance to our understandings and interactions. Figure I.1 illustrates how cultural psychotherapy emphasizes these three interactive and at times overlapping perspectives. Without any one of these three perspectives, cultural psychotherapy's understanding of the psychotherapeutic process is incomplete.

At this point, a general equation for developing cultural psychotherapy is proposed:

cultural psychotherapy = individual factors × relational factors × contextual factors.

This equation highlights the need to include all three factors. This equation may be used to evaluate any of our interventions or clinical formulations, research hypotheses/methods, or any psychological concept. In looking at Figure I.1, it can also be seen that some parts of these factors tend to overlap, just as parts of Omar's communication style could be considered individual, relational, and cultural. Although much of cultural psychotherapy stems from this contextual epistemological model (**knowledge = object × subject ×**

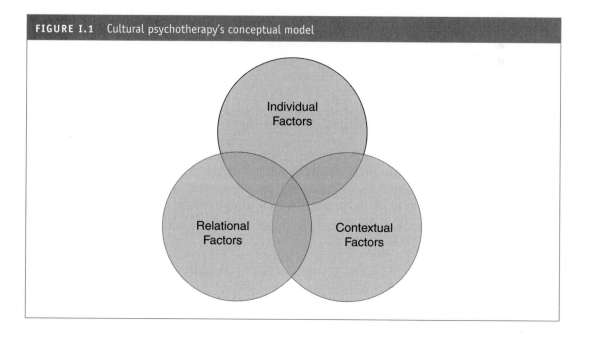

FIGURE I.1 Cultural psychotherapy's conceptual model

Individual Factors

Relational Factors

Contextual Factors

context), it is important to highlight that additional factors (e.g., genetic, neurological) are likely to be considered.[4] Another implication of this equation is that culture and context are not equivalent; culture is more than the context. Culture manifest itself within individuals (e.g., cultural variables), relationships (e.g., they way people interact) and contexts (e.g., sociocultural processes). However, not all is a shared cultural meaning; some are unique individual or relational variables. Yet much of what is contextual is cultural.

An important corollary of this equation is that cultural factors are ever present, not just for ethnic minorities but for all. Initially, it might have been easier to recognize culture in ethnic minorities, as I, too, selected an interethnic couple to illustrate cultural psychotherapy's core ideas; however, we are all embedded in specific contexts that give meaning to our experiences. Thus, cultural psychotherapy recommendations are also applicable to people of the dominant culture (e.g., White Americans). The three-phased cultural psychotherapeutic model, which is described below, is an attempt to systematize and organize these ideas.

THE THREE-PHASED CULTURAL PSYCHOTHERAPEUTIC MODEL

Cultural psychotherapy develops an integrative framework that attempts to complement current psychotherapeutic approaches by emphasizing the need to consider individualistic, relational, and contextual elements not only during the psychotherapeutic process[5] (Chapters 1–3, 7), but also in the way we theorize (Chapter 5) and conduct psychotherapeutic research (Chapter 6) and in the world beyond psychotherapy (Chapter 8). Given this emphasis on complementing and coherently benefiting from different approaches, a wide variety of theories, disciplines, and models inform cultural psychotherapy (e.g., psychodynamic; dialectical behavioral therapy; neuroscience; three-staged trauma recovery models, particularly Judith Herman's [1992] model; anthropology; economy; social psychology; acceptance and commitment therapy, etc.). Nevertheless, these diverse ideas are organized through the three-phased cultural psychotherapeutic model that includes the following three phases: (1) addressing basic needs and symptom reduction, (2) understanding clients' experiences, and (3) fostering empowerment.

Although the three-phased cultural psychotherapeutic model is presented in "phases," it is important to underscore that these phases are not independent of each other as there is much overlap. What happens in one phase has an effect on what happens in the others. In my previous work (e.g., La Roche, 2002; La Roche & Christopher, 2010; La Roche & Tawa, 2011), I described this psychotherapeutic model in terms of "stages." However, I have found that the term *stage* seems to convey a rigid, stepwise sequence of the psychotherapeutic process that is far from the fluidity that in fact characterizes psychotherapy.

It is also important to emphasize that some individuals may spend very little time in the first phase and move quickly to the second or third phase.[6] Others will stay in the first or remain in the second phase, never reaching the third phase. Clearly, there is much variability in the way clients use therapy. Furthermore, it is likely that some individuals benefit from some phases more than others. For example, it could be hypothesized, following Blatt's (1992) or Triandis's (1994) conceptualizations, that individuals who are more *introjective* (preoccupied with establishing and maintaining autonomy and self-definition) and/ or *individualistic* (understand themselves in terms of self-attributes and pursuing individual goals) benefit more from the first phase, while more *anaclitic* (preoccupied with issues of relatedness) and/or *collective* (understand themselves in relation to others and seek group goals) benefit more from the second phase. Clearly, research is needed to explore the specific contributions of individual differences in each phase. Nevertheless, this point underscores the need for therapy to adjust to the characteristics of each client in relation to the therapist and context.

However, if there is so much fluidity and complexity within the psychotherapeutic process, the question arises of why it is useful to order this process through phases at all. The clinical answer is that each phase has a set of preconditions that are required for clients to meet if they are to deal with the typical issues at certain therapeutic times. For example, it is necessary for clients to develop a relationship with the therapist in order for this dynamic to be used therapeutically as suggested in the second phase of cultural psychotherapy. The therapeutic relationship does not emerge immediately; it takes time to develop and time for clients to trust it and benefit from it. Most clients and therapists can only establish a therapeutic relationship after interacting and getting to know each other for a while. In addition to the development of a therapeutic relationship, there are other conditions for Phase II and several conditions for Phase III. These conditions are specified in the second and third chapters of the book.

The first phase—addressing basic needs and symptom reduction—focuses on meeting clients' needs/goals and assuaging their most prominent symptoms. Omar and Sophie came to therapy because they wanted to define their relationship (end it or move in) and reduce the number of arguments they had. Much of treatment during this phase focused on using cognitive behavioral strategies to identify triggers for their conflicts and help them develop alternative ways to respond to silences. The assumptions of an individualistic framework are fundamental for this phase. Thus, the general equation of cultural psychotherapy during this first phase can be reformulated as

$$\text{Phase I} = \text{individual factors}^2 \times \text{relational factors} \times \text{contextual factors.}$$

The quadratic factor (**individual factors^2**) is not intended to reflect an exact quantity; it instead aims to illustrate the importance of individualistic factors during this first phase of treatment. Similarly, during different phases, other factors are considered. Furthermore, each of these variables (i.e., individual, relational, or contextual factors) is not an absolute value; rather, they change depending on how important they are for clients. For example, although individualistic factors were underscored during the first phase with both Sophie and Omar, I may have emphasized these more with Omar because they were more important for him, while with Sophie I may have highlighted relational variables that were more relevant for her. The emphasis given to each variable is a function of how important these are for a client.

The second phase—understanding clients' experience—explores and enriches clients' narratives through the psychotherapeutic relationship. The goal of this phase is to develop a better understanding of how important experiences have marked our lives. Omar and Sophie learned not only how their past relationships (e.g., Sophie's parents' divorce) influenced their current lives, but also how the therapeutic relationship was affecting their lives (including my own identification with their issues). Many of the basic ideas of the second phase are informed by relational approaches (Boston Change Process Study Group

[BCPSG], 2010; Jordan, 2010; Wachtel, 2008) and neuropsychological ideas (e.g., Schacter, 1992; Westen & Gabbard, 2002a, 2002b). This emphasis on relational issues **(relational factors[2])** during the second phase can be illustrated through the following equation:

$$\text{Phase II} = \text{individual factors} \times \text{relational factors}^2 \times \text{contextual factors}.$$

The third phase—fostering empowerment—aims to increase clients' abilities to understand and consequently transform their social contexts. During this phase, contextual factors are emphasized (**contextual factors[2]**). As Omar and Sophie deepened their knowledge about the Palestine-Israel conflict and their religions, they were better able to respond to these influences. They not only learned more about each other's backgrounds and ways of relating but also collaborated with similar couples (Muslim/Jewish) to support a partnership between Israel and Palestine, particularly in helping Palestinian refugees. The third phase, thus, can be illustrated as:

$$\text{Phase III} = \text{individual factors} \times \text{relational factors} \times \text{contextual factors}^2.$$

However, after all conditions (i.e., for Phases II and III) are met, the psychotherapeutic process does not unfold in a linear fashion (first phase followed by second phase and finished with the third); instead, it is more fluid, complex, and cyclical. After all conditions are met, some clients/therapists may simultaneously or intermittently focus on issues typical of the first, second, and/or third phases.

CULTURAL PSYCHOTHERAPY'S THEORY OF PSYCHOTHERAPEUTIC ACTION

Just as with any theory of psychotherapeutic action, cultural psychotherapy must describe both what changes in psychotherapy and also the strategies used to pursue those changes. "What changes" in psychotherapy refers to the general objectives of treatment and the factors that change, while the "strategies used" refers to the specific techniques employed to accomplish change (Gabbard & Westen, 2003). The main therapeutic factors (objectives) that change in each phase are emphasized in this introduction, while subsequent chapters (Chapters 1–3, 7) describe the different techniques or specific clinical recommendations necessary for this change to occur.[7]

The three-phased cultural psychotherapeutic model assumes that during each phase a distinct mechanism of therapeutic action is underscored that supports the utility of depicting the psychotherapeutic process with phases. In the first phase, the primary aim is to improve clients according to their needs and characteristics. The therapeutic factors or change resides within the client. Successful individualistic treatments are described through some of the following therapeutic outcomes: increased insight, enhanced self-awareness, self-organization, self-coherence, self-actualization, enhanced self-esteem levels, improved coping strategies (distraction techniques or relaxation), optimal levels of emotional regulation, increased psychological flexibility, or balanced levels of serotonin or dopamine.

	Main Factors That Change	**Psychoneurological Systems Emphasized**	**Psychological Functions Targeted**	**Psychotherapeutic Paradigm Emphasized**
Phase I Addressing basic needs and symptom reduction	Individual change	Explicit systems or conscious processes	Increased ability to regulate affect, psychological flexibility, and problem solving	Individualistic paradigm (CBT, existential psychology, psychoanalysis, etc.)
Phase II Understanding clients' experience	Relational change	Implicit systems or unconscious processes	Enhanced ability to develop fulfilling relationships	Relational paradigms (e.g., feminism, object relations)
Phase III Fostering empowerment	Contextual change	Not known	Enhanced empowerment	Contextual or ecological paradigms

TABLE I.1 Characteristics of the Three-Phased Cultural Psychotherapeutic Model

During the second phase, the client's main therapeutic objective is to develop more fulfilling relationships, in which case the therapeutic change resides within relationships. One of the most relevant tools to accomplish this goal is the use of the psychotherapeutic relationship (Jordan, 2010; Wachtel, 2008). Finally, cultural psychotherapy comprises a third phase focusing on empowerment, which is often neglected within the traditional psychotherapeutic literature. This involves a deeper understanding of contextual influences coupled with an enhanced ability to comprehend and transform sociocultural contexts (Ivey, 1999; Roysircar, 2009). In this third phase, a central therapeutic objective is to change the context. See Table I.1 for a summary of the characteristics of the three phases of cultural psychotherapy.

NEUROSCIENCE INFLUENCES: EXPLICIT AND IMPLICIT SYSTEMS

There is a growing consensus among neuroscientists that human thought involves at least two types of memory, explicit and implicit (Schacter, 1992, 1995, 1998). Explicit memory[8] involves the retrieval of information—childhood memories, facts, or ideas—that is intentional and conscious. Implicit memory[9] refers to memory that is observable in behavior but not consciously brought to mind (Schacter, 1992, 1995, 1998); it is one way in which the influences of past experiences are expressed in subsequent task performance—unintentionally and without conscious recollection of a learning episode (Schacter, 1995).

In reality, neuroscience talks about explicit and implicit memory. In this book, however, the explicit and implicit terms are broadened to systems as a means to include many processes (e.g., perception, beliefs, attitudes, attention, motivation), not solely memory. These distinct psychoneurological systems are in play during each phase of cultural psychotherapy. During the first phase, however, explicit systems are underscored, while in the second phase implicit and explicit systems are highlighted.

Given that explicit systems are conscious, while implicit systems are unconscious, I often use these terms interchangeably (e.g., implicit/unconscious). Nevertheless, it is important not to confuse cultural psychotherapy's use of the word "unconscious" with the way the word is used in the traditional psychoanalytic literature. For the psychoanalyst, the unconscious is a place filled with repressed desires, memories, or thoughts. All that is vanished from consciousness is stored in the unconscious, and many of these repressed desires end up influencing our lives; thus, a central goal of psychoanalysis is to make this repressed content conscious. In contrast, I use the term unconscious to refer to the mind as a giant processer that quickly and quietly manages large amounts of data, which is necessary to keep human beings functioning. Through our unconscious, we are able to size up the world, and in turn, recognize danger, which influences our goals and at times motivates decisions around actions (Wilson, 2002). Many of the processes we ordinarily conduct are automatic and do not require conscious attention. Cultural psychotherapy argues that not all of what resides in the unconscious (or implicit systems) is repressed; it is simply that the human mind is too complex to simultaneously process all mental processes in a conscious manner (Schacter, 1992; Wilson, 2002).

Piaget (1954) revolutionized our thinking about infants' meaning making by demonstrating that rather than verbally categorizing objects as older children do, infants make meaning of an object from what they can do with it. There are no balls or spoons but things that are "throwable" or "mouthable." This is reminiscent of Garcia Marques's depiction in his classic book *One Hundred Years of Solitude* of the origins of Macondo:[10] "The world was so recent that many things lacked names, and in order to indicate them it was necessary to point."

Meanings often have a significant sensorimotor ("it was necessary to point") component, which is akin to procedural memory in adults (Tronick & Beeghly, 2011). Procedural memory refers to the "how to" do certain activities, such as throwing a ball or riding a bike—processes that are not possible to explain verbally but are learned (Schacter, 1992, 1995, 1998). However, more relevant to the psychotherapeutic process than physical activities are relational procedural memories (implicit systems) of the ways we relate, such as unarticulated social rules (often preverbal). These implicit systems continue across the life span to shape our experiences without us fully acknowledging, articulating, or understandings their influence (BCPSG, 2010; Ivey, 1999; Stern, 1995; Stolorow & Atwood, 2002; Wachtel, 2008).

The basic goal of the first phase of cultural psychotherapy along neuroscientific lines is to underscore the role of explicit functions such as enhancing self-awareness, increasing psychological flexibility, learning new coping strategies, or enhancing affect regulation skills. While some implicit processes are evident from the onset of therapy, and implicit and/or relational change can occur in the first phase (and even in the first session), it is only as therapists glean more information about their clients that they can systematically and more effectively address implicit systems or even know that they are changing.

In the second phase of cultural psychotherapy, therapists tap into implicit or unconscious systems that are not explored in depth in the first phase. Many implicit meanings or unconscious processes are not especially susceptible to change by interpretation, insight, psychoeducation, learning emotional regulation skills (e.g., relaxation), or other verbal strategies that are typical of the first phase. Instead, they are mainly changed through noninterpretative and nonverbal means of feeling understood, test passing, rupture/repair processes (see Chapter 2), or other relational experiences. What goes on procedurally or implicitly is largely a matter of how the words, gestures, metaphors, intonations, subtle interactions, and other nonverbal cues are used within the psychotherapeutic relationship (implicit systems/unconscious), rather than what is in fact said (explicit systems/conscious). Explicit and implicit memories are distinct and not necessarily correlated; instead they process information as parallel systems (Barry, Naus, & Rehm, 2006).

Furthermore, neuroscience studies are also finding that there is a relative degree of functional and neuroanatomical independence between implicit and explicit systems (Gabbard & Westen, 2003; Schacter, 1995, 1998). This could further support the idea that it might be beneficial to specify therapeutic actions (i.e., objectives and techniques) within different phases of treatment. For example, studies of clients with brain damage suggest that explicit and implicit systems rely on different neural mechanisms (Schacter, 1995). In noting these neural correlates, however, I do not hope to explain grief or love through the limbic system, but to inform our interventions and theories according to mind-brain interactions.

It is also important to note that distinguishing between explicit and implicit systems is a psychoneurological finding that is also influenced by a medical cultural taxonomy (Cushman, 1995; Gergen, 2010). Classification systems (e.g., conscious versus unconscious, explicit–implicit, mind–body, object–subject, matter–spirit, white–black) are constructed through cultural categories that organize and give meaning to scientific findings. Cultural categories are a reflection of the prevalent beliefs of a particular time and place. Currently, many of our psychotherapeutic taxonomies are highly influenced by the medical model (Cushman, 1995; Gergen, 2010), which emphasizes an objective, decontextualized, and fragmented view of the "individual." Perhaps in a different time and place what we call explicit and implicit could have different meanings and emphasis. Consistent with this idea is the fact that no studies (that I know of) have examined (or even considered) underlying neurofunctional processes responsible for contextual change. It is not surprising that neurological findings responsible for contextual changes have been neglected from a literature that overlooks this possibility.

However, neuroscience has advanced many studies that support the idea that culture shapes both explicit and implicit systems (Dovidio, 2009). Furthermore, cultural psychotherapy emphasizes the need to understand explicit and implicit systems in relationship to specific contexts. The context gives meaning to both explicit and implicit systems. One of the basic assumptions is that different cultures promote distinct child-rearing practices that lead to implicit relational systems that influence meanings (e.g., different cultural variables), social interactions, and narratives (La Roche, 1999; Tronick & Beeghly, 2011). However, research noting the impact of culture is not limited to child-rearing practices. Culture is continuously and relentlessly shaping our emotions, cognitions, and lives through explicit and implicit messages. An explicit message is information that we are aware of, and implicit is information that we do not notice but that has an effect on our behavior.

In the United States, we are surrounded every day by explicit and implicit messages linking some attributes with good (e.g., white skin = good; black skin = bad) (Dovidio, 2009; Steele & Aronson, 1995; Weisbuch et al., 2009). It is not that we choose to make positive associations with the dominant group; we are conditioned to do so. Just opening the newspaper or turning the TV on, we are immediately bombarded by explicit and implicit messages about the meanings of race, religion, gender, and many other attributes (Dovidio, 2009; Steele & Aronson, 1995; Weisbuch, Pauker & Ambady, 2009). Unfortunately, we are often not aware of the influence these messages have in our lives. Cultural psychotherapy aims to clarify these messages. For example, the psychologists Claude Steele and Joshua Aronson created a well-known and now classic experiment to test the toxic effects of what they called "stereotype threats." They asked a group of African American students to take 20 questions of the Graduate Record Examination, the standardized test used for entry into graduate school. When the students were asked to identify their race on a pretest questionnaire, that simple act was sufficient to prime them (with an implicit message) with all the negative stereotypes associated with African Americans' academic achievement. As a result, the number of questions they answered correctly was cut in half. In contrast, a similar group (controlling for IQ and previous results on the GRE) that was not asked about their race performed significantly better than the first group. The detrimental effects of these stereotype threats during a lifetime of exposure are often catastrophic. Cultural psychotherapy aims to enhance clients' understanding of these social forces and the development of strategies that will not only inoculate them but also allow them to transform these toxic influences (see Chapter 3 for more details on how to accomplish this goal). While the impact of context on behavior is an important premise of cultural psychotherapy, it also holds that we can influence our contexts.

Neuroscience studies find that sustained exposure to a set of cultural experiences can change neural functioning. An emerging literature suggests that fundamental cultural values (e.g., individualism and collectivism) influence the neural networks activated when recognizing and thinking about others (Park & Huang, 2010). The study of the "cultural brain" is a critically important, growing area of research that demonstrates the influence of cultural processes in sculpting the brain (Park & Huang, 2010). It is not that there are permanent neuroanatomical or neurofunctional racial differences between groups, but rather that social and cultural processes have the power to influence neural functions, which, in turn, affect our behavior. Far from being deterministic, cultural psychotherapy underscores the tremendous flexibility and hope contained in the new data on brain plasticity (Eberhardt, 2005). Again, this emphasizes the bidirectional influence of the person and context. By exploring both molar and molecular processes, we may find better ways to understand how these processes intersect, which will lead us to develop more effective therapeutic strategies.

CULTURAL PSYCHOTHERAPY'S RESEARCH STRATEGIES

Cultural psychotherapy asserts that there are multiple understandings for similar processes and many valid strategies/methods to know. Cultural psychotherapy emphasizes the need to use diverse methodological and interdisciplinary research approaches to address psychotherapeutic questions. Rigorous/objective research strategies (randomized control trials, laboratory studies) and qualitative ones (e.g., phenomenological studies, content analyses) are encouraged to explore specific questions.

Cultural psychotherapy, however, underscores the need to contrast results using not only different methodologies, but also samples from different cultures (including, e.g., socioeconomic status, gender orientation, race, and ethnicity). By contrasting samples from different backgrounds, we start exploring what may be universal (nomothetic) from what is particular (ideographic) in our psychological interventions. Nevertheless, cultural psychotherapy consistently proposes the need to consider nomothetic findings as working hypotheses when applied to individuals. As already noted, not all Muslims would equate loving someone to "surrendering," as Omar did with Sophie. However, the levels of endorsement or lack thereof are important pieces of clinical information that are useful in designing culturally sensitive interventions (see Chapter 6). It is essential that we constantly assess our ideas and continue to learn from our clients, ourselves, therapeutic relationships, and contexts. The aim of cultural research is to gain information about clients, relationships, and contexts as well as how these factors interact.

The need to study questions through multimethods and in different cultures is consistent with the epistemological idea that what we know is influenced by the observers' attributes (researchers/clinicians and participants/clients) and the observation process (e.g., laboratory study, psychotherapeutic relationship) as well as by the context in which the research takes place (e.g., during certain times and places some variables/questions are underscored while others are overlooked). The relative validity of some research methods is dependent upon the cultural context. Thus, it is important that research incorporates individual, relational, and contextual variables. Not including any one of these may lead us to develop incomplete or even erroneous understandings.

Cultural psychotherapy's research approach leads us to develop many hypotheses for one question. However, through the systematic use of the scientific method, many hypotheses could lose credibility. Cultural psychotherapy is currently attempting to create guidelines to seek, organize, and assess available scientific evidence (La Roche & Christopher, 2008, 2009) or even how we define scientific evidence. Much work still remains to be conducted in this area.

Cultural Ethics

Cultural psychotherapy acknowledges that within the psychotherapeutic session we are constantly making decisions that reflect specific social values and/or have ethical meanings. Cultural psychotherapy emphasizes the need to become aware of these values and their consequences. If we do not make these assumptions explicit, they will end up narrowing our views and possibilities. Underlying this approach is the belief that many perspectives inform our understandings and decisions. Diversity and complexity can enrich our lives if presented in an appropriate environment. However, diversity and complexity are values that also need to be questioned by both therapists and clients.

In principle, cultural psychotherapy openly endorses social justice, which is defined here as actively advocating for the well-being of all, not just clients or their immediate context; but, in practice, each client in fact decides what is important for him or her. It is not for cultural psychotherapists to impose our social justice stances upon others. Instead, clients need to decide what they value and what is good for them. The clinicians' role is to clarify these decisions. Therapists must respect and avoid influencing clients' decisions and limit themselves to presenting options that emerge within the session.

Although during the first phase most clients and clinicians may never directly discuss the ethical implications of their decisions, it is increasingly important to do so as they learn more about their cultural contexts. Clients and therapists learn that they can in fact have an impact in their cultural contexts. An enhanced awareness of this power entails a gradual increase in social responsibility. Cultural psychotherapy does emphasize the influence of social forces but in doing so it does not intend to minimize individual responsibility. That is, the impact of social forces does not exonerate us from making "bad" decisions. In fact, as we become aware of our social influences, we become increasingly responsible for our acts.

To close this chapter, I provide a summary of some of the basic assumptions of cultural psychotherapy for review.

BASIC ASSUMPTIONS OF CULTURAL PSYCHOTHERAPY

1. The race and/or ethnicity of an individual does not determine the existence of any psychological characteristic. Cultural psychotherapy emphasizes the need to measure cultural variables rather than to assume psychological characteristics, according to the ethnicity and race of a person. Cultural variables include ethnicity and race as well as gender orientation, gender, disability status (e.g., deaf, blind), socioeconomic status (SES), religious background, and discrimination experiences, among other variables. Cultural psychotherapy argues that a more thorough consideration of cultural variables can increase the efficacy and effectiveness of our psychotherapeutic interventions.

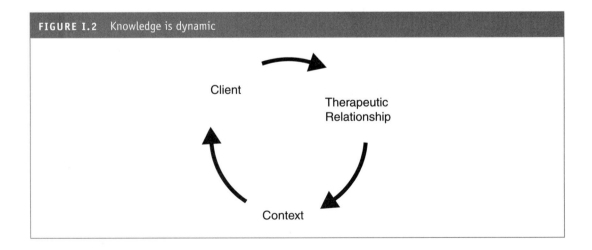

FIGURE I.2 Knowledge is dynamic

2. Cultural variables are herein defined as meanings that are overall more frequent in one cultural group (e.g., ethnic, religious, gender orientation) than others. Nevertheless, there is much variability amongst individuals within each cultural group.

3. All psychological processes (e.g., assessment, research) and concepts (e.g., meaning, narratives, self-concept) are more thoroughly understood as a result of the interaction of individualistic, relational, and contextual variables. Culture manifests itself in each of these three levels.

4. Each of these factors (individual, relational, and contextual) interacts and at times overlaps with the others, transforming and being transformed by them, which emphasizes the dynamic nature of knowledge (see Figure I.2).

5. Cultural psychotherapy aims to complement current psychotherapeutic approaches by providing an integrative framework that allows therapists to formulate clients' individualistic, relational, and contextual variables as well as providing therapists with specific treatment and assessment recommendations.

6. Cultural psychotherapy proposes an integrative, three-phased psychotherapeutic model in which individualistic assumptions highly inform the first phase, while the second phase underscores relational assumptions, and the third phase emphasizes a contextual/ecological understanding.

7. Cultural psychotherapy emphasizes the need to consistently consider explicit and implicit systems in a systematic manner throughout the psychotherapeutic process.

8. Cultural psychotherapy seeks not only individual change (emphasized during the first phase) but also relational change (second phase) and contextual change (third phase).

9. Cultural psychotherapy highlights the need to bring interdisciplinary research methods that combine multiple disciplines (clinical, ethnographic, mathematical, epidemiologic, etc.) to the study of psychotherapeutic processes as well as to continue questioning and refining the research strategies used to glean data.

10. Given that we are all embedded in specific and increasingly interconnected contexts, it is impossible to remain neutral when social injustices occur. Injustices affect us all. In theory, cultural psychotherapy emphasizes the importance of social justice, not just individual or relational justice. Nevertheless, clients are ultimately the ones making decisions about what is right or wrong for them.

11. Given that we all have multiple cultures and live in context, it is important to note that cultural psychotherapy is applicable not only to ethnic minorities but to each and every one of us.

12. The development of cultural psychotherapy is an ongoing conceptual and integrative process based on clinical data and empirical evidence from diverse fields, but it still requires significant research to confirm and support many of its assumptions. This book is the first systematic effort to coherently describe these ideas.

Notes

1. Gender, as noted by feminist authors, is an extremely powerful variable that influences our understandings. Cultural psychotherapy attempts to underscore the influence of gender as well as that of many other cultural variables.
2. I reluctantly use the term *White*—given its common usage—to encompass a wide range of diverse individuals (e.g., Irish, Italian, Scottish) living in the United States who are part of the dominant culture, speak English, and trace their background to a European country.
3. In this chapter, when I refer to the Palestine-Israel conflict, I alternate mentioning one or the other first (Israel or Palestine), as it was very important for Omar and Sophie to do so during our sessions.
4. For factors to be included in this model, they need to have clear psychotherapeutic effects. To date and to the best of my knowledge, it is still unclear to me, for example, how changing our DNA can be used to improve clients' behaviors.
5. In this book, when I discuss the "psychotherapeutic process," it is also meant to include the processes of assessment, formulation, consultation, and supervision.
6. All phases are important, and the movement from one phase to the next is a gradual and qualitative one. It is more aptly true to say that a client is mostly dealing with issues typical of the second phase and moving to the third phase, than that the client is in the second phase and will soon cross the line to be in the third phase. There are no clear-cut demarcations between phases.
7. Each of these clinical recommendations is assigned two numbers to allow for easy reference. The first number reflects the phase number (and chapter number) and the second the clinical recommendation number. For example, clinical recommendation 2.3 is the third clinical recommendation of Phase II and it appears in Chapter 2. The clinical recommendations for addressing cultural differences start with the number 4 and appear in Chapter 4. Thus, clinical recommendation 4.5 refers to the fifth recommendation in Chapter 4, "addressing cultural differences." When a letter appears with a number it refers to a prerequisite of a phase. For example, 3a refers to the first prerequisite of Phase III, which appears in Chapter 3.
8. There are two main types of explicit memories—generic and episodic. Generic (previously called semantic) refers to the general knowledge of facts (e.g., names, meanings of words), and episodic refers to specific autobiographical incidents (e.g., a visit to a grandparent).
9. Similarly, there are two types of implicit memories. Procedural memory refers to the "how to" do certain activities, such as the motor memory of throwing a ball or riding a bike. Procedural meanings are encoded in a sensorimotor language rather than a verbal one (Schacter, 1995, 1998; Tronick & Beeghly, 2011). The second type involves associative memory, which refers to the associations that guide mental processes and behavior outside consciousness.
10. Macondo is the fictional town in which the protagonists of *One Hundred Years of Solitude* live.

References

American Psychological Association. (2003). Guidelines on multicultural education, training, research, practice, and organizational change for psychologists. *American Psychologist, 58,* 377–402.

Ballou, M., Matsumoto, A., & Wagner, M. (2002). Feminist ecological theory. In M. Ballou & L. Brown (Eds.), *Rethinking mental health disorders: Feminist perspectives* (pp. 99–141). New York: Guilford.

Barry, E., Naus, M., & Rehm, L. (2006). Depression, implicit memory, and self: A revised memory model of emotion. *Clinical Psychology Review, 26*(6), 719-745.

Blatt, S. J. (1992). The differential effect of psychotherapy and psychoanalysis with anaclitic and introjective patients: The Menninger Psychotherapy Research Project revisited. *Journal of the American Psychoanalytical Association, 40*(3), 691–724.

Boring, E. G. (1957). *A history of experimental psychology* (2nd ed.). New York: Appleton-Century-Crofts.

Boston Change Process Study Group (BCPSG). (2010). *Change in psychotherapy: A unifying paradigm.* New York: Norton.

Brown, L. S. (1994). *Subversive dialogues: Theory in feminist therapy.* New York: Basic Books.

Cole, M. (1998). *Cultural psychology: A once and future discipline.* Cambridge, MA: Harvard University Press.

Cushman, P. (1995). *Constructing the self, constructing America: Studies in the cultural history of psychotherapy.* New York: Addison-Wesley.

Dovidio, J. (2009). Racial bias, unspoken but heard. *Science, 326,* 1641–1642.

Eberhardt, J. (2005). Imaging race. *American Psychologist, 60*(2), 181–190.

Freud, S. (1974). *Repression.* In *Standard edition* (Vol. 14, pp. 143–158). Newark, DE. Hogarth Press. (Original work published 1915)

Gabbard, G., & Westen, D. (2003). Rethinking therapeutic action. *The International Journal of Psychoanalysis, 84*(4), 823–841.

Gadamer, H. (1975). *Truth and method.* New York: Seabury Press.

Geertz, C. (1973). *The interpretation of cultures.* New York: Basic Books.

Gergen, K. (2010). The acculturated brain. *Theory & Psychology, 20*(6), 795–816.

Gold, J., & Wachtel, P. (2006). Cyclical psychodynamics. In G. Stricker & J. Gold (Eds.), *A casebook of psychotherapy integration* (pp. 79–87). Washington, DC: American Psychological Association.

Griner, D., & Smith, T. (2006). Culturally adapted mental health intervention: A meta-analytic review. *Psychotherapy: Theory, Research, Practice, Training, 43*(4), 531–548.

Heine, S. (2008). *Cultural psychology.* New York: Norton.

Helms, J., Jernigan, M., & Mascher, J. (2005). The meaning of race in psychology and how to change it: A methodological perspective. *American Psychologist, 60,* 43–50.

Herman, J. L. (1992). *Trauma and recovery: The aftermath of violence from domestic abuse to political terror.* New York: Basic Books.

Herrnstein, R. J., & Murray, C. (1994). *The bell curve: Intelligence and class structure in American life.* New York: Free Press.

Hinton, D., & Good, B. (2009). *Culture and panic disorder.* Stanford, CA: Stanford University Press.

Huey, S., & Polo, A. (2008). Evidence-based psychosocial treatments for ethnic minority youth. *Journal of Clinical Child & Adolescent Psychology, 37,* 263–301.

Ivey, A. (1999). Psychotherapy as liberation: Toward specific skills and strategies in multicultural counseling and therapy. In J. Ponterotto, J. M. Casas, L. A. Suzuki, & C. M. Alexander (Eds.), *Handbook of multicultural counseling.* Thousand Oaks, CA: Sage.

Ivey, A. (2000). *Developmental therapy: Theory into practice.* Sunapee, NH: Microtraining Associates.

Jordan, J. (2010). *Relational-cultural therapy.* Washington, DC: American Psychological Association.

Kleinman, A. (1988). *The illness narratives: Suffering, healing and the human condition.* New York: Basic Books.

Kluckhohn, C. (1959). *Mirror for man: A survey of human behavior and social attitudes.* New York: Premier Books.

La Roche, M. (1999). Culture, transference, and countertransference among Latinos. *Psychotherapy, 36,* 389–397.

La Roche, M. (2002). Psychotherapeutic considerations in treating Latinos. *Harvard Review of Psychiatry, 10,* 115–122.

La Roche, M., & Christopher, M. S. (2008). Culture and empirically supported treatments: On the road to a collision? *Culture and Psychology, 14,* 333–356.

La Roche, M., & Christopher, M. S. (2009). Changing paradigms from empirically supported treatment to evidenced-based practice: A cultural perspective. *Professional Psychology: Research & Practice, 40*(4), 396–402.

La Roche, M., & Christopher, M. S. (2010). Cultural diversity. In J. C. Thomas & M. Hersen (Eds.), *Handbook of clinical psychology competencies.* New York: Springer.

La Roche, M., & Tawa, J. (2011). Taking back our streets: A clinical model for empowering urban youths through participation in peace promotion. *Peace and Conflict: Journal of Peace Psychology, 17*(1), 4–21.

Lau, A. S. (2006). Making the case for selective and directed cultural adaptations of evidenced-based treatments: Examples from parent training. *Clinical Psychology Science and Practice, 67,* 295–310.

Markus, H. R., & Kitayama, S. (1991). Culture and the self: Implications for cognition, emotion, and motivation. *Psychological Review, 98,* 224–253.

Marsella, A., & Pedersen, P. (1980). *Cross-cultural counseling and psychotherapy: Foundations, evaluation, ethnocultural considerations, and future perspectives.* New York: Pergamon.

McGoldrick, M., & Giordano, J. (1996). Overview: Ethnicity and family therapy. In M. McGoldrick, J. Giordano, & J. Pearce (Eds.), *Ethnicity & family therapy* (2nd ed.). New York: Guilford.

Na, J., Grossmann, I., Varnum, M. E. W., Kitayama, S., Gonzales, R., & Nisbett, R. E. (2010). Cultural differences are not always reducible to individual differences. *Proceedings of the National Academy of Sciences, 107,* 6192–6197.

Park, D. C., & Huang, C. (2010). Culture wires the brain: A cognitive neuroscience perspective. *Perspectives on Psychological Science, 5*(4), 391–400.

Piaget, J. (1954). *The construction of reality in the child* (8th ed.). New York: Basic Books.

Roysircar, G. (2009). The big picture of advocacy: Counselor, heal society and thyself. *Journal of Counseling & Development, 87,* 288–294.

Schacter, D. L. (1992). Understanding implicit memory: A cognitive neuroscience approach. *American Psychologist, 47,* 559–569.

Schacter, D. L. (1995). Implicit memory: A new frontier for cognitive science. In M. S. Gazzaniga (Ed.), *In the cognitive neurosciences.* Cambridge, MA: MIT Press.

Schacter, D. L. (1998). Memory and awareness. *Science, 280,* 59–60.

Shweder, R. (1973). The between and within of cross-cultural research. *Ethos, 1,* 531–545.

Shweder, R. A. (1990). Cultural psychology: What is it? In J. W. Stigler, R. A. Shweder, & G. Herdt (Eds.), *Cultural psychology: Essays on comparative development* (pp. 1–43). Cambridge, UK: Cambridge University Press.

Slife, B., & Wiggins, B. (2009). Taking relationship seriously in psychotherapy: Radical relationality. *Journal of Contemporary Psychotherapy, 39,* 17–24.

Steele, C., & Aronson, J. (1995). Stereotype threat and the intellectual test performance of African Americans. *Journal of Personality and Social Psychology, 69,* 797–811.

Stern, D. (1995). *The motherhood constellation: A unified view of parent-infant psychotherapy.* New York: Basic Books.

Stolorow, R. D., & Atwood, G. E. (2002). *Contexts of being: The intersubjective foundations of psychological life.* New York: Analytical Press.

Sue, D., Ivey, A., & Pedersen, P. (2007). *Theory of multicultural counseling & therapy.* Mason, OH: Cengage Learning Press.

Sue, W. S., & Sue, D. (2008). *Counseling the culturally diverse: Theory and practice* (5th ed.). Hoboken, NJ: John Wiley.

Triandis, H. C. (1994). *Individualism and collectivism.* Boulder, CO: Westview.

Tronick, E., & Beeghly, M. (2011). Infants' meaning-making and development of mental health problems. *American Psychologist, 66,* 107–119.

Wachtel, P. (2008). *Relational theory and the practice of psychotherapy.* New York: Guilford.

Weisbuch, M., Pauker, K., & Ambady, N. (2009). The subtle transmission of race bias via televised nonverbal behavior. *Science, 326,* 1711–1714.

Westen, D., & Gabbard, G. (2002a). Development in cognitive neuroscience: I. Conflict, compromise, and connectionism. *Journal of the American Psychoanalytic Association,* 1–49.

Westen, D., & Gabbard, G. (2002b). Development in cognitive neuroscience: II. Implications for theories of transference. *Journal of the American Psychoanalytic Association,* 50–98.

Wilson, T. (2002). *Strangers to ourselves: Discovering the adaptive unconscious.* Cambridge, MA: Harvard University Press.

Zimbardo, P. (2008). *The Lucifer effect: Understanding how good people turn evil.* New York: Random House.

Phase I

Addressing Basic Needs and Symptom Reduction

Our greatest glory is not in never failing, but in rising every time we fall.

—Confucius

The ultimate measure of a man is not where he stands in moments of comfort and convenience, but where he stands at times of challenge and controversy.

—Martin Luther King, Jr., *Strength to Love,* 1963

Most of the clients we meet during the first phase of cultural psychotherapy face enormous challenges. They come to us devastated by various crises and injustices and it is important for us to consider not where they are in their lives at this moment but what they can become. As clinicians, our main goal is to meet our clients' chief complaints, while ensuring that their basic needs are addressed and that their most prominent or painful symptoms are ameliorated. At times, we find that even during the most adverse of times, people will in fact shine and grow.

Phase I of cultural psychotherapy starts when clients walk through our door and it ends when they terminate therapy. Throughout the duration of treatment, we must continue to address their goals and ensure that they are safe and stable. Thus, at some level cultural psychotherapy treatment always underscores the first phase. Although some clients during the first sessions may report being ready and motivated to explore the meaning of their experiences in depth (Phase II) or to transform cultural contexts (Phase III), in my clinical experience this is rarely the case. Most clients present with specific goals in mind (e.g., reducing panic symptoms, improving their marital relationship) and will promptly end psychotherapy once these goals have been met.

Much of the treatment during the first phase underscores the need to change explicit or conscious meanings rather than exploring or addressing implicit ones. It is not infrequent, however, that an enhanced understanding of implicit systems occurs within the first session(s). Nevertheless, the process of exploring and systematically understanding implicit systems is more thorough during the second phase than the first.

The duration of the first phase may be one session, or it may never be completed even after many years. Its length is mostly dependent upon the severity of clients' symptoms, motivations, and needs. When symptoms are more severe and refractory, they require more time to treat. Even after clients have advanced to Phase II or III, they may return to deal with issues of the first phase (e.g., if their symptomatology reemerges). Paramount to the transition from the first to the second phase of cultural psychotherapy is an underlying foundation of optimal affect regulation to ensure that clients are able to cope with the intense feelings evoked as they review in detail their experiences during Phase II.

The goal of this chapter is to provide clinicians with concrete clinical recommendations to help them assist clients in dealing with issues typical of the first phase of cultural psychotherapy. These Phase I recommendations are diverse, but they all share the rationale of emphasizing the client's individual characteristics, while not overlooking relational and cultural factors as they emerge. Thus, the first phase of cultural psychotherapy can be illustrated as

$$\text{Phase I } = \text{ individual factors}^2 \times \text{ relational factors } \times \text{ contextual factors.}$$

There is much variability among clients, and a "one-size-fits-all" model is unrealistic. However, I have underscored 14 clinical recommendations for the first phase of cultural psychotherapy. This list is not intended to be exhaustive and does not include all possible interventions. Clearly, many other clinical strategies are useful, but these 14 clinical recommendations are particularly illustrative of the basic concepts or principles of the first phase of cultural psychotherapy.

CLINICAL RECOMMENDATIONS FOR PHASE I

1.1   Chief complaints need to be understood in a culturally sensitive manner.

1.2   The goals and structure of psychotherapy are established as soon as possible.

1.3   Safety and basic needs are always a priority.

1.4   Establish a culturally sensitive therapeutic relationship.

1.5   Stay in the experiential level.

1.6   Learn and use clients' language.

1.7   Understand clients' formulations of problems in a culturally sensitive manner.

1.8   Use indigenous healing practices to address symptoms.

1.9   Use evidenced-based psychotherapies.

1.10   Encourage culturally sensitive lifestyle changes.

1.11   Learn and use clients' cultural context.

    1.12   Address cultural and demographic differences.

    1.13   Conduct cultural assessments and diagnoses.

    1.14   Enhance affect regulation and psychological flexibility.

Each of these clinical recommendations is discussed in detail next.

1.1 Chief Complaints Need to Be Understood in a Culturally Sensitive Manner

The first task of cultural psychotherapy is to understand clients' chief complaints, which are defined as the main reasons clients seek psychotherapy. However, it is also necessary to understand their chief complaints in depth and in a culturally sensitive manner (Kleinman, 1988; La Roche, 2002; Lewis-Fernandez & Diaz, 2002; Sue, Fujino, Hu, Takeuchi, & Zane, 1991). This is crucial because worldviews and life experiences affect not only the way in which clients organize and express their chief complaints and symptoms, but also their emotions, cognitions, and the personal meaning of illness. Not making an effort to understand the cultural values underlying clients' chief complaints may lead to situations in which they feel misunderstood and consequently drop out of treatment. Sue et al. (1991) found in their landmark study that more than 50% of ethnic minorities do not return to a second appointment. One of the main reasons for this high dropout rate is the lack of fit between clients' and therapists' goals. Sue et al. (1991) found that many clients wanted to address one set of issues, while their therapists had other goals in mind. Imagine for a moment that you go to a store and ask the clerk for a hat but she repeatedly shows you pants. Would you return to that store? Similarly, many of us would not return to a clinician who does not address our issues in a culturally sensitive manner. Consider the following four clinical examples:

1. Usha and Von are a recently married young Indian couple that came to the United States two years ago and were studying at a prestigious business school in Massachusetts. They said they came to therapy because they were no longer able to get along with Sid, who was Usha's previous boyfriend.

2. Antoine is a 35-year-old married Haitian man who sought therapy after he started experiencing severe panic attacks. Antoine said he came to therapy because his doctor asked him to do so.

3. Mike is a successful White American businessman who recently wed a young Vietnamese woman named Hanna after meeting on a business trip. He brought her to therapy because he wanted her to participate in a "ménage à trois."

4. Mayra is a 7-year-old Dominican girl who reported "being trash," because she was not as light skinned as her sister and classmates.

In the case of Usha and Von, I found out that Sid—Usha's first boyfriend—was also a family friend. Her family and Sid's had been "friends" for generations in a wealthy area of Bombay. Not talking to each other constituted disloyalty to a long history of family friendship. Von completely agreed with his wife's sense of family duty. He believed it was imperative to mend their friendship with Sid. Together, the three of us planned strategies to accomplish this goal. Questioning Usha's motives could have been received as an insult to her family and likely would have caused them to disengage from therapy. As it was, they had already dropped out of treatment with another therapist. The previous therapist had questioned whether she had feelings for Sid, rather than first exploring the meanings of family relationships. By assuming a Westernized view of the situation, the previous therapist ignored an important cultural element.

Antoine was a gentle Haitian man who had lived in Boston for 10 years. He had a stoic look and did not believe that psychotherapy could help him. He often reminded me that he was only in treatment because his primary care provider (PCP) had asked him to meet with me. About three months before his initial visit, he started experiencing frequent and severe panic attacks. He seemed unmoved when I explained to him that there are effective psychological techniques to decrease his panic symptoms. He repeated that the only reason he was seeing me was that his PCP had asked him to do so; thus, we agreed to meet for a trial of four sessions and address his PCP's concerns. After four sessions he would decide if he needed further treatment.

It was a different story for Mike and Hanna. They did not return for a second appointment. During the initial session, I expressed *my belief* that she had the right to decide whether or not to participate in her husband's sexual encounters and that his failure to respect her wishes was tantamount to exploitation. Hanna explained that she loved Mike and added that her family was counting on her. Her marriage would allow others in her family to immigrate to the United States. I expressed my view that she did not have to do anything she did not feel comfortable with and explained that there are laws that allow her to choose in which activities to engage, even if married. I emphatically added that sometimes the U.S. Citizenship and Immigration Services expedited cases in which women were being exploited or abused; in short, she could still have a chance to become a citizen without doing the things Mike wanted. I ended the session by giving her the names and telephone numbers of attorneys who specialized in such cases. Needless to say, Mike did not bring Hanna to a second appointment. In hindsight, I believe I should have further explored her cultural values (family loyalty) and tried to establish a therapeutic alliance before questioning her marriage in such an emphatic manner. From a very young age, Vietnamese children are taught the concepts of obligation and shame. They are reminded throughout their lives that their duty toward their parents and family comes before their own needs (Leung & Boehnlein, 1996).

In the case of Mayra, we explored her feelings of sadness arising from her skin color. Her eyes would immediately well up as we explored the meanings ascribed to her dark skin. She would describe the preferential treatment her "white" sister (Marta) received. Her parents and grandparents would repeatedly remark on Marta's beauty and neglect to say anything nice about her. Marta was nicknamed "*Bonita*" (pretty) and Mayra was nicknamed "*Negrita*" (blackie). Although *Negrita* in Spanish does not have the same pejorative meaning that it has in English, her nickname spread among her classmates who started picking on her. In tears, Mayra would explain that she was not as beautiful as Marta and did not look like an actress or pop star, and thus she concluded that she was "trash." In the Dominican culture, there are more than 40 words (e.g., *Indio, Taino, Mulato,* and

Moreno) that describe the countless shades of skin color (Mella-Mejias, 1992). The large number of words is reflective of the importance that skin color plays in the Dominican Republic. Lighter skin is highly valued and darker skin such as Mayra's is undervalued (Mella-Mejias, 1992).

1.2 The Goals and Structure of Psychotherapy Are Established as Soon as Possible

By the end of the first session, it is necessary for clients and clinicians to have an agreed-upon set of psychotherapeutic goals that allows clients to understand what to aim for and what to expect from the psychotherapeutic process (Sue & Sue, 2008). For example, with Usha and Von the goal was to explore ways in which they could reach out to Sid and avoid family conflict. In the case of Mayra, we decided together that the primary aim would be to reduce her feeling of being "trash." In addition to goal setting, defining the structure of treatment, which includes the frequency, length, and time of sessions, is essential. For example, with Antoine we agreed to meet every Thursday for 50 minutes from 2:00 to 2:50 p.m.

Structure is not limited to frequency, length, and time as it can also include setting up basic policies (limits of confidentiality, no-show policy, emergency procedures, payment schedules, etc.) and completing all required forms. It is necessary to immediately inform clients about these policies to avoid misunderstandings, while at the same time providing clients with information that may influence their decision on whether to continue treatment. For example, many times clients, especially those of minority status, are concerned about who will have access to the information they share in treatment. They want to know if others in their community will find out what they say. Undocumented individuals may worry about the risk that their information will be leaked to the Department of Homeland Security or the U.S. Citizenship and Immigration Services. These fears are heightened among ethnic minorities and others who have traditionally been marginalized or oppressed by dominant groups. If such matters are presented or discussed up front, it may help them feel comfortable enough to come back for a second session.

Many diverse and underserved clients are concerned about financial issues; they worry about how to pay for psychological treatment. Will managed care or government-subsidized health entities (e.g., Medicaid) really pay? Will these fee arrangements hold? The idea that managed care companies (government or private) will pay for their care is often met with skepticism. This is not surprising as in the past the system has often not been supportive of their needs; thus, why should it now be different? Thus, it is important to explain the payment structure (e.g., for managed care companies) and expectations (co-payments) as early as possible. I have also found it useful to predict problems (e.g., you may unexpectedly receive a "bill or something that looks like a bill") and have plans to address such issues. For example, I often preemptively state that "if you receive bills, please bring them to therapy and together we will deal with the managed care company." The first impulse for many clients who receive a large bill, particularly if they are having financial problems, is to drop out of treatment. Discussing these concerns openly and directly, however, makes clients feel more at ease and able to focus on discussing more personal issues.

Aside from the logistical aspects of psychotherapy, it is also important that treatment boundaries be explained and established at the beginning of treatment. Therapists should clarify personal policies of self-disclosure and be explicit in conveying that therapy precludes any other form of social relationship. Defining this contract clearly and early on will help decrease the likelihood of receiving personal invitations from clients to family parties and social gatherings, or being given expensive gifts. When working with clients from different cultural backgrounds, it is important to understand that they may take offense if a therapist does not accept a gift or does not attend a family event, because it is customary in some cultures to extend such invitations to or bestow such tokens on important people in their lives. Clarifying these boundaries up front helps to minimize the negative repercussions of refusal.

1.3 Safety and Basic Needs Are Always a Priority

If clients report safety concerns (e.g., suicidality, homicidality, substance abuse, domestic violence), clinicians need to immediately make these issues a priority. In these instances, clinicians may need to become more directive and structured. The need to establish effective precautions (e.g., detailing and rehearsing emergency plans, hospitalizations) cannot be emphasized enough. Depending on the specific cultural beliefs of clients (e.g., familism, spiritualism, allocentrism), it is often useful to identify their resources (e.g., extended family, church) as means to design a safety plan that is culturally sensitive and stems from their contextual assets (Christopher & Skillman, 2009).

During the first phase, it is necessary to prioritize symptoms, goals, and needs (Linehan, 1993). An important aspect of prioritizing symptoms is assessing safety and addressing those issues first, followed by the most troubling symptoms (e.g., impulsivity, sleep disturbance, academic problems) that are interfering with clients' day-to-day functioning. Although it is necessary to continuously explore the influence of different stressors (e.g., discrimination, marital problems, or poverty) on clients' functioning, this exploration should not discourage the need to immediately and directly intervene as needed. Interventions that provide immediate relief and/or alleviation of the "problem" are very effective during the initial segment of treatment. For example, Johanna is an elderly African American widow who had suffered from insomnia for many years and explained that every evening she drank several cups of black coffee. I explained that caffeine often leads to insomnia and encouraged her to stop drinking coffee after 6:00 p.m. or switch to decaf. This direct recommendation was beneficial immediately; it allowed her to sleep for longer periods of time. These fast results also increased my credibility to address other, more complicated emotional issues.

Second to safety issues, clients' basic needs (e.g., food, shelter, health) also need to be addressed quickly. These issues may be overlooked by inexperienced clinicians who assume that this is not within their clinical purview. In many contexts (particularly with immigrant clients), clinicians can be extremely helpful in providing them with information on how to start meeting their basic needs (e.g., seeking social security benefits, or what to expect from their new culture, etc.). If basic needs are not addressed, it may be difficult for psychotherapy to proceed to the next phases (La Roche, 2002; Maslow, 1969). During the early stages of Phase I, clinicians should make referrals to case managers who have expertise in linking clients to services (e.g., pursuing food stamps, seeking social security). It is important to note the ways in which clients address their basic needs, for this may also be illustrative of the ways in which they deal with other matters in their lives; it may be reflective of explicit or implicit systems. For example, some clients may not seek services (e.g., food stamps) even though they are hungry because they feel hopeless or fear their efforts may be to no avail. This last point illustrates that even as case management issues are addressed, clinical issues are present (e.g., psychological hopelessness). A clinical understanding of these emotional barriers makes case management more effective.

1.4 Establish a Culturally Sensitive Therapeutic Relationship

The psychotherapeutic relationship is the means by which a clincian and a client engage with each other and work to create a beneficial change in the client. This engagement needs to occur in a culturally sensitive manner. Three characteristics of this relationship are: it is acceptable initially to take an expert stance, maintain solidarity with clients' struggles, and a dialectic therapeutic stance is useful. Although good therapeutic relationships have many characteristics (e.g., empathy, agreement with goals), I emphasize only these three, as they are largely distinctive of cultural psychotherapy and to the first phase. It is also important not to confuse the therapeutic relationship with the therapeutic alliance (Bordin, 1979), which is a client's belief that she or he can work with a therapist, while the therapeutic relationship is the way therapists and clients work together.

It Is Acceptable Initially to Take an Expert Stance

Often at the beginning of psychotherapy, clinicians take a more active, objective, and structured approach. Clinicians can suggest direct strategies for clients to solve some problems. Consistent with this initial expert stance is the delivery of psychoeducational information that normalizes or explains clients' conditions (e.g., muscular tension, stress, sexual dysfunction) and the employment of behavioral directives (e.g., diaphragmatic breathing, improving diet, reducing caffeine intake). During this first phase, many behavioral techniques (e.g., exposure, systematic desensitization) and cognitive strategies (e.g., monitoring self-talk) are extremely useful.

Furthermore, some culturally diverse groups, particularly many Asians and Latinos, are accustomed and expect their PCPs, teachers, or other professionals to tell them what to do. If this expectation is not met, it may decrease clinicians' credibility (Sue & Sue, 2008). Additionally, in the beginning phase of treatment clinicians and clients do not know each other, so it is difficult for them to talk about relational issues. Instead of exploring their interactions, clients and therapists collaborate in pursuing some formal goals.

While therapy is a collaborative relationship, there are often power dynamics in play. It is important to acknowledge these issues from the outset so they can be effectively addressed. For example, the employment of behavioral therapeutic strategies entails a significant power differential between clients and therapists, where clinicians are construed as the experts and clients the novices. An increased awareness of the effects of this perceived power differential provides a unique opportunity to further understand clients' experiences and how psychotherapy mirrors society's power dynamics. This mirroring is also an opportunity to start exploring the influence of context in clients' lives.

Consistent with culturally competent models that emphasize an awareness of power differentials (e.g., Sue, Ivey, & Pedersen, 2007), it is hoped that therapeutic relationships will evolve toward egalitarian ones (Phase II); or ones in which clients lead the therapeutic process (Phase III). While this is rarely the case during the first phase of psychotherapy, it does not mean that clients are discouraged from leading the sessions. On the contrary, cultural psychotherapy encourages clients to begin leading their treatments as soon as they are ready or willing to do so.

Finally, at the beginning of the therapeutic relationship, clients often follow their prescribed cultural roles and norms, and their behaviors are highly influenced by social expectations. Therapists are often perceived according to clients' cultural and social expectations of what a "doctor" of a particular race, age, or gender is supposed to be. Nevertheless, even these social or cultural scripts can reveal much of what clients expect. By interpreting these cultural meanings, therapists can infer important implicit meanings (e.g., how to deal with authority) that can be addressed more effectively in later phases.

Maintain Solidarity With Clients' Struggles

Cultural psychotherapy is not neutral. In the face of injustice, cultural psychotherapists do not remain silent. Comments that affirm therapists' commitment to diversity, against discrimination, and in favor of social or economic justice are required from the onset of psychotherapy. If this commitment is not clearly communicated either implicitly or explicitly, many clients will avoid talking about diversity, discrimination, or injustice. Furthermore, some clients may believe that their experiences of social injustice are irrelevant to the psychotherapeutic process and that they should focus on more important inner matters or past family experiences.

A Dialectic Therapeutic Stance Is Useful

To establish an appropriate working alliance, it is first recommended that therapists take a dialectic stance in which they validate clients' struggles and simultaneously (or gradually) point toward areas for growth and change (Linehan, 1993). By maintaining an awareness of the need to both validate and promote change, therapists are able to intervene in ways that maximize the possibility that clients will really take in what is being said. Statements that first validate clients' experience—radical acceptance—increase the likelihood that they will listen to therapists' suggestions (Linehan, 1993; Roemer & Orsillo, 2009). The goal of radical acceptance is for clients to feel as though their therapists are standing with them, not in opposition to them (Linehan, 1993).

1.5 Stay in the Experiential Level

In the first phase of psychotherapy, we have access to only a limited amount of information that is provided by clients' self-report (explicit meanings) and communicated by nonverbal behaviors. It is often helpful to stay in the here and now of the therapeutic relationship rather than inferring implicit meanings. This consideration can be translated into the following three clinical recommendations. First, it is helpful to make reflective statements in which the content of comments are clarified. Second, it is useful to note nonverbal responses (e.g., tearing of the eyes), and third, to contrast these nonverbal cues with explicit statements.

During the first few sessions (Phase I), it is often too early to effectively infer implicit meanings (e.g., identify relational procedural memories). Furthermore, many of the issues addressed during this first phase only require explicit and declarative information. For example, Usha and Von wanted and needed direct and concrete suggestions to befriend Sid. At this point, it was unnecessary to explore unconscious processes. Although it is likely that implicit meanings were underlying their issues, it was not necessary to explore them to accomplish Usha and Von's initial treatment goals. After a few sessions, Usha and Von successfully befriended Sid, and they reported no longer requiring treatment.

1.6 Learn and Use Clients' Language

Not knowing a client's primary language significantly impairs the psychotherapeutic process. It is ideal when clinicians are fully knowledgeable of clients' languages, particularly their native language. Since languages are loaded with emotional meanings, semantic translations are often not accurate. The intonations or the context in which a sentence or word is said can change the meaning in one language but not necessarily in another. Furthermore, some emotional issues are more readily accessible through one language[1] and thus can be more easily described by the client in one language over another. For example, Pepe is a married Mexican American man who spoke English when discussing his homosexuality but switched to Spanish when talking about family issues. Pepe was unable to communicate in Spanish about his homosexuality. His father had often reminded him that being homosexual is one of the worst sins that could happen to a "macho." In contrast, when speaking English, he could not find the words or gestures to convey his strong family attachments. Thus, my ability to understand and speak both English and Spanish allowed me to help Pepe access his emotions for both his family and homosexual experiences.

While this clinical recommendation to "learn and use clients' language" plainly applies to language fluency, it is also applicable to the words and symbols (narrative style, metaphors, intonation, proverbs, and even gestures) that clients use to communicate (Sue, 1998; White & Epston, 1990). For example, exploring the meanings of "trash" for Mayra opened additional dimensions of understanding that allowed her to revise her basic assumptions. Even as a 7-year-old, Mayra was able to realize that her definition of trash (because of her dark skin color) was highly influenced by the cultural assumptions of beauty (e.g., only Whites are beautiful). To reach this understanding, it was helpful for Mayra to describe many specific experiences that led her to feel like trash. As she became increasingly aware of the meanings ascribed to her skin color, she was able to question and revise them.

She gradually learned to laugh at the "stupid" assumption that only Whites are good or beautiful. Mayra realized that she could create her own meanings and deal with imposed cultural meanings in a different manner. Meanings that are explored (e.g., only Whites are beautiful) are more likely to be questioned and changed than those that remain unchecked or implicit. Furthermore, clients learn that they do not have to endorse dominant cultural assumptions. By helping Mayra see her many positive attributes (e.g., being a good student, having close friends, and excelling in kickball), she realized she was much more than just the color of her skin and eventually saw her own skin color as beautiful, too.

When clinicians learn their clients' language, they can more accurately access their clients' world, which enhances communication, credibility, empathy, and the therapeutic alliance. Similarly, a growing number of clinicians are incorporating the use of proverbs (Andres-Hyman, Ortiz, Añez, Paris, & Davidson, 2006; Otto, 2000) as means to connect and speak clients' language. While the accurate use of words, gestures, proverbs, or other communicational symbols allows clients and clinicians to connect more effectively, an inappropriate use of words and gestures is likely to lead to disruptions. If an interpreter is added to this process, it is very possible that it will increase the risk of misunderstanding. For this reason, psychotherapists should use interpreters with caution. In fact, I think interpreters should only be used in the psychotherapeutic process as a last resort.

From the onset of therapy, clinicians should strive to learn and understand their clients' verbal as well as nonverbal language. Words, expressions, and sentences can convey idiosyncratic messages—implicit meanings. The radical implication of this recommendation is that even if a client and therapist are from the same cultural background, they need to keep exploring their understandings rather than assuming similarities. Just because they share the same cultural background does not mean they share the same dictionary.

While individuals develop their own sets of words, gestures, and symbols, these are also highly shaped by their cultures. This is particularly important because it has repeatedly been found that different cultural groups have preferred styles for reporting their concerns. Some groups have culturally specific idioms of distress (Lewis-Fernandez & Diaz, 2002) that can be pathologized by others who do not recognize them. For example, research shows that some Asian clients prefer to first discuss somatic complaints, such as stomach pains and headaches (Kleinman, 1988; Sue & Sue, 2008), rather than intrapsychic issues. Unfortunately, this has led some clinicians to believe that Asians are not psychologically sophisticated (Sue & Sue, 2008). Thus, it is imperative for therapists to know the culture of clients so that differences are not understood as deficits. Although no one single clinician will ever learn all the subtle cultural distinctions that exist within different cultures, it is imperative that therapists continuously strive to learn more about their clients' cultures.

1.7 Understand Clients' Formulations of Problems in a Culturally Sensitive Manner

The *Diagnostic and Statistical Manual of Mental Disorders (DSM–IV;* American Psychiatric Association, 1994) and the *DSM–5* (soon to be published) include a short appendix called "Cultural Formulation" that sketches a systematic method to evaluate the contribution of culture in the mental health assessment. Unfortunately, this effective system is not well-known and furthermore is rarely used despite its tremendous clinical potential. At times, it almost seems as if this cultural appendix is buried or even hidden behind hundreds of diagnostic labels. Many of the ideas developed in this chapter (e.g., learning clients' languages, using cultural tools) stem from the *DSM*'s cultural formulation section and from the contributions of the originators of this system (Kleinman, 1988; Lewis-Fernandez & Diaz, 2002).

Consistent with cultural formulation, cultural psychotherapy holds that as clients start to describe a problem, it is also useful to explore their explanation as to why the problem occurred, including when the problem started, how it evolved, and why the client sought help at this particular time (American Psychiatric Association, 1994; Kleinman, 1988; Lewis-Fernandez & Diaz, 2002). These explanations reflect both individual and cultural influences. Although we all develop theories to make sense of our problems, some clients hide these explanations because they fear being stigmatized. We return to the case of Antoine to more fully examine this point.

Antoine was a 35-year-old hardworking married Haitian man experiencing severe panic attacks. It took a month of therapy before he was able to trust me enough to start talking about his Voodoo beliefs and practices, which were essential to understanding his panic attacks. Even then, he would only mention Voodoo very briefly and would quickly remind me that he attended a Catholic church on Sundays. Nevertheless, he believed that everyone has spirits and we all have a special relationship with one spirit that owns our head. This spirit is called the *Iwa*.[2]

Many of Antoine's experiences in the United States had been filled with ridicule and fear. He had been stigmatized and marginalized by people who did not understand the roots of his beliefs. Antoine had learned the hard way that it was better to avoid talking about himself and his background, particularly about his spiritual beliefs, even though these were central to his identity.

Antoine denied being ill and denied having panic attacks, which he attributed instead to the rage of his *Iwa* over his affair with his brother's wife. He said he was being punished by possession for disrespecting his family. Antoine said despite his love for his family and his desire not to disrespect them, he had been unable to end the affair even after multiple attempts. As a result of his self-reported weakness, he feared his *Iwa* would end up killing him. Antoine explained that when his *Iwa* "possessed" him, first he would start feeling short of breath, then his heart would start pounding, and then he would choke and fear that his end had come.

By consulting a *Houngan*,[3] we learned that Antoine was not in danger of dying, as he had feared; however, he would continue to be "tortured" as long as the affair lasted. He was being possessed because he was not listening to a message that was being conveyed to him: He needed to stop the affair. He had ruptured the balance between his family and the spirit world and he now had to restore it. Like Antoine, many Haitians believe that mental illnesses emanate from the supernatural world and Voodoo holds the solution to these problems. It is not unusual for Haitians to use their belief in God or Voodoo gods (*Loa*)[4] to explain their joys and suffering, poverty and wealth, health and illness, and hopes and fears (Bibb & Casimir, 1996). Often, healing only occurs after a good or bad *Loa* or one's *Iwa* is appeased.

During one session, Antoine nervously described how his *Iwa* was about to possess him. He said it started because he was having sexual fantasies about his brother's wife, Jenny, and then the shortness of breath and heart palpitations set in. Nevertheless, the symptoms got no worse and nothing more serious happened. He was not possessed or punished by his *Iwa* (or using my psychological vocabulary, he did not experience a panic attack). Furthermore, as predicted by the *Houngan,* he did not die.

Throughout psychotherapy and consistent with Antoine's beliefs, I referred to his symptoms as *Iwa* related rather than panic related. Even though I saw his symptoms as consistent with those of panic disorder, I used Antoine's cultural vocabulary and understanding. After Antoine realized that he would not die "for his sins," we explored ways to more effectively cope with his *Iwa* (panic). One strategy devised during these sessions was to pray and/or visualize his family as means to debilitate temptation (his sexual desires). He hoped these visualizations would reduce his intense sexual thoughts and desires.

While Antoine acknowledged that he loved having sex with Jenny, he said he also enjoyed her company and conversation. This led to the realization that he might be able to resolve his problem by talking to her. To his surprise, Jenny revealed that she too wanted to end the affair, as it was also making her feel ill. Together, they discussed ways to exorcise their demons. They agreed to avoid being alone, and, when together, they agreed to talk about Jesus or their respective children, particularly if they felt the odor of any bad *Loa.* They also considered visiting a *Houngan* who could perhaps cleanse them of their desires through some specially prepared ointment. This proved unnecessary because they were able to end the affair on their own. Soon afterward, Antoine started to provide financial help to his brother, whose rug business was about to go bankrupt. As he supported his brother, he started to feel more empowered to control his *Iwa* (panic).

In exploring clients' formulations of their symptoms or problems, much can be learned about the way they make sense of the world and themselves. In this process, it is important to identify not only their vulnerabilities but also their strengths. For example, Antoine's love for his family was an important asset for treatment. His desire to do well by his brother was an important element in leading to his recovery from his *Iwa* possessions/panic attacks. Effective treatment plans will address vulnerabilities through strengths. As we will see in the next two sections, clients' formulations of their problems are the foundation for the design of therapeutic interventions that are consistent with their cultural beliefs and experiences.

1.8 Use Indigenous Healing Practices to Address Symptoms

Antoine's case illustrates how an understanding of the cultural formulation led us to integrate indigenous practices (e.g., prayers, *Houngan, ointments*) with standard psychological techniques as means to control his panic attacks. Indigenous practices are strategies developed within each culture to address specific problems. Most cultures have developed different types of healing strategies. For example, many Buddhists use relevant healing ceremonies, such as anointing with lustral waters or yoga meditation; among Latinos, spiritual healing is sought through going to church services, lighting a votive candle, or reciting the rosary; among Native American groups, participation in traditional ceremonies such as sweat lodges is employed; most Islamic groups repetitively recite Allah's name in a ritual called *dhikr,* to bring about a peaceful state of mind; in Japan, Morita therapy teaches the importance of attentional control (Maeda & Nathan, 1999). (For further discussion of the incorporation of traditional healing into treatments, see Gone, 2009, 2010). Similarly, in the United States many nontraditional practices are emerging (e.g., the new age movement, crystals, massages) that should not be disregarded because their techniques have not been tested scientifically. In psychotherapy, it may be useful to explore what clients found useful or not about nontraditional healing strategies so that the useful elements can be included in treatment while eliminating the less useful ones. It is not unusual for clients to have first employed indigenous healing practices before seeking psychotherapy, which they sought only as a last resort.

In Antoine's case, exploring his understandings of his *Iwa* possession/panic attacks may have been crucial for his decision to remain in treatment. As a result of this enhanced understanding, he benefited not only from indigenous healing practices, but from cognitive behavioral strategies as well (there are more examples of such integration in the next section). In therapy, Antoine learned to identify panic attack triggers (e.g., sexual wishes) as well as to monitor his bodily sensations (e.g., increased heart rate, shortness of breath), which allowed him to know when *Iwa* possession/panic attacks were roaming and thus when it was important for him to pray. Had this strategy not worked, I may have, for example, suggested adding breathing exercises into his prayers.

1.9 Use Evidenced-Based Psychotherapies

One of the main goals in the first phase of cultural psychotherapy is to reduce clients' symptoms. To accomplish this, clinicians must use the most effective strategies at their disposal. Research shows that evidenced-based psychotherapies (EBPs) may be some of the most effective strategies to address specific constellations of symptoms or mental health disorders. EBPs are particularly effective if they have been culturally adapted to the clients' cultural group and tailored to their individual characteristics (Huey & Polo, 2008; Smith, Domenech-Rodriguez, & Bernal, 2010).

EBPs are often criticized as manualized cookbooks that need to be rigidly followed to ensure fidelity and efficacy. In actuality, the vast majority of EBPs emphasize the need to adapt these interventions to the characteristics of a given client, including their cultural characteristics. For example, a recent update of EBP guidelines (American Psychological Association, 2006) repeatedly underscored the need to adjust clinical recommendations to the characteristics of clients and their cultural contexts. To highlight this point, I describe some of the fundamental research on the nature and treatment of panic disorder (Barlow, 2002), and then discuss how it was adapted to Antoine's cultural characteristics.

A substantial body of research finds that clients experiencing panic symptoms have catastrophic cognitions that can initiate or exacerbate panic attacks. Catastrophic cognitions, in essence, are beliefs that something bad will happen if they have certain experiences (e.g., if their heart beats too fast, or they cannot breathe or are dizzy). As a result, clients suffering from panic disorders have very sensitive appraisals of bodily sensations (interceptive conditioning), such as heart palpitations or shortness of breath, that are construed as signs of imminent death (i.e., heart attack), loss of control, or going crazy (Clark & Beck, 1988; Ottaviani & Beck, 1987). Three of the main interventions with evidence-based treatments for panic disorder (Barlow, 2002) are described below with notes on how they were adapted to Antoine's cultural characteristics.

First, a central therapeutic aim of most panic disorder treatments is for clients to learn that they can in fact control panic symptoms (Barlow, 2002). To accomplish this goal, they need to understand how the presence of catastrophic cognitions perpetuates the panic cycle. This first goal is often accomplished through the provision of information that teaches them that their panic symptoms are not deadly as they fear. For example, scientific information about the fight-or-flight[5] response to normalize panic responses is standard treatment practice. In Antoine's case, however, I emphasized the information provided by a *Houngan,* as Antoine did not believe my scientific techniques to be useful or my understandings credible.

Second, EBPs for panic disorders aim to teach clients a set of skills to effectively monitor and control symptoms and accurately appraise situations (both internally and externally). Antoine learned to identify when his *Iwa* was going to start punishing him (i.e., as he sensed that he was having shortness of breath, that his heart was pounding faster, or that he had sexual fantasies), and then learned to use prayers or visualizations of his family to control these physical responses. Instead of prayers and family visualizations, most EBPs would have emphasized progressive muscular relaxation, guided imagery, or breathing exercises.

It is also important to note that social cues may have different meanings in different contexts. What is considered important, problematic, catastrophic (triggered for panic symptoms), or even healing in one culture can be construed very differently in another (Hinton & Good, 2009). Cultural beliefs about functional somatic symptoms are an important source of catastrophic cognitions about anxiety symptoms. If anxiety symptoms are interpreted as indicative of the presence of a culturally specific distress syndrome, multiple catastrophic cognitions may result. For example, if a Cambodian considers anxiety symptoms, such as dizziness, as the start of a *khyâl* attack (in which *khyâl* and blood are thought to rush upward in the body to cause various bodily disasters), or a Puerto Rican believes that shakiness is the start of an *ataque de nervios* (in which it is thought that the nerves are in poor shape, which may result in loss of control, asphyxia, and other disasters), multiple catastrophic cognitions may result (Hinton & Good, 2009).

The third and the crux of most EBPs for panic disorder is repeated exposure to the feared internal stimuli and/or agoraphobic situation.[6] Much is accomplished therapeutically once clients know (and particularly after they have experientially known) that they will not die from a panic attack and that they can confront these internal (e.g., sexual fantasies, fast heartbeat) or external situations (e.g., seeing Jenny at a family gathering).

Findings with different ethnic groups (e.g., Lester, Resick, Young-Xu, & Artz, 2010; Markowitz, 2010) suggest that traditional exposure treatment (initially suggested by Barlow, 2002) is not well tolerated by many ethnic minorities, who end up dropping out of treatment. In contrast, a more gradual and mindful approach can be more effective in decreasing panic symptoms. In Antoine's case I did not employ a traditional systematic exposure treatment. Instead, I used many of the basic elements of panic treatment (including exposure) in a manner consistent with Antoine's beliefs. For example, in the session described above (in which he feared he was going to have an *Iwa* possession/panic attack because he had been thinking of Jenny), he learned to tolerate these symptoms. As Antoine understood that he was not going to die, his anticipatory anxiety decreased. In Voodoo, it is through prayer and good acts (supporting his brother's business) that people become strong enough to rid themselves of the influence of bad *Loas*.

Research suggests that one of the most important benefits of EBPs is that they contain certain therapeutic ingredients to ameliorate specific symptoms. For example, exposure to intense emotions in such a way that the client learns to tolerate the affect and use more adaptive ways of reacting has repeatedly been found to be effective in treating panic symptoms (Fairholme, Boisseau, Ellard, Ehrenreich, & Barlow, 2010; Otto, Powers, & Fischmann, 2005; Wilamowska et al., 2010). However, EBPs continue to have important limitations, such as limited empirical validity among minority populations or questionable efficacy with comorbid conditions (Westen, Novotny, & Thompson-Brenner, 2004). Cultural psychotherapy attempts to benefit from the existence of specific therapeutic ingredients to solve some problems but does so by underscoring the need to adapt these interventions to clients' individual characteristics and cultural context.

Many clients of diverse cultural backgrounds do not adhere to standardized treatment recommendations because these are not perceived as culturally valid. For example, some authors (Miranda et al., 2005) have noted that the traditional EBP treatments for panic disorder are heavily aligned with European and North American values of individualism, autonomy, and rational thinking. Such values are often at odds with those of harmony, family, and spirituality that are deeply embedded in Asian, Latino, African, and Arabic cultures. It is clear that in some cases (as in Antoine's) standard EBPs require significant cultural modifications to be accepted, implemented, and therapeutic.

Although I have emphasized similarities between EBPs and indigenous cultural practices, significant differences exist. Antoine believed he had been cured because his *Iwa* no longer needed to punish him for upsetting the balance between his family and the spirit world. EBP researchers would argue that Antoine had learned how to manage his panic symptoms more effectively. Clearly, the healing practices of some cultures may be untranslatable. Even in these situations, however, EBPs can be used to inform and offer alternative therapeutic interventions to deal with specific problems. Similarly, indigenous healing practices can be used to inform and offer alternative ideas to cope with clients' particular issues.

1.10 Encourage Culturally Sensitive Lifestyle Changes

Research has consistently found that certain lifestyles dramatically improve our physical and mental health. If we exercise, socialize, eat appropriately, abstain from drugs (including cigarettes), and avoid abusing alcohol, we will very likely live healthier, longer, and more productive lives. Often, however, when in treatment, we explore the presence of these lifestyles, and we do so according to our own cultural biases. We may ask our clients about how frequently they walk, jog, or go to the gym but may forget to ask them how often they dance salsa or regathon, or practice Tai Chi. If we can step outside of our own cultural box, we may be more effective in assessing and then encouraging healthy behaviors.

Furthermore, it is also important that we understand the barriers that hinder positive lifestyle changes. For example, we may encourage parents to let their children play in public parks as means for them to run and jump (exercise). However, some inner-city parks have become centers for drug dealing and gang recruitment. In these instances, parents would be wise to *not* follow their clinicians' prescriptions. It is therefore important that clinicians take into account clients' environmental contexts as well as individual cultural characteristics before making suggestions for lifestyle changes.

The encouragement of healthy lifestyles is crucial during the first phase of cultural psychotherapy as these can immediately increase clients' sense of well-being. Unfortunately, promoting healthy lifestyles or providing information is not enough. Information by itself is insufficient for behavioral change. Although most people will completely agree with the need to improve their lifestyles (and clients decide what changes they want), few will in fact change them just because they have received all the pertinent information. In fact, most already know the basics of a good lifestyle (e.g., exercise, diet).

Therefore, providing clients with information about improving their lifestyles needs to be followed with an assessment of their motivation to change (Prochaska & Norcross, 2010). The ultimate goal is to encourage action, maintain the change, and then prepare them to prevent relapse into old behaviors. Throughout this process, the cultural context plays an important role not only in encouraging change but also in increasing or decreasing the risk of relapse. For example, a clinician may encourage a client to eat healthier, but if they are of a certain cultural background, for example, Puerto Rican, it may be impossible to convince them to give up their rice and beans (daily staple) for salad (extremely discouraged). An enhanced awareness of these powerful cultural influences is necessary to effectively promote change.

1.11 Learn and Use Clients' Cultural Context

In psychotherapy, the client is often the unit of analysis. However, cultural psychotherapy argues that a focus solely on one client's functioning is insufficient; rather, it is necessary to understand individuals as embedded in their relationships and communities. This seems particularly true for individuals who define themselves in relation to others (individuals high on allocentrism). This is the case with many diverse clients (e.g., Asian or Latino), who describe themselves in relational terms and whose life stories are anchored within a social network (Boyd-Franklin, 2003; La Roche, 1999, 2002; La Roche & Turner, 1997). Similarly, feminist authors (e.g., Jordan, 2010) suggest that the "self-in-relation" is an essential characteristic of our human condition.

To explore this relational understanding, it is useful to inquire about clients' family and social environments through an ethnographic history, family genogram, looking at family photographs, viewing Facebook or Myspace (or other Internet sites), and/or asking about relevant "family stories" or cultural stories as well as exploring community resources and social networks (Kleinman, 1988; Lewis-Fernandez & Diaz, 2002). It is not surprising when questions directly related to clients' individual history are often answered in abrupt short words (particularly during initial visits), while those about family or close friends are often elaborated upon. Relational questions often evoke intense feelings that reveal not only the structure and dynamics of their social networks but also much of their struggles/goals and cultural expectations.

An effective strategy to explore clients' relationships, particularly those of adolescents, is to navigate through their favorite websites (e.g., Myspace, Facebook, favorite games, avatars). This is a unique opportunity for therapists to see clients' family (pictures and videos) and even experience clients' relationships unfold as they read and write e-mails or text each other. Additionally, specific places of significance to the person can also be viewed through Google Earth. For example, if a client was bullied or abused in a specific place, viewing that place on the computer can induce intense emotions. This exposure can provide a unique therapeutic opportunity to teach the client to modulate intense emotions, if they are paired with affect regulation strategies.

Furthermore, the cultural context of many diverse clients is not only different from that of most Whites but often also more complex. Diverse clients may simultaneously live in multiple cultures (e.g., English vs. Spanish worlds). For example, Sam, a Puerto Rican adolescent, may act cool at school, behave tough in the streets, be sweet and protective with his younger sisters, and be devoted in his church. It is important for clinicians to access these different worlds and explore clashes between different contexts and expectations. Often these clashes create much confusion and anxiety. Psychological flexibility is necessary to reconcile these diverse and at times conflictive contexts.

A useful strategy to explore the broader sociocultural picture involves comparing contexts (school vs. home vs. street) and situations in which clients have experienced social injustices with contexts and situations in which they have not. For example, in some instances clients' experiences of discrimination in the United States can be contrasted with their experiences while living in or visiting other countries or other ethnic neighborhoods. Identifying the differential effects of each context promotes an understanding of how symptoms are exacerbated by adverse social conditions. This enhanced awareness can allow clients to gradually place some responsibility for their problems on society rather than shouldering it entirely by themselves. This strategy allows them to recognize a political and socioeconomic dimension to their misfortunes (key to the third phase of cultural psychotherapy).

1.12 Address Cultural and Demographic Differences

The meanings of important cultural characteristics such as race, ethnicity, gender, and religion should also be discussed during the first phases of psychotherapy (see Chapter 4 for a more thorough review). As differences between therapists and clients become more prominent, it becomes more important to discuss them (La Roche & Maxie, 2003). Exploring and addressing cultural differences provides an opportunity to examine the psychotherapeutic relationship as well as a way to examine how the sociocultural context influences the psychotherapeutic process (La Roche & Christopher, 2009; La Roche & Maxie, 2003).

It is extremely important from the onset that clients feel and know they can openly discuss their cultural differences with the clinician. Unfortunately, in our Western culture when we talk about cultural differences with others, it seems we automatically access stereotypes and stigmas and therefore feel we are walking on eggshells. To move away from the stagnating effects of cultural stereotypes, it is often helpful for clinicians to directly address the possible influence of differences upon entering the therapeutic relationship. For example, it may be useful to inquire early in treatment about any concerns, fears, or expectations clients may have because their clinician is from a different race, gender, religion, culture, or sexual orientation. Although most clients may decide to first discuss other issues, the message conveyed with this initial comment is that cultural issues are relevant and that they can be discussed at any point in treatment (see Chapter 4 for a more extensive discussion of this issue).

1.13 Conduct Cultural Assessments and Diagnoses

A cultural assessment is an ongoing and dynamic process that starts when clients and therapist meet (e.g., telephone call) and ends only at termination. Throughout this time, clinicians are always in the process of further understanding clients. These assessments are approximations of clients' realities. Only rarely (if ever) are complete descriptions of clients possible. Efforts to understand them should not end because there is a diagnosis that matches their symptoms. Les Havens (1986), a Harvard psychiatrist, spoke eloquently about clinicians' need to remain "surprised" in therapy and encouraged efforts to continuously view clients in new ways. This inquisitive attitude enriches assessments, diagnoses, and clinical formulations and energizes interventions.

Cultural psychotherapy is consistent with the *DSM–IV* (American Psychiatric Association, 1994) appendix on cultural formulation, which emphasizes the importance of including clients' socioeconomic and cultural contexts in diagnostic assessments. Mental health disorders are culturally patterned; culture gives meanings to symptoms, and if these cultural meanings are not explored, we miss an important part of clients' lives. In contrast, when therapists complement their traditional diagnostic understandings with sociocultural issues, the result is not only a more comprehensive understanding of our clients but also one that is less pathologized (Lewis-Fernandez & Diaz, 2002). These more complex understandings can lead clinicians to develop more culturally competent interventions. For example, if a clinician had not considered Antoine's Haitian cultural background, it is likely that his "*Iwa* possessions" would have been diagnosed as psychotic experiences. He could have been prescribed antipsychotic medications, and he could even have been hospitalized.

The *DSM-IV* (American Psychiatric Association, 1994) is often described as having originated from an atheoretical orientation. However, many (e.g., Barlow, 2009; Hinton & Good, 2009) note that the *DSM* is highly influenced by biological assumptions that are currently dominant within the scientific community (and psychopharmacological companies). A reflection of this biologic influence is that many mental health disorders, such as panic disorder, are described as universal with little variation across cultures. It is not surprising then that during the last decade as this biologic understanding became more prevalent, the percentage of people seeking psychopharmachological treatment increased while the percentage of people seeking psychotherapy decreased (Hinton & Good, 2009).

Even though I suggested psychopharmacological treatment, Antoine did not even entertain this option as it was not within the realm of his cultural and religious beliefs. Instead, he felt that his symptoms were caused by his affair and his *Iwa*'s displeasure with how he was operating in his life. This example illustrates the need to design treatments based on his cultural beliefs. If I had not incorporated his beliefs, it is very likely that Antoine would have also rejected my treatment efforts. To him, the meanings of his symptoms were not located within his brain but between the people and cultural symbols of his community.

If clinicians cannot adapt their formulations and treatments to their clients' understandings of their symptomatology, then it is likely that many will fall through the cracks, be misdiagnosed, or drop out of treatment. For example, most inpatient units have a larger number of ethnic minorities than Whites (Snowden & Cheung, 1993; U.S. Department of Health and Human Services, 2001), which may be partly due to cultural misunderstandings and misdiagnoses.

For example, consider the case of an 8-year-old Cambodian girl, who was brought to the emergency room with a 104° Fahrenheit fever. The physicians discovered many burns on her back and immediately reported the family to the department of social services. The child seemed to have experienced significant abuse—having been purposefully burned—and neglected. (How could the girl's parents have waited so long before bringing her to the hospital?) After a social worker explored the incident, however, she discovered that the family—far from neglecting the child—had in fact been attempting to heal her. They had been trying to cure her through the practice of "coining" or *cao gio* (pronounced phonetically as *cao-gi-O*), which literally means to "scrape fever away." Coining is an alternative form of healing most commonly practiced in Southeast Asia. Coining involves rubbing heated oil on the skin, most commonly the chest, back, or shoulders, and then vigorously rubbing a coin over the area in a linear fashion until a red mark is seen. This is believed to allow a path by which a "bad wind" can be released from the body. This "wind" is believed to be the cause of an illness (Hinton, Pich, Marques, Nickerson, & Pollack, 2010). Advocates use this method to treat a variety of minor ailments including fever, chills, headache, colds, and cough. Given the parents' concern for the well-being of their daughter, the charge of neglect was dropped; but the charge of abuse was not so easy to dismiss. The social worker argued, however, that the parents had done what they thought best according to their cultural beliefs. Consequently, no charges were pressed.

Although this family was fortunate to have a caseworker who was versed in culturally competent strategies as she effectively explored cultural differences, what about the many other families who had not been so fortunate? How many families have been separated or even destroyed because their cultural differences were misconstrued as deficits? How many may have been condemned with criminal charges because their cultural characteristics were misunderstood by the legal system? It is undeniable that diagnoses have powerful legal, psychological, religious (sinful or not), political, and economic effects. Only as we thoroughly incorporate the cultural context into the process of diagnosis will we be able to more accurately and fairly portray and treat our clients' characteristics.

1.14 Enhance Affect Regulation and Psychological Flexibility

An important goal throughout the psychotherapeutic process is enhancement of clients' affect regulation, an effort that extends from the first treatment session to the last. Affect regulation is defined as clients' ability to control their emotions and feelings in different situations. Clients can always learn new and better ways to regulate affects. Rather than dredging up the same strategies they have always used, clients are encouraged to try different psychoeducational strategies, indigenous healing practices, EBPs, and other CBT (cognitive behavioral therapy) skills that gradually increase their ability to regulate their affect. As a result, clients develop a broader repertoire of strategies to increase their psychological flexibility.

Psychological flexibility is defined as the ability to distance oneself from current mindsets and consider other possibilities (Kashdan, 2010). This is a meta-level processing mode that cultural psychotherapy tries to create as a default. If psychological inflexibility is a key cause of psychopathology (Ehrenreich, Fairholme, Buzzella, Ellard, & Barlow, 2007; Hinton, Hofmann, Pollack, & Otto, 2009), then psychological flexibility is integral to psychological health and emotion regulation. It allows clients to create a new adaptive processing mode (Kashdan, 2010; Kok & Fredrickson, 2010).

Psychological flexibility is a crucial skill, particularly for immigrants or clients who are less acculturated and dealing with different and complex contexts. Clients must reconcile multiple cultural views, contexts, and interpretations to approach different problems. Additionally, they have to learn a new social and geographic location, learn to switch languages, and learn to deal with different ideas about proper behavior and social interaction. Affect regulation and psychological flexibility are often intertwined and interconnected. Often, the more affect regulation we have, the more psychological flexibility we develop and vice versa.

While increased psychological flexibility and affect regulation are key, they are frequently not enough. If psychotherapy focuses solely on these strategies, then other social, economic, and cultural issues are missed. Sometimes, the underlying cause (e.g., experiences of discrimination, poverty) that triggered or exacerbated the symptoms remains unchanged. This lack of change makes it more likely that clients relapse. Thus, even though the initial chief complaints may have been attenuated, it may be appropriate to remain in psychotherapy to ensure that clients will not relapse. For those clients who decide to remain in psychotherapy, it may be beneficial to explore their narratives and contexts in a more in-depth manner. This is discussed in the next chapter on Phase II of the three-phased cultural psychotherapeutic model. However, more the rule than the exception is that many clients decide to conclude psychotherapy after their chief complaints are met.

Notes

1. Neuroscience explains that languages may constitute somewhat independent systems in themselves.

2. *Iwa* is a spiritual mass made up of departed family members. Their purpose is to advise, warn, and interact with loved ones still residing in the physical world. If a loved one

chooses to ignore a departed spirit, this is considered a dangerous action. Honoring the spirit of the departed is a deeply felt ritual in the Voodoo religion.

3. *Houngan* is the term for a male priest in the Voodoo religion in Haiti (a female priest is known as a *Mambo*). It is the *Houngan's* role to preserve rituals and songs and maintain the relationship between the spirits and the community as a whole (although some of this is the responsibility of the community as well). The *Houngan* are entrusted with leading the service of all of the spirits of their lineage.

4. The *Loa,* also called the Mysteries and the Invisibles, are a central part of Voodoo. They act as intermediaries between human beings and the creator (*Blondie* or *Bon-Die*—meaning "Good-God"), not unlike saints and angels in Catholicism. Voodoo practitioners do not, however, as Catholics do, simply pray to these intermediaries. The *Loa* represent a great deal more than Catholic icons. Each *Loa* has a unique and developed personality. What they like and do not like is known and honored, and each has distinct rhythms, songs, dances, symbols, and rituals of service associated with it. To avoid persecution for their beliefs, African slaves in Haiti, some Latin American countries, and the southern United States took advantage of the similarity between saints and *Loa* and used the former to represent the latter. Today, many saints have become *Loa* in their own right, which leads to the development of Voodoo syncretic beliefs.

5. In standard treatments for panic disorder, clients are taught about the nature and function of fear and its nervous system substrates. The fear response is presented as a normal and generally protective state that enhances our ability to survive and compete in life. Panic attacks are conceptualized as inappropriate fear reactions arising from spurious but otherwise normal activation of the body's fight-or-flight nervous system. Like other fear reactions, they are portrayed as alarms that stimulate us to take immediate defensive action. Because we normally associate fight-or-flight responses with the presence of danger, panic attacks typically motivate a frantic search for the source of threat. When none is found, affected individuals may look inward and interpret the symptoms as a sign that something is seriously wrong with them (e.g., "I'm dying of a heart attack" or "I'm losing my mind").

6. To change maladaptive anxiety and fear behaviors, clients are taught to engage in graded therapeutic exposure to cues they associate with panic attacks. The exposure component of standard treatments (called interceptive exposure) focuses primarily on internal cues—specifically, frightening bodily sensations. Exposure to external cues (traditional situational exposure) is often not systematically addressed in standard treatments, although as clients begin to apply the techniques they have learned, they are encouraged to gradually reenter situations they have been avoiding.

References

American Psychiatric Association. (1994). *Diagnostic and statistical manual of mental disorders* (4th ed.). Washington, DC: Author.

American Psychological Association. (2006). Evidence-based practice in psychology: APA presidential task force on evidence-based practice. *American Psychologist, 61,* 271–285.

Andres-Hyman, R., Ortiz, J., Añez, L., Paris, M., & Davidson, L. (2006). Culture and clinical practice: Recommendations for working with Puerto Ricans and other Latinas(os) in the United States. *Professional Psychology: Research and Practice, 37,* 694–701.

Barlow, D. (2002). *Anxiety and its disorders: The nature and treatment of anxiety and panic.* New York: Guilford.

Barlow, D. (2009). Foreword. In D. Hinton & B. Good (Eds.), *Culture and panic disorder.* Stanford, CA: Stanford University Press.

Bibb, A., & Casimir, G. (1996). Haitian families. In M. McGoldrick, J. Giordano, & J. K. Pearce (Eds.), *Ethnicity and family therapy* (2nd ed.). New York: Guilford.

Bordin, E. S. (1979). The generalizability of the psychoanalytical concept of the working alliance. *Psychotherapy: Theory, Research, and Practice, 16,* 252–260.

Boyd-Franklin, N. (2003). *Black family in therapy: Understanding the African American experience.* New York: Guilford.

Christopher, M. S., & Skillman, G. D. (2009). Exploring the link between self-construal and distress among African American and Asian American college students. *Journal of College Counseling, 12,* 44–56.

Clark, D. M., & Beck, A. T. (1988). Cognitive approaches. In C. Last & M. Larsen (Eds.), *Handbook of anxiety* (pp. 362–385). New York: Pergamon.

Ehrenreich, J. T., Fairholme, C. P., Buzzella, B. A., Ellard, K. K., & Barlow, D. H. (2007). The role of emotion in psychological therapy. *Clinical Psychology: Science and Practice, 14*(4), 422–428.

Fairholme, C. P., Boisseau, C. L., Ellard, K. K., Ehrenreich, J. T., & Barlow, D. H. (2010). Emotions, emotion regulation, and psychological treatment: A unified perspective. In A. M. King & D. M. Sloan (Eds.), *Emotion regulation and psychopathology: A transdiagnostic approach to etiology and treatment.* New York: Guilford.

Gone, J. P. (2009). A community-based treatment for Native American historical trauma: Prospectus for evidence-based practice. *Journal of Consulting and Clinical Psychology, 77,* 751–761.

Gone, J. P. (2010). Psychotherapy and traditional healing for American Indians: Exploring the prospects for therapeutic integration. *The Counseling Psychologist, 38,* 166–235.

Havens, L. (1986). *Making contact.* Cambridge, MA: Harvard University Press.

Hinton, D. E., & Good, B. (2009). *Culture and panic disorder.* Stanford, CA: Stanford University Press.

Hinton, D. E., Hofmann, S. G., Pollack, M. H., & Otto, M. W. (2009). Mechanisms of efficacy of CBT for Cambodian refugees with PTSD: Improvement in emotion regulation and orthostatic blood pressure response. *CNS Neuroscience and Therapeutics, 15*(3), 255–263.

Hinton, D. E., Pich, V., Marques, L., Nickerson, A., & Pollack, M. H. (2010). Khyâl attacks: A key idiom of distress among traumatized Cambodia refugees. *Culture, Medicine and Psychiatry, 34,* 244–278.

Huey, S., & Polo, A. (2008). Evidence-based psychosocial treatments for ethnic minority youth. *Journal of Clinical Child & Adolescent Psychology, 37,* 263–301.

Jordan, J. V. (2010). *Relational-cultural therapy.* Washington, DC: American Psychological Association.

Kashdan, T. B. (2010). Psychological flexibility as a fundamental aspect of health. *Clinical Psychology Review, 30*(7), 865–878.

Kleinman, A. (1988). *Rethinking psychiatry: From cultural category to personal experience.* New York: Free Press.

Kok, B. E., & Fredrickson, B. L. (2010). Upward spirals of the heart: Autonomic flexibility, as indexed by vagal tone, reciprocally and prospectively predicts positive emotions and social connectedness. *Biological Psychology, 85*(3), 432–436.

La Roche, M. (1999). Culture, transference, and countertransference among Latinos. *Psychotherapy, 36,* 389–397.

La Roche, M. (2002). Psychotherapeutic considerations in treating Latinos. *Harvard Review of Psychiatry, 10,* 115–122.

La Roche, M., & Christopher, M. (2009). Changing paradigms: A cultural perspective of empirical supported treatments and evidenced based practice. *Professional Psychology Research & Practice, 40,* 396–402.

La Roche, M., & Maxie, A. (2003). Ten considerations in addressing cultural differences in psychotherapy. *Professional Psychology: Research and Practice, 34,* 180–186.

La Roche, M., & Turner, C. (1997). Self-orientation and depression levels among Dominicans in the United States. *Hispanic Journal of Behavioral Sciences, 19,* 479–488.

Lester, K., Resick, P. A., Young-Xu, Y., & Artz, C. (2010). Impact of race on early treatment termination and outcomes in posttraumatic stress disorder treatment. *Journal of Consulting and Clinical Psychology, 78*(4), 480–489.

Leung, P. K., & Boehnlein, J. (1996). Vietnamese families. In M. McGoldrick, J. Giordano, & J. K. Pearce (Eds.), *Ethnicity and family therapy* (2nd ed.). New York: Guilford.

Lewis-Fernandez, R., & Diaz, N. (2002). The cultural formulation: A method for assessing cultural factors affecting the clinical encounter. *Psychiatric Quarterly, 73,* 271–295.

Linehan, M. M. (1993). *Cognitive behavioral treatment of borderline personality disorder.* New York: Guilford.

Maeda, F., & Nathan, J. (1999). Understanding taijin kyofusho through its treatment, Morita therapy. *Journal of Psychosomatic Research, 46,* 525–530.

Markowitz, J. C. (2010). IPT and PTSD. *Depression and Anxiety, 27*(10), 879–881.

Maslow, A. (1969). *Towards a psychology of being.* Princeton, NJ: Van Nostrand.

Mella-Mejias, R. (1992). *Ponencias desde la universidad.* Santo Domingo: Publicación de la Universidad Central de la República Dominicana.

Miranda, J., Bernal, G., Lau, A., Kohn, L., Hwang, W. C., & LaFromboise, T. (2005). State of the science on psychosocial interventions for ethnic minorities. *Annual Review of Clinical Psychology, 1,* 113–142.

Ottaviani, R., & Beck, A. T. (1987). Cognitive aspects of panic disorder. *Journal of Anxiety Disorders, 1*(1), 15–28.

Otto, M. W. (2000). Stories and metaphors in therapy. *Cognitive and Behavioral Practice, 7,* 166–172.

Otto, M. W., Powers, M. B., & Fischmann, D. (2005). Emotional exposure in the treatment of substance use disorders: Conceptual model, evidence, and future directions. *Clinical Psychology Review, 25*(6), 824–839.

Prochaska, J. O., & Norcross, J. C. (2010). *Systems of psychotherapy: A transtheoretical analysis* (7th ed.). Pacific Grove, CA: Brooks/Cole.

Roemer, L., & Orsillo, S. M. (2009). *Mindfulness- and acceptance-based behavioral therapies in practice.* New York: Guilford.

Smith, T., Domenech-Rodriguez, M., & Bernal, G. (2010). Culture. *Journal of Clinical Psychology in Session, 67*(2), 166–175.

Snowden, L., & Cheung, F. (1993). Use of inpatient mental health services by members of ethnic minorities groups. *American Psychologist, 45,* 347–355.

Sue, D., Ivey, A., & Pedersen, P. (2007). *Theories of multicultural counseling & therapy.* Mason, OH: Cengage.

Sue, S. (1998). In search of cultural competency in psychotherapy and counseling. *American Psychologist, 53,* 440–448.

Sue, S., Fujino, D. C., Hu, L., Takeuchi, D. T., & Zane, N. W. S. (1991). Community mental health services for ethnic minority groups: A test of the cultural responsiveness hypothesis. *Journal of Consulting and Clinical Psychology, 59*(4), 533–540.

Sue, W. S., & Sue, D. (2008). *Counseling the culturally diverse: Theory and practice* (5th ed.). Hoboken, NJ: John Wiley.

U.S. Department of Health and Human Services. (2001). *Mental health: Culture, race, and ethnicity— A supplement to* Mental Health: A Report of the Surgeon General. Rockville, MD: Author.

Westen, D., Novotny, C. M., & Thompson-Brenner, H. (2004). The empirical status of empirically supported psychotherapies: Assumptions, findings and reporting in controlled clinical trials. *Psychological Bulletin, 130,* 631–663.

White, M. J., & Epston, D. (1990). *Narrative means to therapeutic ends.* New York: Norton.

Wilamowska, Z. A., Thompson-Hollands, J., Fairholme, C. P., Ellard, K. K., Farchione, T. J., & Barlow, D. H. (2010). Conceptual background, development, and preliminary data from the unified protocol for transdiagnostic treatment of emotional disorders. *Depression and Anxiety, 27*(10), 882–890.

Phase II

Understanding Clients' Experiences

> *Listen, Paula. I'm going to tell you a story, so that when you wake up you*
> *will not feel so lost.*
>
> —Isabel Allende, *Paula,* 1995

Sitting by Paula's[1] hospital bed in Madrid and waiting for any sign of improvement as her daughter lies in a coma caused by a rare blood disease, Isabel Allende, in *Paula* 1995), begins to tell the story of her life, offering her own past to her ailing daughter. As she narrates her life, Allende starts to make sense of her experiences and gradually becomes stronger to cope with Paula's imminent death. Allende illustrates a truth about human nature that the second phase of cultural psychotherapy addresses: Our most painful losses are reworked and ameliorated by the understanding and sharing of our stories. In other words, the telling of our stories deepens meaning and promotes healing.

Through this exploration and sharing, the psychotherapeutic relationship becomes the central unit of analysis and an element of therapeutic action. The following equation is used to describe the second phase of cultural psychotherapy:

$$\text{Phase II} = \text{individual factors} \times \text{relational factors}^2 \times \text{contextual factors.}$$

Clearly, the quadratic emphasis on relational factors (relational factors[2]) is not an exact quantity but a means to underscore and represent the importance of the therapeutic relationship during Phase II. This emphasis on the psychotherapeutic relationship is similar to that of many authors who find that the therapeutic relationship makes a significant and consistent contribution to the outcomes for all types of psychological treatments (Norcross, 2010; Wampold, 2010).

An enhanced understanding of the therapeutic relationship allows treatment to focus on explicit (conscious, declarative, or verbal issues) and implicit systems. This means that issues can be both discussed and played out in the here and now of the therapeutic relationship. The possibility to explore issues that are being experienced within the psychotherapeutic relationship allows therapists and clients to understand and treat more complex and automatic responses/affects (implicit systems) than during the first phase. This enhanced understanding of implicit systems is an important characteristic of the second phase of cultural psychotherapy.

In this chapter, I describe four prerequisites that clients have to meet to thoroughly review their lives in cultural psychotherapy. I then review 10 clinical strategies that can further our understanding of clients' experiences. Both the prerequisites and the strategies are illustrated and discussed with the help of the following clinical illustration.

Case Illustration Part 1: Helen

I began treating Helen, a gentle, soft-spoken 54-year-old African American woman who was unemployed and newly separated. She was recently released from an inpatient unit, after an overdose prompted by the discovery that her husband was having an affair with her best friend. After a few months of cognitive behavioral therapy (CBT),[2] Helen's depression had abated and she had become more functional. However, as Helen's symptoms improved, she repeatedly mentioned a need to discuss one of her most painful life experiences—not her ex-husband's affair, but rather the time when she was taken away from her grandparents in South Carolina.

When she was 2 years old, her grandparents had rescued her from her biological mother, who was abusing drugs and neglecting her, often leaving her unattended. Helen reported that after being saved by her grandparents, she lived "a blessed life" for the following six years. However, this happy time was interrupted when her mother came back "clean" and took her away. The separation from her grandparents was traumatic, and adjusting to being one of four children was painful. Helen repeatedly described how she felt "invisible" in her new home, as if she did not exist. During therapy, she explored her feelings of invisibility and the many ways in which these feelings had resurfaced throughout her life, particularly with her ex-husband, with her daughters, and most recently in treatment with her therapist. She often described me, her therapist, as being "unavailable and tired."

PREREQUISITES TO THOROUGHLY REVIEWING CLIENTS' EXPERIENCES

The second phase of cultural psychotherapy often begins when clients' primary symptoms subside and they are ready to describe their lives in detail. Some clients may never reach this phase because they are not ready, do not want to, or drop out before they are able. Fortunately, for Helen, this was not the case. From the onset of treatment, she was eager to talk about the traumatic separation from her grandparents, husband, and significant others. However, it was necessary to wait until certain conditions were met (e.g., she was not suicidal) before the process could begin. The act of narrating one's life is not risk free and often evokes intense emotions that can end up dysregulating clients. Emotional dysregulation entails psychological pain (e.g., enhanced symptoms of anxiety, flashbacks, substance use, or suicidal ideation) that leads some clients to avoid further exploration (e.g., prematurely dropping out of psychotherapy, feelings of numbness, substance use). For these reasons, clinicians must ensure that clients have met the following four prerequisites before they journey into Phase II: (2a) no recent psychological crises, (2b) sufficient levels of emotional regulation, (2c) a safe and trusting psychotherapeutic relationship, and (2d) the ability to confront their therapists. These four conditions are discussed in turn. Each prerequisite is identified with a number after the phase number.

2a. No Recent Psychological Crises

The first condition for clients to safely and thoroughly share their stories in treatment is that they have not suffered any recent psychological crises. This condition is easily assessed by inquiring about their histories of hospitalization, substance abuse, domestic violence, and so forth. Clearly, if clients are presenting with an immediate crisis, it is not appropriate to explore emotionally painful past experiences as this could intensify emotional pain and cause further emotional dysregulation. Instead, it is crucial that treatment focus on ensuring safety (as underscored by Phase I) and stabilization. For example, should Helen have had active suicidal thoughts, it would not have been appropriate to discuss the separation from her grandparents. Instead, it would have been important to develop emergency and/or safety plans.

Moreover, it is necessary to consider not only the primary client but also the impact of others within clients' intimate circles (e.g., spouses, children, parents), as the psychotherapeutic process may also affect them. It is not rare, for example, that spouses become more depressed or anxious as their partners explore past emotional wounds. In some cases, revisiting the past leads clients' spouses to dysregulate (e.g., become violent or depressed). It is crucial that therapists consider the different factors that could affect clients' safety.

2b. Sufficient Levels of Emotional Regulation

Before clients share their stories in a thorough manner, they must have an appropriate level of emotional regulation to cope with the intense affects and thoughts that arise when difficult experiences are retold. Emotional regulation is the ability to modulate intense affects. Although different psychotherapeutic models use different terms (e.g., homeostasis, affect regulation, self-control) to describe similar processes, it can be suggested that for most psychotherapies emotional regulation is a core therapeutic concept (Westen, 1988). Many clients who have attained this goal no longer desire to seek treatment and may appropriately terminate. However, for some clients, such as Helen, it is not enough to gain an improved ability to control symptoms (i.e., reduced depressive symptoms); in such cases, it is also necessary to understand the issues underlying the symptoms. With Helen, decreasing her suicidal ideation would not be enough. She needed to make sense of her life through further exploration or she would be at continued risk for relapse. As in the case of Isabel Allende, the act of identifying and articulating salient and powerful life stories is an important component of achieving emotional strength.

A simple strategy to assess clients' levels of emotional regulation is inquiring about their psychological functioning or symptomatology (e.g., increased nightmares, mood changes, poor appetite) after a session in which they narrated difficult experiences. Frequent check-ins allow therapists to assess whether clients' functioning is deteriorating in relation to their narration and self-exploration. For example, as Helen described her abrupt separation from her grandparents, she experienced intense feelings of loss and grief. I repeatedly monitored changes in her symptomatology, particularly depressive symptoms and suicidal ideation between sessions. I feared that her disclosures could dysregulate her and lead her to relapse and restart experiencing severe depressive symptoms. Although at times she reported being anxious and depressed, she was able to effectively use therapy and CBT skills to control an escalation of her depressive symptoms. A thorough review of clients' experiences can only proceed if clients can control their symptomatology.

It is important to continuously assess emotional regulation as well as to repeatedly teach and rehearse coping and self-regulation strategies (e.g., relaxation, distraction techniques). A significant therapeutic accomplishment comes when clients learn that even after disclosing traumatic/difficult experiences and being dysregulated by this narration, they realize that they can in fact return to a self-regulated state (Herman, 1992). As clients learn to self-regulate and feel increased capacity to move back and forth between affectively charged and relaxed states, they are often energized to explore additional experiences.

2c. A Safe and Trusting Psychotherapeutic Relationship

For clients to share their life stories, memories, and dreams, treatment must be experienced in a safe environment where they can explore core issues in the presence of an intimate other (Winnicott, 1965). For this feeling of safety to emerge, ruptures between therapist and client must be repaired. Ruptures occur frequently—often quietly and inadvertently. Clients develop trust in their therapists as they are able to negotiate these misunderstandings or mistakes. Furthermore, as a result of these repeated reparations, clients believe and experience their therapists as having their best interests in mind (and therapists should in fact always have their clients' best interest in mind!).

Two assumptions are implicit in cultural psychotherapy's understanding of "ruptures/repairs." First, ruptures, impasses, strains, or empathic failures are unavoidable. Inevitably, therapists will misunderstand or convey meanings that do not match those of their clients. This is particularly true because cultural psychotherapy emphasizes the need to explore differences. Second, in the process of repairing such ruptures, if it is done correctly, significant growth can result. Clients and therapists can learn to clarify misunderstandings (repair) in ways that not only acknowledge differences, but also view them as assets. Often, it is not what is said but the way it is said that has a therapeutic effect. The way a rupture is repaired is often more important than the rupture itself. Furthermore, as connections are repaired, there is an opportunity to develop new or more complex meanings.[3] A broader and more complex array of meanings allows clients to have more flexibility in responding to their relationships and contexts.

If therapy occurs in a group setting, it is necessary that the group be experienced as a safe and cohesive environment and that members achieve an enhanced sense of belonging. Similarly, it is also important that the therapist feels safe, connected, and engaged with the client and is able (has sufficient awareness, skill, and cultural knowledge) to address issues in a culturally competent manner (Sue & Sue, 2008).

2d. Ability to Confront Their Therapists

Related to the rupture/repair process is the ability of clients to confront their therapists. Often during the first phase of cultural psychotherapy, therapists provide clients with psycho-educational information (e.g., how losses can increase depressive symptoms), clinical advice (e.g., sleep hygiene strategies), or interpretations that are often gratefully taken in by clients. However, as therapy proceeds, clients realize that this information is colored by their therapists' particular perspective. As clients recognize their therapists' singular perspective, they are able to question and enrich it. At times, clients may confront therapists about differences in perspective. Cultural psychotherapy fosters clients' ability to question their therapists. As clients are increasingly able to question therapists' comments and views, they rehearse skills that may move them closer to challenging society's power arrangements (see Chapter 3). Cultural psychotherapy emphasizes the need to explore and, when necessary, challenge different cultural perspectives—including and often starting with those of therapists. Nevertheless, this does mean that all clients challenge their therapists, but that they have developed at this phase the ability to question therapists' perspectives and construct their own views.

During the second phase, it is common for clients to construe therapists as part of the establishment and become critical of their educational, socioeconomic, and political privileges (La Roche, 1999). These responses can be particularly difficult with some ethnic minorities and may temporarily transform the therapeutic relationship from a positive to an adversarial relationship (see Chapter 4). This response is not solely a reflection of clients' relational history, but also of their experiences of injustice (e.g., poverty, discrimination; La Roche, 1999). Such feelings should be explored and understood. Unfortunately, therapists may respond negatively to these confrontations and become defensive. Furthermore, therapists may go as far as invalidating clients' feelings. Clinicians treating individuals of different cultural backgrounds need to be sensitive to their own feelings, cognitions, and cultural biases to prevent them from being expressed (La Roche, 1999; La Roche & Maxie, 2003). Underlying this statement is the assumption that we all have cultural biases that need to be acknowledged and explored (Sue & Sue, 2008).

CLINICAL RECOMMENDATIONS FOR THE SECOND PHASE

After clients meet the four prerequisites discussed above, they can begin to explore their life experiences in more depth. What follows are 10 clinical strategies that can be used for this exploration. These strategies are merely suggestions, as none of them by themselves is essential; rather, some will be more applicable to one client than to another. Furthermore, each of these recommendations needs to be adapted to the unique characteristics of each client, therapist, and context. Finally, these 10 clinical recommendations complement each other and are not presented in order of importance.

2.1   Understand the therapeutic relationship as more than the sum of the characteristics of clients and therapists.

2.2   Start by exploring clients' lives, not only their problems.

2.3   Examine the complex and changing nature of meanings.

2.4   Address the cultural influences of explicit and implicit systems.

2.5   Continue to develop a culturally sensitive therapeutic relationship.

2.6   Explore and expand meanings.

2.7   Allow the therapeutic relationship to become emotionally charged.

2.8   Understand that ruptures are inevitable.

2.9   Make contact.

2.10   Use clients' renewed sense of vitality.

2.1 Understand the Therapeutic Relationship as More Than the Sum of the Characteristics of Clients and Therapists

The psychotherapeutic relationship is more than the sum of its parts—more than clients and therapists put together. Once the client and therapist experience treatment as a relationship, they are in the second phase of cultural psychotherapy. As two people repeatedly interact, they form a relationship that is not explicable by an understanding of either participant in isolation. This idea can be illustrated with the following expression:

Therapeutic relationship > clients' characteristics + therapists' characteristics.

What this clinical recommendation emphasizes is the need to understand the therapeutic process through a relational framework. In contrast to the first phase in which the client is the basic unit of analysis, during the second phase the psychotherapeutic relationship becomes the central unit of analysis. No longer can any of the therapeutic processes, sentences, or gestures be understood solely as an emanation of clients' characteristics or history; a relational perspective is needed to understand each and all of these. Although the therapist and client "relate" from the onset of treatment, the initial relationship is qualitatively different from the one that is established after many encounters. As they gather information from each other, the client and therapist learn to respond in an increasingly complex manner. Through multiple and in-depth interactions, they negotiate the direction of treatment and learn each other's idiosyncratic styles (including explicit and implicit systems). Furthermore, as therapy progresses, each member of the therapeutic relationship is increasingly able to recognize the moves or intentions of the other person. Gradually, each word or gesture accrues a meaning that is only understandable because of its relational history.

As clients share their experiences, an important transformation occurs when they start to feel the influence of the therapeutic relationship (e.g., clients imagine what they will share in therapy and how the therapist will respond). This stands in contrast to the first phase, in which what they discuss in therapy mostly relate to events outside the four walls of the session. As the therapeutic relationship progresses, it becomes a mutual regulation process involving both client and therapist. This new mutual regulatory process is distinct from that of either the client or the therapist. As therapist and client learn to influence each other, they negotiate ways to communicate, deal with ruptures, and develop strategies to repair them. The defining characteristic of this mutual regulation process is its bidirectional nature. In addition, these exchanges occur at multiple levels (e.g., explicit and implicit, verbal and nonverbal). Some studies (Beebe & Lachman, 2002) trace the development of these mutual regulation processes to the mother-infant relationship. This mutual regulation process underscores the need to understand the therapeutic process as occurring within a relationship and not solely within the individual seeking treatment.

Although it is impossible to draw a clear line demarcating when the first phase ends and the second phase starts, there is a qualitative difference that emerges from the therapeutic relationship. Whereas in the first phase the focus is mostly on the client's symptoms, goals, or needs, in the second phase the therapeutic relationship becomes more complex, reciprocal, and emotionally charged. This is what allows for the discussion of a higher-risk exploration of the client's life and relationships.

2.2 Start by Exploring Clients' Lives, Not Only Their Problems

Cultural psychotherapy aims to obtain a more complete picture of clients' lives as well as their problems. Clients are encouraged to discuss not only their symptoms (e.g., depression or suicidal ideation) and life situations that led to those symptoms, but also the goals and experiences that pre-dated their problems (e.g., Helen's life with her grandparents, her grandchildren, her previous job). This broader understanding allows clients and their therapists to contextualize their problems. Ultimately, this exploration may lead them to identify additional resources to cope with the challenges they face.

Helen, for example, came to therapy after a hospitalization due in part to her distress over how her husband left her for her best friend. But discussion of that trauma was interspersed with important conversations about her daughters and granddaughters, her dreams of becoming an attorney, sunny days in South Carolina, and her love for animals. Often, clients are better prepared to examine their psychological pain after describing some positive aspect of their lives. After Helen described her "blessed life" in South Carolina, she talked about how her life "disappeared" when she was betrayed by her husband and best friend. After that she felt "invisible" and wanted to die. She had no energy to do anything and stayed in bed all day. After a few weeks of absences, she was fired from work. She had enjoyed her job, where she had many close friends, for more than a decade. Furthermore, during this time one of her daughters stopped talking to her (she blamed Helen for her father's abandonment). To further aggravate the situation, her youngest (and unmarried) daughter became pregnant.

2.3 Examine the Complex and Changing Nature of Meanings

Meanings are the way we construe and make sense of our experiences (Bruner, 2002). Narrating life stories entails an exploration of the way clients construct meanings in the world. Although meanings are explored from the onset of psychotherapy, they are explored in even more depth during the second phase of cultural psychotherapy. Meanings are the result of both implicit and explicit systems[4] and contain both verbal and nonverbal elements.

One of the main goals of the second phase of cultural psychotherapy is to understand implicit systems. It is difficult to do so in the first phase because symptom stabilization comes first. Also, the therapeutic relationship is only beginning to grow and often there is not enough reliable information. Implicit systems are better understood once therapists and clients get to know each other, particularly as some interactions repeatedly and almost automatically unfold within the psychotherapeutic relationship. In contrast, during the first phase much of what is processed is explicit. Clients describe events, relationships, and injustices that have clear, declarative, and semantic content. Although an enhanced understanding of clients' implicit systems becomes increasingly therapeutic as the psychotherapeutic exploration expands, the importance of explicit systems does not diminish during the second or third phases of cultural psychotherapy. Furthermore, explicit and implicit systems are interwoven and have a synergistic therapeutic effect. As clients' implicit systems are better understood, similarly explicit systems are also better understood.

To explore clients' implicit systems, it is useful to examine how they respond to significant life events. As clients describe important experiences in their lives, it is possible to identify common themes, relational patterns, and expectations about others as well as assumptions about the context in which they live (e.g., feelings of invisibility, people who are not responsive to their needs). To promote this exploration, it is often helpful to involve not only their own understandings (including thoughts and feelings), but also the responses of their significant others. Implicit systems often constrain people's experience by filtering information in a narrow manner and by endlessly repeating similar relational patterns (Cortina & Liotti, 2007). For example, Helen had come to believe that she could not have an impact on people, as she was not able to do so with her mother and husband.

Another way to explore clients' implicit systems is to inquire about relevant somatic sensations. Often implicit memories are not verbal or symbolic, but are registered and expressed through bodily sensations. The lack of a vocabulary for these affects makes it challenging to express them in words.

Also, it is useful to explore events occurring in the here and now of the therapeutic relationship. Some authors (e.g., Westen & Gabbard, 2002a, 2002b) suggest that interactions occurring after the therapeutic relationship has deepened (when it is characterized by greater intimacy or an emotional bond between the therapist and client) are more reflective of clients' implicit systems than the ones occurring in the first phase. The feelings evoked by the therapeutic relationship during the second phase are often more intense than those in the first phase. Thus, it is challenging to explore implicit systems during the first phase of treatment. Furthermore, implicit systems are often played out in psychotherapy rather than talked about. I will elucidate these ideas with more of our case illustration.

Case Illustration Part 2: Helen

After a few months of treatment, Helen complained that I seemed tired and did not appear to be paying attention to her, which made her feel invisible. I asked her to describe what she was feeling and she said, *"You look tired,"* and immediately added, *"When you look tired, it makes me feel as if you are not here with me."*

This interaction had occurred on a number of previous occasions, and in past sessions we had agreed that I would acknowledge whether I was feeling tired or not. This time, I was not tired. As she further described her feeling that I was not paying attention to her, she reported having the following memory.

"I am about 9 years of age and I am at my mother's apartment. It is loud," she said.

"What are you hearing?"[5] I asked.

"I hear my mother screaming at Joan [a 6-year-old sister]. *She is crying. I hear Mickey* [a 5-year-old brother] *and Tommy* [who is 4 years old] *running and jumping all over the place. I think they are in trouble. I think they broke something. The heater is on, it is making some crackling noises . . . it is still so cold. I am so damn cold. I am freezing cold. I do not like being cold . . . It is so cold."*

"It is so cold," I repeated empathically.

"I also see the apartment," continued Helen. *"It is very small, and it is messy. There is crap all over the floor, the dishes are not clean, it is a mess, and it smells. Somebody has just puked, maybe Mickey, he is always sick and I know my mother is expecting me to clean the mess, but I don't want to, I really don't want to, I am so cold, I just want to hide somewhere so that she will not see me . . ."*

"It is so cold," I repeated.

Her eyes welled up and she said, *"I just wanted to hide and cry. I did not want to clean up someone else's mess."* In tears, Helen said, *"I did not want to clean anymore, all I wanted was to be with my grandparents. I wanted to hug my Grandma and Grandpa, just a hug. I was lonely and trapped in that horrible, smelly hole, like now, I am trapped and alone, but in a different hole. My fucking husband left me for that bitch . . . he is now fucking her and not me."*

Helen had begged her mother to return her to her grandparents just as she had begged her husband to come back. Both had said no. She had no power. She was invisible. She had asked her mother again and again until she screamed at her, *"Ungrateful child! Don't you love your Mama?"*

Helen often felt like an ungrateful child that just wanted to cry and die. Nobody cared about her. Why should she keep trying? She felt invisible and hopeless. Would it not be easier to die? Helen did not want to continue to live trapped, alone, and invisible in a smelly and noisy apartment. Her apartment was now as "smelly and messy" as her mother's had been.

These memories in turn triggered new memories of invisibility and not being heard, which included some instances in therapy. Many of these memories could be related to her first years with her mother. In therapy, Helen learned that she did not expect people to hear her. As a result of this expectation, she would sometimes not even try to talk. She would just stay silent as if hiding behind a noisy radiator.

The process of understanding implicit systems is often painstakingly slow and resembles putting together a complex puzzle of countless affects, bodily sensations, experiences, narratives, memories, and cognitions. However, unlike a puzzle, the process of understanding implicit systems does not end.

2.4 Address the Cultural Influences of Explicit and Implicit Systems

Meanings are inseparable from the sociocultural context in which they are created (Bruner, 2002; Shweder, 1995). Our meanings are anchored in multicultural values that provide us with a range of themes, symbols (verbal and nonverbal), affects (implicit and explicit), and values (e.g., individualism, heterosexuality, time orientation) from which we construct our lives. Some meanings or cultural variables are more prominent than others in certain groups and times. Thus, contexts reinforce explicit and implicit messages. Tronick and Beeghly (2011) describe how the parenting practices of specific cultural groups affect infant development. Culture-specific parenting practices can reinforce certain infant relational patterns (e.g., implicit systems) and cultural values and variables (e.g., both implicit and explicit systems) that are consistent with a certain culture.

In any given culture, some meanings are dominant, while others are marginalized. Cultural psychotherapy asserts that it is crucial to examine the cultural nature of our meanings because society has reinforced—often implicitly—many of our goals and values. Additionally, whatever does not match dominant sociocultural values is considered "less than" and is often overlooked. For example, in American culture we are expected to work hard, make money, and look attractive, while so-called "alternative" lifestyles (gay/lesbian, single, living in communion with nature) are discouraged and seen as second class.

Many clients who do not endorse dominant values are more hesitant to share their core beliefs (e.g., Antoine in the first chapter not wanting to discuss his beliefs about Voodoo) than clients who share dominant values. On the one hand, they may desperately want to share their beliefs—as with any important experience—but on the other, they fear they will reveal too much. They fear that therapists may end up thinking less of them or not understand them. This ambivalence is not solely a result of clients' resistance, but also of past cultural experiences (e.g., racism, cultural marginalization).

Although the powerful impact of social situations, systems, and culture has been thoroughly and repeatedly documented (e.g., Richard, Bond, & Stokes-Zoota, 2003), this does not mean that culture is destiny. In fact, we can author and edit our understandings (White & Epston, 1990). To accomplish this, however, we must first recognize the powerful influence of systems, culture, and situations (Zimbardo, 2008) in shaping our explicit and implicit systems. Second, we need to explore and question these understandings. Finally, we need to consider and decide whether we will accept, modify/enrich and/or develop alternative meanings (see Chapter 3 for a more extensive explanation of this process).

2.5 Continue to Develop a Culturally Sensitive Therapeutic Relationship

The establishment of a culturally sensitive therapeutic relationship is an ongoing process that does not stop because a working alliance has been formed between the client and therapist. The therapeutic relationship during the second phase has many culturally sensitive characteristics. I underscore two: (1) *the dialectic therapeutic stance,* and (2) *therapists' opportunity to more frequently share their experiences.* I underscore these two characteristics not because they are exhaustive or unique to the therapeutic relationship, but because they are helpful to differentiate the first phase from the second. There are additional characteristics (e.g., positive regard, feedback) that are equally psychotherapeutic but not unique from the other phases.

The Dialectic Therapeutic Stance

The therapeutic process is enriched when therapists show an active interest in and acceptance of clients' experiences (Rogers, 1961; Stolorow & Atwood, 2002) and areas of growth (Linehan, 1993). This dialectic stance aims to both understand and extend clients' experience or action (Linehan, 1993; Roemer & Orsillo, 2009). It cannot be emphasized too strongly that therapists' acceptance of clients' sense of reality (e.g., individual, relational, and contextual) or what Marsha Linehan (1993) called "radical acceptance" is of inestimable importance in establishing the therapeutic alliance and creating a climate that fosters growth. Threats to clients' construction of reality can lead to disruptions in the psychotherapeutic process (Stolorow & Atwood, 2002; Linehan, 1993). However, the second phase tilts slightly toward more challenge and in pointing out areas of potential growth than the first phase, which focuses more on support.

Although empathy and acceptance are crucial throughout all phases of the psychotherapeutic process, they are often not enough to facilitate change. Rather, therapists also need to challenge clients and encourage them to explore painful issues that are otherwise avoided (Roemer & Orsillo, 2009). Clinicians must be continuously alert to clients' cues of disavowed affect that are not fully admitted into their subjective world (e.g., anger, sadness).

A central goal in the second phase of cultural psychotherapy is the exploration of painful experiences in the context of a supportive therapeutic relationship. During the second phase, the psychotherapeutic relationship becomes both the thermometer that indicates the tolerated levels of exploration, challenge, or support (e.g., examining in detail painful memories) and the thermostat that helps to modulate affects. The balance between support/exploration is anchored within the relationship; both client and therapist continuously assess whether the affects being addressed are manageable. Furthermore, through the therapeutic relationship clients learn to regulate themselves. As clients describe painful experiences, they use the therapeutic relationship to work out their issues. The empathy, feedback, and positive regard (to name a few) provided within the therapeutic relationship are crucial therapeutic ingredients (Norcross, 2010) that allow clients to regulate their affects. Furthermore, the way therapeutic dyads negotiate their relationship (e.g., ruptures/reparations strategies, affect regulation) is also an important therapeutic ingredient that clients can generalize to other relationships (Norcross, 2010; Tronick & Beeghly, 2011).

Therapists' Opportunity to More Frequently Share Their Experiences

During the second phase of cultural psychotherapy, therapists can disclose their feelings/thoughts about the therapeutic relationship more frequently than during the first phase. These comments should be grounded in the therapists' own experience; they need to be genuine. In contrast, during the first phase some levels of neutrality and anonymity are justified for several reasons. First, therapists are mainly focused on addressing clients' chief complaints (e.g., job-related conflict, depressive symptoms, marital problems). The personality or issues of the therapist are not useful in addressing the clients' specific goals, particularly if it is short-term therapy. Also, during the first phase clients and therapists have yet to create an emotional bond, while in the second phase the emotional connection is almost a condition for it to be successful. During the second phase, neutrality can be interpreted as distance and/or coldness. Finally, in the era of "Google," anonymity is hard enough to maintain outside of the gradual and progressive offering of appropriate personal information. On one occasion, for example, a client greeted me after a week away with the following question: "How did your presentation at the APA go?" He had Googled me and found out that I had an important presentation at an American Psychological Association conference.

Therapist self-disclosure is controversial within the field (Linehan, 1993; Roemer & Orsillo, 2009), for it is crucial that clients' issues and cultural assumptions remain at the forefront of therapy. Cultural psychotherapy suggests that some limited disclosures are most useful in the second phase for some of the reasons discussed above. For example, I have at times decided to share the fact that I too have lost a significant loved one as means to reduce the distance with a client who feels that her pain is insurmountable or unreachable. Disclosing personal information and being genuine entail significant risks. For example, enhanced therapeutic transparency could result in the therapist's needs dominating a session. My client could want to take care of me or make sure I had fully dealt with the grief related to my father's death. My rule of thumb is that I only disclose meaningful personal information if I think it is therapeutically beneficial for a client and I have myself dealt with it. Often, I check with peers to ensure that this is the case.

One strategy to avoid some of the therapeutic challenges mentioned above is for clinicians to frame their experiences using language that conveys that their perspective is just one of many, rather than an absolute or objective truth. Comments such as "What occurs to me . . ." or "I am thinking that . . ." are particularly reflective of this point.

Furthermore, some therapists—unaware of their own cultural standards—may impose their own metrics on their clients. This cultural insensitivity, despite all good intentions, may hinder the therapeutic process. For example, many Latinos do not look into people's eyes as a sign of *respeto* (deference toward authority; Marin & VanOss-Marin, 1991). At times, this cultural difference may be misconstrued as a deficit, a sign of low self-esteem, or shyness (La Roche & Shriberg, 2003).

As clients get to know their therapists, this knowledge elicits certain feelings, fantasies, or memories while it inhibits others (Gabbard, 1996). Given the personality and activities of therapists, some narratives are evoked frequently (e.g., talking about cultural differences), while others are avoided (e.g., anger or sexual issues). Clearly, it is imperative that therapists always explore not only their clients' blind spots but also their own.

As therapists share their experiences about the therapeutic relationship, clients may more clearly understand and experience the bidirectional nature of the psychotherapeutic relationship. This enhanced understanding may in turn help them realize that they have an impact not only on the therapist but also on others. To accomplish this goal, it is often useful to explain how clients have influenced us, by making comments such as "From you I have learned . . ." or "Since you explained . . ." This enhanced awareness can help clients make the transition into the third phase of cultural psychotherapy. Once clients learn that they can influence their therapists, they realize they can also have an effect on others and ultimately on their cultural contexts.

2.6 Explore and Expand Meanings

Cultural therapists continuously attempt to explore and extend clients' meanings. The goal is to help them expand their stories, to see that there is more to them than what they had assumed, that there are potentials not yet realized and feelings not given their fair due (Wachtel, 2008). It is not that clients' perceptions are necessarily "wrong"; it is just that meanings could be further understood.

A central goal of the second phase of cultural psychotherapy is for clients (and therapists) to move beyond the idea that we must have a single unified narrative. In a time in which myriad worldviews, values, and perspectives are emerging, it is useful to explore alternative frameworks. To accomplish this goal, a psychotherapist uses language that frames comments as "and/or" rather than "either/or" (Wachtel, 2008). Additionally, the therapist can ask the client to imagine how people from different groups, times, or history would have handled similar experiences. This may help clients understand that many alternative and even conflicting worldviews coexist in our society, and these are not necessarily mutually exclusive. Therapists use tentative language (e.g., I think that . . .) so clients understand that there is no absolute psychological truth, but rather multiple approximations of it. Furthermore, clients need to know that what therapists say can be questioned because it is a result of their particular experience.

It must be emphasized that the setting fostered in cultural psychotherapy needs to be experienced as safe enough to contain multiple and separate meanings. The coexistence of multiple and conflicting understandings is anxiety provoking in itself. Also, some meanings are emotionally loaded (e.g., homicidal desires) and/or politically incorrect (e.g., racism, homophobia). Exploring these ideas/feelings can increase clients' levels of anxiety.

The development of new or more complex meanings is an important therapeutic goal throughout all phases in cultural psychotherapy as it enhances psychological flexibility. When clients develop more complex meanings, they are able to decide how to respond to their relationships/environments rather than repeating automatic responses/cognitions/affects (implicit systems). In Helen's case, the assumption that "nobody will listen to me, so why should I even talk" needed to be questioned. Once she understood that this belief was highly influenced by her past experiences of abandonments, she could be more flexible in creating alternative meanings.

Many of these meanings are learned early on—during the preverbal and presymbolic stages of infant development—and remain unarticulated within implicit systems. Much of the psychotherapeutic process entails an enhanced understanding of these implicit systems. Cultural psychotherapy aims to make explicit what is implicit. The psychotherapeutic goal of explicating implicit systems is not the same as traditional psychodynamic authors' goal of making the unconscious conscious. The difference is that implicit systems are not necessarily a result of repression and consequently implicit systems are not made conscious by lifting repression.

2.7 Allow the Therapeutic Relationship to Become Emotionally Charged

As the therapeutic relationship evolves, the affective bond between therapist and client intensifies. This can cause the therapeutic relationship to become intensely emotional, highly charged, and deeply personal for both participants. During the second phase, the therapeutic process is expected to be bidirectional. Clients' responses are increasingly enriched by the information that unfolds within the therapeutic relationship. Therapists' emotions, reactions, and understandings become an integral part of the psychotherapeutic process. These reactions are often more honest and less politically correct, which may further fuel the intensity of a session. Often during this phase, clients may question or confront their therapists. For example, I had encouraged Helen to question me whenever she felt I was not listening to her or seemed tired. Although initially she did so very timidly, she was gradually able to do so more frequently and assertively.

Safran and Muran (2000) talk about the need to explain to clients why it is useful to monitor their feelings with their therapists. Consistent with these ideas, therapists in the second phase encourage clients to thoroughly monitor and report on their feelings and thoughts as they interact with others and with the therapist. This relational monitoring helps clients identify relational patterns and their underlying implicit systems.

Given the heightened emotions that characterize the second phase, it is crucial to pay ever more careful attention to the boundaries of the therapeutic relationship. Secure boundaries create a safe environment in which the psychotherapeutic process can grow. In contrast, a psychotherapeutic relationship without clear boundaries will crumble. Furthermore, therapists need to constantly formulate and think about the goals and direction of psychotherapy, assuring that the goals of the client are paramount.

As therapists contribute to the exchanges occurring within the therapeutic relationship, they are also inevitably pulled in and influenced by these interactions. For both therapists and clients, this constitutes a unique opportunity to learn as they are immersed in each other's emotional worlds. However, self-awareness (including an understanding of cultural biases) and/or supervision are particularly important at this time, as therapists can easily get caught up in this rapid and increasingly intense back-and-forth. During this phase, the feeling and even the language of therapy can change from "I," "me," or "you" to "we," "us," and "our." One of the most powerful experiences shared by therapists and clients in this period is the feeling that "we" are together, journeying into a world of alternatively rich and dreaded possibilities.

2.8 Understand That Ruptures Are Inevitable

As the psychotherapeutic process evolves, it is inevitable that ruptures in the psychotherapeutic relationship occur. Although from the onset of the relationship there are minor ruptures and repairs, sooner or later therapists fail to meet their clients' *major* needs or expectations, and/or re-create their primordial fears (Kohut, 1984; Safran & Muran, 2000; Stolorow & Atwood, 2002).

Although ruptures occur in all types of therapies, they are perhaps more likely in cultural psychotherapy because it emphasizes differences (e.g., ethnicity, socioeconomic status, or sexual orientation). In emphasizing differences, cultural psychotherapy runs the risk of creating misattunements that are exacerbated further by the emotional intensity of the second phase. In contrast to this emphasis on differences, most psychotherapists neglect to address cultural differences at all (Maxie, Arnold, & Stephenson, 2006).

Ruptures can destabilize the therapeutic relationship and modify the normal state of mutual regulation. Without ruptures, paradoxically, therapeutic growth is reduced. Furthermore, it is important to underscore that ruptures are not necessarily impasses. Instead, if there is a solid therapeutic relationship, they are opportunities for growth and an efficient way for clients to develop new or more complex explicit systems. Although exploration of cultural differences opens the door for empathic failures, it can also be a gateway for therapeutic progress because differences can enrich and energize the psychotherapeutic process. In contrast, a focus on commonalities can lead to a stagnant understanding of reality. Therapeutic dyads based on similarities assume that some questions are irrelevant (e.g., we are both Irish Catholic, so we do not need to talk about race or religion). The psychotherapeutic process may lose potency if cultural differences are ignored.

In this book I use the term *impasse* to refer to an accumulation of multiple ruptures in which clients do not feel sufficiently supported or understood and in which psychological exploration has come to a halt. Impasses are often exacerbated by frequent, prolonged, and unrecognized ruptures in which therapists consistently misunderstand clients' emotional needs (Stolorow & Atwood, 2002). Impasses are often described as a single event, but in reality they are ongoing chains of exchanges. Furthermore, impasses are not necessarily high-intensity episodes—as in the clinical example in this chapter. Although the causes of impasses are varied (see Figure 2.1), in this book I underscore the cultural component.[6] Ruptures between therapists and clients are often amplified by erroneously interpreting cultural differences as deficits. Consequently, the progress of therapy partly depends on therapists' awareness of their own cultural beliefs and biases (Sue & Sue, 2008). A co-investigation of these differences can transform the therapeutic stalemate into a more complex and culturally sensitive dialogue.

To best illustrate some of cultural psychotherapy's components (6, 7, 8, and 9), let us return to the case of Helen.

Case Illustration Part 3: Helen

After a few months in psychotherapy, Helen reported being angry with me because I seemed indifferent to her pain. She said, *"You know sometimes when you seem tired, like right now, you don't seem to be listening to me. It's almost as if I weren't here, like I don't exist. . . . You may nod but you just don't seem to get what I am really saying. It is almost as if I am back with my mother. . . . Do you know what I mean?"*

I did not feel it was necessary to explain again (I had already done so at the beginning of the session) that I was tired, so in an attempt to be empathic I stated, *"Sometimes it seems as if you fear that I am not listening to you and that reminds you of when you lived with your mother."*

(Continued)

(Continued)

Helen stared at me intently and went on to say, *"It is not only that. We have already talked much about my mother. . . . This is about you. Sometimes* [looking at me], *I wonder if you get what I am saying. No, no, you don't seem to get it. Do you even see what I am now trying to say to you?"*

"It seems like you are wondering if I can understand you," I said.

"It is more than that, no, I don't think you get what I am saying. . . . I don't know if you see me."

"It seems like you are wondering if I can really see you," I said, attempting to be empathic.

"Here we go again! Have you been listening to what I just said to you!," Helen exclaimed, as I automatically nodded. [Clearly, we clinicians also have our own implicit systems!] *"You don't really care about me!"* exclaimed Helen.

"I don't really care about you?" I asked gently.

"Yes!" Helen said, *"You are not taking me seriously. I have been questioning you during the last few sessions and what you say is so . . .* [in a pronounced sarcastic tone] *ever so gently not completely true. . . . Enough BS! You are so damn nice that it is pissing me off! Damn, there, I am so glad to finally say that! Damn, you are so damn nice that it is driving me crazy! Something else is going on! Just spit it out!"*

"I am so sorry if you think I am too nice," I automatically started saying but caught myself uttering these words and noticed how Helen frowned in profound disbelief. I was repeating the same thing!

She responded with her angriest look after which we both erupted into laughter. As we laughed, I felt connected to her. I then realized that I had been avoiding this connection and emotional exchange. Although the content of my comments was an accurate reflection of her responses, these did not contain my signature, my identity. I was not completely there.

Having made contact, Helen then pressed further and asked, *"What's going on?"*

2.9 Make Contact

Although I could have elected to say something technical such as "What do you think is going on?" I decided to explore and share my feelings about the therapeutic relationship. When clients and therapists "make contact" in a manner that includes their thoughts, feelings, and behaviors (Boston Change Process Study Group [BCPSG], 2010; Lyons-Ruth & Members of the Change Process Study Group, 1998), it is an opportunity to transform explicit and implicit systems. These "moments of meeting" can be important in reorganizing procedural and affective experiences within a relational context (Stern, 2004). In addition to these relational elements, cultural psychotherapy emphasizes the need to include the cultural context in order to effectively build a bridge between people and in fact "make

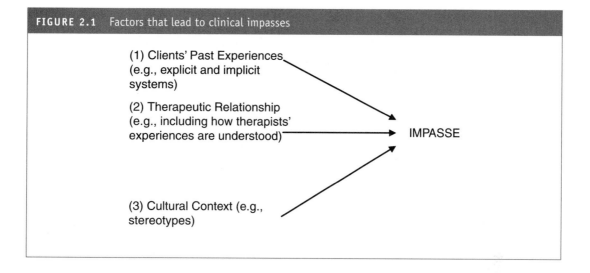

FIGURE 2.1   Factors that lead to clinical impasses

contact." From the process of entering into another person's subjective experience, something new emerges from something old. According to a growing number of authors (e.g., Jordan, 2010; Mitchell, 1988; Norcross, 2002, 2010; Wampold, 2001, 2010), this connection is one, if not the main, curative ingredient of psychotherapy.

Helen's question, "What's going on?" was an opportunity to further this connection. However, to effectively do so I also had to explore and acknowledge my contribution to this interaction. I wondered why I was so distant with her. I enjoyed working with her, but I realized that I feared she would get angry and abandon treatment. Why? I noticed that my own personal limitations (e.g., fear of rejection, and fear of outbursts of anger) were restricting the range and effectiveness of my interventions. However, this was not the whole story. I noticed that the influence of a larger cultural dynamic seemed relevant. As I ventured further, I realized I was worried about losing an African American client. I feared that if she ended treatment abruptly or sought treatment from another clinician, then the staff at my clinic could gossip about my inability to treat African Americans. Some people might even suggest that I am racist. I was surprised that these thoughts crossed my mind. I did not remember having them prior to the exchange with Helen. Indeed, this fear was new, and the heightened tension between Helen and me suddenly seemed related to escalating conflicts between Latinos and African Americans. Racial tensions had not only erupted in Helen's community but also within my workplace. The clinic's budget was being cut and fears of layoffs were rampant. As a result, it appeared there was a fracture in the clinic's staff and two newly formed camps emerged. One group was composed of African Americans and the other of Latinos, while Whites and Asians seemed to fade into the background. I struggled, as I wanted to continue relating to all of my coworkers/friends; however, via my relationship with Helen, I feared I would make a clinical mistake that could jeopardize my interactions with one or the other camp. As a result of this fear, I was more cautious (more intellectual, less emotional, and less me). Once I became cognizant of my own fears, I sought a way to effectively use them in treatment.

Case Illustration Part 4: Helen

When Helen asked me, *"What's going on?"* I responded, *"At times, I too am afraid. I am afraid that I may say something insensitive that offends you because I am not getting it, because I am Latino and you are African American and now more than ever these differences seem particularly intense. I feel that I have to be more careful in not offending you and that may be making me be more distant with you."*

Helen nodded and agreed that at times I did not get what it was like to be Black, and what it was like to live in the projects, and yes, I did seem distant. By simply reflecting her comments, I was leaving myself out of the therapeutic interaction. I acted like an object, like a mirror, and did not include myself in my comments. It finally surfaced that, indeed, it was not all about her past issues with her husband, mother, or grandparents. She too was afraid of saying something inappropriate, something racist in the "here and now" of the therapeutic relationship even though many times she was so enraged at me and Hispanics in general.

"At times," she said, *"I don't feel that I am good enough to be noticed by you or anyone."* She went on to explain that a few years ago the neighborhood (in which she lives and in which the community health clinic is located) was predominantly African American and *"now the neighborhood is being invaded by your people* [Hispanics]." Helen explained that many of her family members, neighbors, and friends had been evicted (e.g., alleging false drug charges) and in turn Hispanics were given their apartments. Similarly, Helen feared that I preferred my Hispanic clients, just as her mother preferred her younger children or her husband preferred her best friend. In turn, I explained that my fear was that she would think that an African American therapist was more appropriate for her. She laughed and agreed to think about it. I emphasized that it was her decision.

She again asked me why I looked so tired. I explained that I had been working long hours because there had been many emergencies in the community.

"The shootings?" she asked.

"Yes," I said and explained that I often had to be involved in dealing with the aftermath of such crimes.

During the next sessions, we also talked in detail about how I had grown in importance to her and how she cared very much about me. She explained that even though it seemed stupid, she feared that I would soon abandon her as her grandparents, husband, "best friend," and one of her daughters had. She explained that everyone who was important to her had left her, so why would I be different? We discussed and explored in detail her relational expectations (implicit systems) as they unfolded.

In addition, it was important to understand her expectation of being "invisible" as a real relational and contextual experience rather than solely as a by-product of "deeper" or "inner" issues (e.g., unconscious dynamics, object relations, relational schemes, learned behavioral patterns, or even implicit systems). It would have been easy to explain our current interactions solely through an understanding of her past issues, but doing so would have neglected important relational and contextual elements that were unfolding in the here and now. The psychotherapeutic relationship provided us with a unique opportunity to explore in detail some of her implicit systems. However, it was also crucial to acknowledge my contribution in this process as well as that of the context.

In exploring the contextual view, I disclosed that I had heard of and witnessed an increasing number of clashes between African Americans and Latinos, and that I was even more fearful that the conflict was spreading to the clinic where I worked. We discussed how the number of shootings in the neighborhood had increased (during the last three months, four teenagers had been murdered). As I shared my view that the neighborhood was on fire, Helen shared her own stories of recent violence and expressed her worry that she or someone in her family would get shot. She also worried that she might be harassed or assaulted by Hispanic teenagers. This led us to discuss how ethnic minorities are depicted on television (e.g., as stupid, poor, and violent), and how we seemed to internalize and fulfill these expectations.

My disclosures strengthened the connection between us and also allowed us to examine contextual cultural forces that otherwise would have been ignored. If not addressed, these issues could have continued to hinder the psychotherapeutic process. Our initial exchange (followed by countless others) allowed Helen to move beyond the belief that I was just another "White Doctor" (even though I am Latino) who would not listen to her. Through these exchanges, I reconnected with her and she was able to see me. Furthermore, after this session the distance between us seemed to have dissipated significantly. Such "moments of meeting" link people and give rise to a state that is more inclusive than what either therapist or client could create alone. As a result, a more complex meaning is derived, which involves both implicit and explicit systems (BCPSG, 2010) and increasingly, particularly during the third phase, the cultural context.

Helen was not the only one who seemed to be positively affected by these developments. The process had a powerful effect on me, too. Even though I continued to work long hours, as I got to know Helen I felt energized. Although the clinical encounter presented in this chapter is of a higher intensity than is necessary to provoke a deeper connection, it provides an opportunity to illustrate the unique dimensions evoked by cultural psychotherapy. In this case, we are reminded that it is insufficient to focus solely on clients' contributions to the clinical encounter (e.g., Helen's experiences of neglect with her mother); it is also crucial to consider the influence of the therapeutic relationship embedded within a cultural context.

In the case of Helen, I emphasized the cultural nature of my fears, but there were other personal attributes in play such as my avoidance of outbursts of anger and rejection fears. In addition, the contexts in which the therapeutic process occurred (e.g., the neighborhood in which the health center is located and the health center itself) also had a powerful impact on the therapeutic process. With Helen, the growing conflict between Latinos and African Americans around us had inadvertently affected our relationship. Similarly, the economic collapse that culminated with the 2008 Great Recession affected us all. This highlights the need for therapists to continuously explore the multiple and interacting personal, interpersonal, and cultural contributions to the therapeutic relationship or else risk the limits that overlooking these aspects can impose upon the therapeutic process.

2.10 Use Clients' Renewed Sense of Vitality

As clients and therapists explore and experience the multiple and complex meanings present in the psychotherapeutic process, they start developing or "authoring" new meanings (White & Epston, 1990). Helen gradually realized that the frequency and intensity of her past experiences of neglect (e.g., experiences with her mother, experiences of discrimination, her therapist's tiredness) contributed to her sense of invisibility. Although these feelings would still frequently appear, she realized she could deal with them in different ways. Just because she "felt invisible" or "less than" did not mean that these feelings were true. Helen came to understand that she could respond differently to these feeling and that she had the power to create alternative plots. However, to do so she not only needed to be aware that she would automatically (implicit) tend to re-create her expectations of not being seen or of being less than but also that she needed to create (explicit) alternative behaviors, narratives, and beliefs. An indicator that implicit systems are changing is when alternative affects emerge (e.g., curiosity, concern) from common triggers (e.g., perception that the therapist is tired) that replace automatic negative affects (e.g., feeling invisible and depressed).

A sense of feeling connected in a relationship with another person fosters a sense of vitality that leads clients to reengage with the world. Furthermore, as new meanings are developed, a renewed sense of hope and possibility is attained. A sense of wholeness and continuity develops that often translates into actions. In psychotherapy, Helen learned that when she felt invisible she could raise her voice, frown, gesticulate, or change her tone of voice.

An enhanced understanding of our lives is an ongoing process that is never completed. Not only because we are endlessly learning, but also because each life cycle entails new conflicts that inevitably challenge, and maybe enrich, our current stories. However, as clients reclaim their history and feel a renewed sense of hope and energy, they often find it important to face and shape their contexts. When they are ready to do so, they move into the third phase of cultural psychotherapy, the "fostering empowerment" phase.

Notes

1. Many authors choose to write their autobiographies as they face extraordinarily horrible tragedies. Out of the many, I chose Allende's not only because of her uncanny ability to tell stories so beautifully but also because Paula was my classmate and friend.

2. Although standard CBT interventions were very helpful in stabilizing Helen's depressive symptoms, particularly her suicidal symptoms, it is not the aim of this chapter to describe these strategies, which are covered in Chapter 1. The main aim of this chapter is to describe the second phase of treatment, that is, understanding clients' experiences.

3. This therapeutic process is not unlike the rupture and repair process in the mother-infant relationship, which is an essential experience for the developmental process (Tronick & Beeghly, 2011).

4. See the introduction for a more thorough review of explicit and implicit systems.

5. As these experiences are described, it is not sufficient to stay in the cognitive realm; it is necessary to thoroughly access random thoughts, affect associations, bodily sensations, sensory information (e.g., smells, tastes, and sounds), and seemingly conflictive images/feelings.

6. Throughout this book, I have aimed to provide individualistic, relational, and cultural elements their fair share of attention. Nevertheless, it is impossible to thoroughly describe all the complex dimensions involved in the psychotherapeutic process. Thus, I have opted to emphasize the cultural elements (in this cultural psychotherapy text), sometimes at the expense of individualistic or relational factors. This does not mean that individualistic or relational processes are less important. On the contrary, they are of crucial importance. Nevertheless, the psychotherapeutic literature has repeatedly emphasized their influence, which makes it less necessary for me to do the same.

References

Allende, I. (1995). *Paula.* New York: HarperCollins.

Beebe, B., & Lachman, F. (2002). *Infant research and adult treatment: Co-constructing interactions.* Hillsdale, NJ: Analytic Press.

Boston Change Process Study Group (BCPSG). (2010). *Change in psychotherapy: A unifying paradigm.* New York: Norton.

Bruner, J. (2002). *Making stories: Law, literature, life.* Cambridge MA: Harvard University Press.

Cortina, M., & Liotti, G. (2007). New approaches to understanding unconscious processes: Implicit and explicit systems. *International Forum of Psychoanalysis, 16,* 204–212.

Decety, J., & Chaminade, T. (2003). When the self represents the other: A new cognitive neuroscience view on psychological identification. *Consciousness and Cognition, 12,* 577–596.

Dovidio, J. (2009). Racial bias, unspoken but heard. *Science, 326,* 1641–1642.

Gabbard, G. (1996). The analyst's contribution to the erotic transference. *Contemporary Psychoanalysis, 32,* 249–273.

Herman, J. (1992). *Trauma and recovery: The aftermath of violence from domestic abuse to political terror.* New York: Basic Books.

Jordan, J. (2010). *Relational-cultural therapy.* Washington, DC: American Psychological Association.

Kohut, H. (1984). *How does analysis cure?* Chicago: University of Chicago Press.

La Roche, M. (1999). Culture, transference, and countertransference among Latinos. *Psychotherapy, 36,* 389–397.

La Roche, M., & Maxie, A. (2003). Ten considerations in addressing cultural differences in psychotherapy. *Professional Psychology: Research and Practice, 34,* 180–186.

La Roche, M., & Shriberg, D. (2003). High stakes exams and Latino students: Toward a culturally sensitive education for Latino children in the United States. *Journal of Educational & Psychological Consultation, 15*(2), 205–223.

Linehan, M. M. (1993). *Cognitive behavioral treatment of borderline personality disorder.* New York: Guilford.

Lyons-Ruth, K., & Members of the Change Process Study Group. (1998). Implicit relational knowing: Its role in development and psychoanalytic treatment. *Infant Mental Health Journal, 19,* 282–289.

Marin, G., & VanOss-Marin, B. (1991). *Research with Hispanic populations.* Newbury Park, CA: Sage.

Maxie, A., Arnold, D., & Stephenson, M. (2006). Do therapists address ethnic and racial differences in cross-cultural psychotherapy? *Psychotherapy: Theory, Research, Practice, Training, 43,* 85–98.

Mitchell, S. (1988). *Relational concepts in psychoanalyses.* Cambridge MA: Harvard University Press.

Norcross, J. C. (Ed.). (2002). *Psychotherapy relationships that work: Therapist contributions and responsiveness to patients.* New York: Oxford University Press.

Norcross, J. C. (2010). The therapeutic relationship. In B. Duncan, S. Miller, B. Wampold, & M. Hubble (Eds.), *The heart and soul of change: Delivering what works in therapy* (pp. 113–141). Washington, DC: American Psychological Association.

Richard, F. D., Bond, C. F., Jr., & Stokes-Zoota, J. J. (2003). One hundred years of social psychology quantitatively described. *Review of General Psychology, 7,* 331–363.

Roemer, L., & Orsillo, S. M. (2009). *Mindfulness- & acceptance-based behavioral therapies in practice.* New York: Guilford.

Rogers, C. (1961). *On becoming a person.* Boston: Houghton Mifflin.

Safran, J. D., & Muran, J. C. (2000). *Negotiating the therapeutic alliance: A relational therapeutic treatment guide.* New York: Guilford.

Shweder, R. A. (1995). Cultural psychology: What is it? In N. Rule Goldberger & J. Bennet Veroff (Eds.), *The culture and psychology reader* (pp. 41–86). New York: New York University Press.

Steele, C., & Aronson, J. (1995). Stereotype threat and the intellectual test performance of African Americans. *Journal of Personality and Social Psychology, 69,* 797–811.

Stern, D. N. (2004). *The present moment in psychotherapy and everyday life.* New York: Norton.

Stolorow, R. D., & Atwood, G. E. (2002). *Contexts of being: The intersubjective foundations of psychological life.* New York: Analytical Press.

Sue, W. S., & Sue, D. (2008). *Counseling the culturally diverse: Theory and practice* (5th ed.). Hoboken, NJ: John Wiley.

Tronick, E., & Beeghly, M. (2011). Infant's meaning-making and the development of mental health problems. *American Psychologist, 66,* 107–119.

Wachtel, P. (2008). *Relational theory and the practice of psychotherapy.* New York: Guilford.

Wampold, B. E. (2001). *The great debate: Models, methods, and findings.* Mahwah, NJ: Erlbaum.

Wampold, B. E. (2010). The research evidence for the common factors models: A historically situated perspective. In B. Duncan, S. Miller, B. Wampold, & M. Hubble (Eds.), *The heart and soul of change: Delivering what works in therapy.* Washington, DC: American Psychological Association.

Westen, D. (1988). Transference and information processing. *Clinical Psychology Review, 8,* 161–171.

Westen, D., & Gabbard, G. (2002a). Development in cognitive neuroscience: I. Conflict, compromise and connectionism. *Journal of the American Psychoanalytic Association, 50,* 1–49.

Westen, D., & Gabbard, G. (2002b). Development in cognitive neuroscience: II. Implications for theories of transference. *Journal of the American Psychoanalytic Association, 50,* 50–98.

White, M., & Epston, D. (1990). *Narrative means therapeutic ends.* New York: Norton.

Winnicott, D. W. (1965). *The maturational process and the facilitating environment.* New York: International University Press.

Zimbardo, P. (2008). *The Lucifer effect: Understanding how good people turn evil.* New York: Random House.

Phase III

Fostering Empowerment

The city, as you see, now shakes too greatly
And cannot raise her head out of the depths
Above the gory swell. She wastes in blight,
Blight on earth's fruitful blooms and grazing flocks,
And on the barren birth pangs of the women.
The fever god had fallen on the city,
And drives it, a most hated pestilence . . .

—Sophocles, *Oedipus Rex*

These lines from the first page of Sophocles' tragedy *Oedipus Rex* (Lind, 1957) underscore the important role the Greek city of Thebes plays in the story, as it is afflicted by illness and burns in fever. Oedipus's initial quest was to emancipate Thebes from this "sickness." Oedipus is ready for this struggle, asking "what I might do or say to save the state." However, it is also important to note the role Thebes plays as a representation of Oedipus's tumultuous state of mind: His quest is not only an attempt to save Thebes but also an effort to heal himself. Similarly, cultural psychotherapy aims both to heal individuals and to change inhumane systems. The first chapters of this book emphasized strategies to ameliorate clients' symptoms. However, individual change is often not enough. In this chapter, I underscore a key and distinct goal of cultural psychotherapy— empowering clients. Empowerment in this book is defined as people's ability to transform their context. Cultural psychotherapy argues that it is necessary to incorporate the context in which symptoms are embedded to be more effective psychotherapeutically and prevent relapse. The following equation of the third phase is used to illustrate this contextual emphasis:

Phase III = individual factors × relational factors × contextual factors².

During the third stage, cultural psychotherapy involves awaking a social consciousness (realistic awareness of one's sociocultural environment and experience) and putting it into action, which gradually leads to a desire to transform and improve oneself and one's context. Unfortunately, the vast majority of clients do not reach this third phase. Furthermore, most psychotherapeutic models do not explicitly encourage empowerment nor do many clients seem invested in changing an unjust context. Is it that our society discourages social awareness and social change? In contrast to this view, cultural psychotherapy consistently aims to emphasize contextual factors. Empowerment issues are not missing from the first and second phases of cultural psychotherapy. Nevertheless, contextual issues are discussed in more depth in the third phase. Below, I illustrate the characteristics of the empowerment phase by examining a group therapy case.

The group in question met for one academic year (from September to June). It was led by a doctoral-level student (John Tawa, a 29-year-old Japanese American) and supervised by me (a 45-year-old Latino clinical psychologist). The adolescent group met weekly at the Martha Eliot Health Center,[1] a community health center located in a poor and dangerous part of Boston. The group consisted of four African Americans (Jojo, his brother Daniel, Julius, and Joe) and two Latino adolescents (Manny and Carlos). The initial goal of the group was to enhance communication skills; however, as the year progressed we found that all six group members had experienced or witnessed significant episodes of violence. The brothers, for example, had been shot at more than twice, and Manny and his family had spent two years in the witness protection program after witnessing and reporting a murder to the Boston police. The first case illustration is drawn from the group's last months, after a relative degree of empowerment had been achieved. For a thorough review of this group therapy example (that includes Phases I and II), please refer to La Roche and Tawa (2011).

Case Illustration Part 1: The Adolescent Group

In a small office, a group of six adolescents (14–16 years of age), led by graduate student John Tawa, worked printing T-shirts with designs they created, reading "Stop the Violence," "Paz (Peace)," and "Black & Latino: One Love" (see Photo 3.1). They listened to hip-hop music as they teased each other for not working hard enough. They wore colorful hooded sweatshirts and some tilted their hats slightly to the side. The jokes stopped, however, when I entered the room and inquired if they could describe their project to a group of "folks" meeting downstairs. The group enthusiastically agreed to do so, particularly after I mentioned the possibility of making their first T-shirt sales.

The group meeting downstairs was the board of the prestigious Harvard Medical School hospital, Children's Hospital Boston.[2] The board consisted of a dozen older men and a handful of women, all White and all elegantly dressed. The president of the hospital, all its vice presidents, and the director of the Martha Eliot Health Center were also present.

After I introduced the adolescents and explained the goals of the group, one brave young man, Julius, stepped up to share his experiences of community violence and his thoughts about what each T-shirt meant to him and his community. Julius eloquently explained that violence hurts not just the injured individual, but also friends, family, and neighbors. Julius paused, and then described how he personally had been harmed by violent episodes in the streets. Right away, and almost interrupting him, Jojo jumped in, and then others shared their experiences and thoughts, while Manny started asking if anyone wanted to buy a T-shirt. Almost all the board members bought several.

The next day, a grant was awarded by the Children's Hospital Boston to start a violence prevention program at the Martha Eliot Health Center. John Tawa and I had submitted a draft of a violence prevention program to the director of the clinic, who had refined it and submitted it to the Harvard board. To this day, this program—although much larger and more sophisticated than the way John and I designed it—continues to serve families victimized by violence. After the adolescent group formally ended, some of its members moved to develop similar antiviolence groups in the community.

PHOTO 3.1 T-shirts designed by the adolescent group

PREREQUISITES FOR THE EMPOWERMENT PHASE

Most clients end treatment before reaching Phase III. Some, however, move to the third phase after developing a relationship with their therapist (Phase II). For clients to proceed to the final phase, they must have (3a) an interest in transforming an unjust social context, and (3b) an enhanced and ongoing knowledge of the cultural context. Again letters after the phase number are used to indicate prerequisites.

3a. Interest in Transforming an Unjust Social Context

As already mentioned, not many clients reach or seem interested in the empowerment phase. Thus, a first condition is for clients and therapists to be motivated to change their social context. If either the therapist or client lacks this interest, it is unlikely that the therapeutic dyad (couple, family, or group) will ever reach this phase. For example, many of my students, perhaps motivated by these empowerment ideas, have unsuccessfully encouraged clients to transform their context. Unfortunately, soon after they started implementing these empowerment strategies, clients began missing appointments. In these cases, there is a disconnect between the goals of the therapist (i.e., interest in fostering empowerment) and those of the client (e.g., interest in assuaging their symptoms), which may have led to these treatments ending prematurely (Sue, Fujino, Hu, Takeuchi, & Zane, 1991).

3b. Enhanced and Ongoing Knowledge of the Cultural Context

For clients to change their context, they must have some knowledge of it. People cannot change what they do not know. Only as Oedipus could "see" was he able to have in impact on Thebes and start healing himself.[3] Learning about one's own context is an ongoing process. From the onset, cultural psychotherapy aims to enhance our contextual knowledge. Fostering empowerment is not limited to the third phase of cultural psychotherapy; however, it is emphasized in this phase.

As mentioned earlier, the context is complex and multilayered. Using an ecological/contextual perspective, it could be divided into three interactive and at times overlapping parts: systems, situations, and actors (Zimbardo, 2008). The term *systems* refers to the larger, or macro social, political, cultural, economic, and political context (e.g., institutions, history, geography, industries) that defines people's social roles, statuses, values, expectations, and so on. "Situations" are the immediate behavioral contexts in which specific social exchanges occur, such as the work or family environment or even the psychotherapeutic session. Situations are defined by social systems. Finally, in cultural psychotherapy the "actors" are the individuals (clients or therapist) who are performing on the stage of life (situations/systems). Using an ecological stance, people can only be understood within systems/situations; their behaviors acquire meaning through them. Systems provide the institutional support, authority, and financial resources that allow situations to operate as they do, and in turn they define people's behavior. However, people's ability to choose is also informed by their genetic, biologic, physical, and psychological makeup.

Contextual (e.g., systems) influences can express themselves through explicit or implicit messages. Explicit messages are clearly defined and expressed (e.g., laws, economic arrangements). Implicit social messages are ideas, values, or feelings conveyed by society in ways that are not completely conscious (e.g., values) (Dovidio, 2009). However, most contextual messages contain both explicit and implicit messages and to some level there is always the possibility to further understand them. Given that explicit messages are clearly defined, they are more easily understood than implicit ones. In psychotherapy, an example of an explicit message is the therapeutic contract (e.g., no-show policies, co-payments, time arrangements). An example of an implicit message in psychotherapy is the power dynamic between clients and therapists or the cultural values and symbols used in the psychotherapeutic dialogue, which include what is said or not, and how it is valued and expressed.

Cultural psychotherapy argues that only as we are able to recognize the power of contextual forces and acknowledge our vulnerability to them will we be in a better position to understand, prevent, and treat pain and "psychopathology." However, social forces are not destiny. As we understand ourselves embedded within these social, cultural, historical, and political systems, we are more effective in controlling our behaviors and situations as opposed to being controlled by them. Cognitive sciences allow us to have a fuller appreciation of the mechanisms involved in this process. Furthermore, as we are able to understand specific situations, we are also able to elucidate social systems that can also be transformed by our situations and behaviors. However, a first and central task for clients is to become aware of contextual influences so that they can increasingly lead the psychotherapeutic process and their lives. The rule of thumb is that the more we know about our context, the more effectively we will be able to transform it. A therapist's level of contextual knowledge—or interest/ability to learn about it—has a significant impact on the empowerment process. As therapists know more about the realities of clients' context, they will be able to assist them in changing it.

EMPOWERMENT CHARACTERISTICS

Once these two conditions are met (which means that all the prerequisites of the second phase have also been met), it can be said that clients are dealing with issues typical of the third phase of cultural psychotherapy. Some clients reach the empowerment phase within a few sessions of treatment, while with others it may take years. The case study I have chosen to present in this chapter illustrates these ideas with a diverse group of adolescents who have a significant history of marginalization (e.g., live in a very poor neighborhood) and live in a community plagued by violence. Despite many obstacles, this group was able to change not only themselves and their clinicians (they definitely influenced John and me), but also our context.

Although a growing number of interventions are being developed to treat adolescents who have experienced violence, most psychotherapeutics aim for individual change and most are designed to reduce related symptoms (e.g., PTSD, depression, anxiety). In contrast, cultural psychotherapy holds that it is not enough to promote individual change; it is necessary to foster cultural and contextual awareness, and transformation. If we just encourage individuals to adapt, this leads to the perpetuation and justification of structural violence, that is, social arrangements in which oppressed groups have disparate access to basic needs, material goods, and political power (Bulhan, 1985; Christie, Tint, Wagner, & Winter, 2008; Freire, 1970; Galtung, 1996; Ivey, 1999). If psychotherapy only encourages clients to adapt to their context, it becomes a supporter of the status quo (Albee, 1986; Cushman, 1995; Gergen, 1991; Prilleltensky, 1999).

This chapter describes a variety of strategies to transform clients' unjust environments. These strategies include behavioral techniques, social psychology, and peace promotion (Christie, 2006), activities that challenge structural violence (e.g., lack of resources addressing violence in our community). Peace promotion in this book is consistent with the growing field of peace psychology (Wagner, de Rivera, & Watkins, 1988), which views peace not merely as the absence of violence but as the building of collaborative relations between people.

In this chapter, I present ideas that aim to empower clients. Presented below are 10 specific clinical recommendations related to the third phase of cultural psychotherapy.

CLINICAL RECOMMENDATIONS FOR PHASE III

3.1   Link contextual influences to clients' lives.

3.2   Clients lead the way.

3.3   Meanings of symptoms are often culturally dependent.

3.4   Cultural differences are assets.

3.5   Awaken to social justice.

3.6   Embrace multiple stories.

3.7   Talking is not enough: Action is necessary.

3.8   Restore connections and encourage new ones.

3.9   Understand that what is local is global.

3.10   Coping with termination issues.

Each of these Phase III clinical recommendations is discussed in turn.

Case Illustration Part 2: The Adolescent Group

During the time the adolescent group met, violence between Black and Latino gangs was increasing. A record number of shootings had occurred and the police were raiding homes in the community. Group members excitedly—or nervously—discussed the most recent incidents of violence. They described the latest shooting and speculated about who pulled the trigger or who would be the next target(s). In the group, they also talked about the dangers of Latino and Black kids being seen together. Members came and left the group alone for fear of being seen with someone of the other ethnicity. After a few months, two subgroups were formed; one composed of the four African Americans and another of the two Latino adolescents. The two groups would often have heated arguments. For example, at one point Carlos commented that "Blacks are violent" and Jojo immediately shot back with "Hispanics are fucking lazy."

3.1 Link Contextual Influences to Clients' Lives

The first task is to identify contextual messages (both explicit and implicit) and then to explore how they influence clients' behavior. The case illustration highlights several explicit and implicit messages affecting the group. It is clear how the teenagers were grouping themselves (i.e., by race, African American and Latino), and they would even explain, "Blacks will stick with Blacks against Hispanics, and Hispanics will stick with Hispanics against Blacks." Furthermore, acting aggressively toward the "other" group also seemed to be a response to explicit neighborhood rules. An example of an implicit social message present is stereotyping, both inside and outside of the group.

Stereotyping is often overlooked as a type of aggression, discrimination, or prejudice in which individuals are deprived of their identity and uniqueness, as a set of generalizations is imposed upon them (e.g., Hispanics are lazy and Blacks are violent) (Fiske, Harris, Lee, & Russell, 2009). Stereotyping is also a result of the power asymmetries designed to control people (Fiske et al., 2009). It reinforces some attributes and neglects others. In this process, people's unique identity is denied, particularly during stressful situations (such as the ongoing gang war between African Americans and Latinos in the case illustration) in which people enact socially prescribed roles (e.g., acting tough). Furthermore, during times of danger people focus and process information that is relevant for their survival. Stereotyping occurs when the "others" (e.g., different racial groups) are assumed to have different feelings, thoughts, values, and purposes in life than their own group does. Commonalities are diminished or erased from awareness. This is accomplished by the psychological mechanisms of intellectualization, denial, and the isolation of affect (Zimbardo, 2008). Human relationships are subjective, personal, and emotional, and to use Martin Buber's terms, they are "I-Thou." This is starkly contrasted by dehumanizing relationships, which are objectifying, analytical, and empty of emotional or empathic content—what Buber would say is "I-It." The misrepresentation of others as subhuman is facilitated by means of labels, stereotypes, discrimination, prejudice, slogans, and advertisements.

As the adolescents explored these stereotypes they were able to recognize that they were replicating immediate neighborhood expectations and also being influenced by the media and the "system" that portrayed them all as hopeless drug addicts who would sooner or later drop out of school and end up in jail. Jojo, a 14-year-old African American group member, said it best, when he commented, "It's almost expected that we kill each other." Thus, the Black and Latino youth in the group began to discuss the ways in which the social structure (e.g., explicit and implicit messages) encouraged dissention among minorities, and it was then that they saw the need for peace among them as a means to combat racism and structural violence.

As clients become increasingly aware of the power of systems, they realize that each situation creates specific demands and roles. The youths started to understand that each situation has a different set of expectations and rules in which behaviors are understood differently (Roccas & Brewer, 2002). This is particularly important with racial minorities whose experiences are grounded in multiple cultural situations, each influencing the way in which they make meaning of the world. For diverse clients (e.g., ethnic minorities, gay/lesbian, religious minorities), psychotherapy offers a unique opportunity to examine the influence of different cultural norms, expectations, and values (White & Epston, 1990). For example, Manny visited his relatives in Puerto Rico during the first few months of attending the group. When he returned, he described the sharp contrast between his experience as a Latino in the United States and his experience in Puerto Rico. As a "light skinned" individual, Manny felt that he tended to be "looked up to" or privileged in Puerto Rico, while in Boston—because of his racial minority status—he was "looked down upon." One of the main goals of exploring a context is to recognize its power. This enhanced contextual awareness allows clients to start transferring their experiences of "shame" or "guilt" for living in poverty or having poor schools onto sociopolitical or economic forces rather than shouldering the responsibility themselves.

Rigid and narrow implicit messages are hurtful not only to ethnic minorities, but also to privileged groups such as White males, who are often considered to be at the top of the socioeconomic and political ladder (see Chapter 5 for a case illustration that involves this idea). Cultural roles demand that men achieve the goals of independence, autonomy, and individualistic competitive achievement. However, the pursuit of this Western male ideal of independence exacts an enormous emotional toll that has been called the gender role strain (Levant, 1995; Pleck, 1995; Pollack, 1998). William Pollack, a prominent psychoanalyst and Harvard author, has written about what he calls the normative trauma of male socialization in which males are forced to disconnect early on from their loved ones (particularly from their mothers). This traumatic separation leads to what Ron Levant has called the normative alexithymia of men schooled in a "strong," stiff-upper-lip, tough, hard masculinity (Levant, 1995). This type of socialization limits their ability to express feelings and establish nourishing egalitarian relationships. Studies find that men's limited ability to develop nourishing egalitarian relationships is detrimental not only to their psychological well-being but also to their physical health (Pleck, 1995).

3.2 Clients Lead the Way

By Phase III, clients have often developed a greater capacity for self-observation and greater tolerance for inner conflict that allows them to increasingly direct treatment. With this empowered appreciation of themselves also comes a changed appreciation of their therapists who are gradually viewed as real people—less idealized—with limitations and idiosyncrasies of their own. As a result of these changes, their interactions are more relaxed and secure (than during the second phase of cultural psychotherapy); there is usually more spontaneity and humor. During the third phase, the therapeutic relationship feels less emotionally charged than during the previous phase. Furthermore, clients become less dependent upon the therapeutic relationship and therapy becomes more open-ended, less structured, and less frequent.

During the first phase of cultural psychotherapy, the therapist leads the sessions. This is particularly true if there are any safety issues (e.g., suicidality, domestic violence, neighborhood violence, child abuse, etc.). Nevertheless, this does not mean that clients are passive. On the contrary, from the onset of treatment cultural therapy encourages clients to continuously lead and evaluate the usefulness of treatment. During the second phase, the therapeutic process becomes more egalitarian, with a gradual shift toward clients leading the process. During the third phase, clients are capable of making suggestions to tackle a wide array of problems or propose ideas to understand issues and conflicts. Culturally competent therapists offer feedback and ideas, and they attempt to contextualize clients' suggestions. Although clients' symptoms still need to be treated, it is also necessary to increasingly understand the meaning of these symptoms as anchored within cultural contexts (Kleinman, 1988).

3.3 Meanings of Symptoms Are Often Culturally Dependent

One of the main characteristics of cultural psychotherapy is its emphasis on understanding symptoms as embedded within cultural contexts. If the context in which the symptoms occur is not considered, our clinical understandings may be inaccurate and/or invalid (Kleinman, 1988). Consider the following case.

Case Illustration Part 3: The Adolescent Group

Julius had been in therapy for three years with different therapists prior to being part of the adolescent group and had been diagnosed as having "conduct disorder," "attention deficit disorder without hyperactivity," "post traumatic stress disorder," and/or "oppositional defiant disorder." He was known to start physical fights (with classmates and teachers) without provocation. He had been suspended numerous times from school and was in danger of being expelled. At the beginning of the group, Julius reported feeling proud that peers and teachers feared him. However, as group therapy progressed, Julius revealed that he needed to "toughen himself up" so that one day he could defend his mother, who was repeatedly beaten by his stepfather.[4] Despite the involvement of the police and the department of social services, the violent climate in the home did not improve. His stepfather continued to beat his mother. Julius felt that it was his duty as the eldest son to "protect the family." In the adolescent group, however, Julius started exploring other means of addressing his stepfather's violence. His direct, forthright behavior with the Harvard Board was indicative of the transformation he was experiencing around the problem of violence in his life.

The story of Julius is consistent with the findings of Andres-Hyman, Forrester, Achara-Abrahams, Lauricella, and Rowe (2007), who eloquently explain how behaviors exhibited by inner-city youth (e.g. attitude, aggression, substance use) are often "adaptive" within a malevolent and oppressive context (e.g., community violence, poverty). Although assaulting peers and teachers is never permissible, it was more therapeutic and less stigmatizing to understand Julius's fighting as less of a "conduct problem" and more as a means of addressing an adverse and violent context.

Cultural psychotherapy aims to describe problems that our clients face (i.e., frequent fights) in conjunction with strengths (desire to protect family). As problems and strengths are explored within the context, new possibilities to address the issues are recognized. In Julius's case, the group suggested strategies to help stop Julius's stepfather's physical violence (e.g., get the pastor involved or call the cops). The group also helped Julius guide the social workers' investigation, which ultimately found that the stepfather was a danger to the family, and had him permanently removed. It was important for Julius to lead this process, as he had been disappointed on numerous occasions by a system he had experienced as being designed only to protect White folks.

3.4 Cultural Differences Are Assets

An increased understanding and validation of clients' cultural differences (e.g., ethnicity, race, socioeconomic status, sexual orientation, religion, etc.) is an important therapeutic goal of the third phase of cultural psychotherapy. The acknowledgment and exploration of differences is often helpful for clients, particularly adolescents, in their identity-building process. In this exploration process, they can become increasingly aware of the different dimensions of their identity as well as the multiplicity of aspects within their context. This enhanced understanding fosters their developmental processes (Erikson, 1993). Unfortunately, there are multiple explicit and implicit contextual messages that construe cultural differences as deficits. Therefore, recognizing and validating cultural differences is often not enough. Consistent with Janet Helms's (1990) racial identity model, during her third phase of immersion/emersion clients are able to develop a sense of pride about their unique features (e.g., skin pigmentation, Spanish accent) by inoculating themselves against the effects of an adverse cultural context that marginalizes and stigmatizes these characteristics and by noting their cultural strengths (see Chapter 4 for a more thorough review of this issue).

3.5 Awaken to Social Justice

Exploring experiences of racism, poverty, or marginalization for the first time or in significantly more depth may dramatically shift clients' worldviews. In the beginning, they may "conform" to the dominant group standards; then, through treatment, they gradually "emerge" in their communities and often reject and even position themselves in opposition to the standards of the dominant group or culture. This is again consistent with Helms's (1990) racial identity model. Therapists can help empower clients by raising their awareness of how contextual issues (e.g., stereotyping, racism) pervade their lives. The goal is to help them address contextual issues about which they were previously unaware or that they had believed were insurmountable. For example, the damaging effects of violence are exacerbated by feelings of hopelessness and alienation that stem from a sense of limited control (e.g., living in a neighborhood in which violence and poverty are pervasive).

Across the United States, adolescents of color (particularly African Americans and Latinos) are often stereotyped to "fit the mold," which happens to be that of violent/aggressive teens. Peers and social media often inadvertently (i.e., via implicit messages) reinforce these stereotypes. It was thus important for John Tawa to explicitly explore stereotypes of young men of color and how they operate to constrain their emotional and identity options. Through repeated discussions of race and racism (often through discussion of films such as *Crash;* Haggis, 2005), the youth began to retell their stories, contextualized by understandings of the ways in which their identities and related emotional experiences are shaped by society.

Achieving a deeper understanding of explicit and implicit contextual messages (e.g., racial stereotypes) may trigger intense feelings of anger, frustration, hopelessness, and sadness (Helms, 1990). The assumptions of a "just world" prevalent in Helms's (1990) pre-encounter phase are shattered by the painful reality of racism, community violence, and/ or socioeconomic inequality.

Occasionally, clients resist talking about their pain because it feels useless and overwhelming. Under such circumstances, it is not surprising that some clients are enraged and may entertain violent fantasies of revenge (e.g., Julius had fantasies about killing his stepfather) that can frighten other group members and their therapists alike. Also, many adolescents may feel overwhelmed by their sadness, and fear not being able to control their emotions when discussing social injustices. Clients and therapists together, within the empathic holding environment of therapy, need to address and discuss such feelings if new meanings are to be construed.

As clients are confronted with the injustices of their context (e.g., unjust socioeconomic environment, discrimination, sexism, community violence, economic inequalities, materialism), they realize that they can refuse to conform to a marginalizing, violent, and oppressive status quo. The empowerment phase is by nature paradoxical; the injustices that have hindered clients' development and growth now fuel their quests to overcome difficulties and seek new challenges. Their struggles gain new meaning and they are motivated by a desire to prevent others from suffering similar misfortunes and deprivations (Bulhan, 1985; Freire, 1970; Herman, 1992; La Roche, 2002).

Clients' enhanced awareness that they can transform their context has ethical implications. For some clients, it becomes a moral imperative to change and improve their contexts, but not for all. After the adolescent group ended, some members decided to be more active while others remained on the sidelines. Julius, for example, went on to develop a violence prevention group at his high school. Although cultural psychotherapy respects clients' decisions to focus only on their own needs, unlike most psychotherapy it at least explores clients' potential to initiate contextual change.

During the third phase, clients seek new challenges that stimulate them (Brown, 1994) and help them increase their sense of power and hope rather than seeking homeostasis. It is quite energizing when clients realize they can change not only parts of themselves, but also their context. However, even though they may have generated some contextual transformations, many of the painful realities of their lives remain unchanged. Some of these injustices can trigger symptoms and take treatment back to the first phase of cultural psychotherapy. After each shooting, it was not rare for the teens in the adolescent group to report increased symptoms of post-traumatic stress disorder (PTSD) that required more attention than our efforts to improve the context.

The quest to overcome difficulties should not overshadow clients' pain, which requires continuous acknowledgment. Marginalization, discrimination, and poverty entail much suffering. If these painful experiences are not acknowledged in psychotherapy, they can cloud assets and hinder further progress. If this pain is not validated, clients will very likely feel misunderstood by their therapists or as if something is missing. As a result, the pain may seem to grow, making them feel increasingly hopeless and helpless.

3.6 Embrace Multiple Stories

As clients progress through the therapeutic process, they learn that they do not need to live with a single story that they have constructed or that has been constructed for them. Rather, they can experience multiple, often contradictory stories within different situations. Through a deeper exploration and understanding of their experiences, adolescents sometimes discover that they can change the trajectory of personal injustices they have suffered by making them the basis for social action (Bulhan, 1985; Herman, 1992; La Roche, 2002). The reaffirmation of multiple experiences is not only empowering; it also facilitates a more integrated self (White & Epston, 1990).

The old beliefs (e.g., implicit systems and messages) that gave meaning to life have been challenged; newly created beliefs (explicit), some bridging conflicting contexts, provide a new and sustaining faith. The main therapeutic goal is to help the client achieve a heightened integration of the old beliefs with the newer ones and therefore a more balanced, realistic and empowered perspective from which to move forward.

3.7 Talking Is Not Enough: Action Is Necessary

The adolescent group had gradually discussed social critiques, and believing that they had the power to do something about these social structural problems was still a large leap for many. Some adolescents expressed doubt about the group's ability to create change in the system, even in their community. As Julius said one day in group, "Nobody will listen to a bunch of Black and Latino kids," and Joe quickly added, "People have been fighting racism for hundreds of years and it's still here."

These comments from Julius and Joe clearly reflect an understanding of contemporary and historical realities of racism, but, simultaneously, a diminished sense of agency to create change. To help group members make this leap, John Tawa and I decided to suggest the group undertake a project that would model some form of community activism. John had previous experience in community activism and knew it was important to explore ideas in an open-ended manner and to draw from the strengths of the group. To further allow the youth to "own" their empowerment process, John decided to ask them how they wanted to take action to fight community violence—which had already been identified as their goal.

After brainstorming and exploring possibilities (e.g., street art, community photography), the group decided on a T-shirt project, designing antiviolence and positive race relations T-shirts and selling them in the community. Many of the youth had an interest in art, and others were skilled at hustling for money. Joe, for example, spent his evenings after school at a local supermarket, helping customers carry bags to their car in exchange for tips. After reviewing many of the levels of influence affecting the group dynamics (La Roche, 2005), John and I agreed that the T-shirt project fulfilled multiple therapeutic ends (enhance self-efficacy, empowerment, self-esteem), the least of which was offering the youth an avenue to earn money as none of them held jobs, despite efforts to find work.

The T-shirt project, however, faced considerable practical and ethical challenges, particularly as it was outside the scope of more traditional group psychotherapy. This project could breach the confidentiality code, as it would require clients to visibly identify as such in order to sell T-shirts. Through consultation with an attorney at the Children's

Hospital Boston, we developed a consent form, which was to be signed by the youths' guardians/parents, that described the project in detail as well as the therapeutic risks. Although we needed to maintain a diagnostic-psychotherapeutic focus internally, we publicly redefined our group as a community action group under the name of Promoting Empowerment and Community Engagement, or PEACE. In addition, all profits earned from selling the T-shirts would be disseminated among the youth. The group leader or health center could not profit, because running a business from the health center would be a violation of ethics codes. The legal consultations were also used as means to inform others in our health center and parent hospital about our work and enlist them as possible allies in our struggle against community violence. Even the attorney we consulted bought a T-shirt.

As clients struggle to improve an unjust context, they not only become increasingly aware of explicit and implicit messages, but also enhance their understandings of explicit and implicit systems. For example, their implicit belief that nothing could be done against racism or violence—as articulated by Julius and Joe—was challenged through their actions, support, and discussions. There are multiple strategies to enhance our understandings of implicit systems, which need not be limited to just "moments of meeting" (Boston Change Process Study Group [BCPSG], 2010; see Chapter 2).

3.8 Restore Connections and Encourage New Ones

One of the most important goals of psychotherapy is to encourage people to connect and develop relationships outside the psychotherapeutic relationship and within their communities. Often, fear, trauma (including discrimination and poverty), and/or violence as well as different psychological problems (e.g., panic attacks, posttraumatic stress disorder, depression) generate not only inner fragmentation but also social isolation and marginalization. One of the advantages of group psychotherapy is that it allows individuals to relate and connect with group members and to use these connections to expand their social networks. From the onset of treatment to termination, both individual and group psychotherapy should aim to do the same. Although strong feelings and even dependence are often transferred to therapists and these strong feelings are useful (particularly during the earlier phases), during the third phase it is helpful to promote independence from the therapist and encourage clients to start new and more fulfilling relationships or restore connections with other ones. The psychotherapeutic process can be used to assess how these relationships are developing and how they could be improved.

3.9 Understand That What Is Local Is Global

When the therapeutic process is understood within clients' context, this may increase not only its effectiveness but also its impact on social systems. After having worked for many years in the community health center, I am often aware of ongoing issues and politics affecting the clinic, such as the various neighborhood and community leaders who were increasingly vocal about the rise in street violence. And it was my good working relationship with the director of the clinic that allowed him to excitedly share with me the fact that the Harvard board was meeting for the first time in the clinic to discuss

Boston's growing violence epidemic. I also knew that the youth in the adolescent group were ready to present their T-shirt empowerment project. My awareness of these situations allowed me to introduce the teenagers to the Harvard board at just the right time. The fact that psychotherapy is embedded in multiple and interacting contexts (e.g., community health center, the Harvard hospital, the community) is not unlike experiences occurring in hospitals, psychoanalytic institutes, or yoga centers. This may be particularly true with inpatient or partial hospital units in which much of what happens within the therapeutic milieu is reflected in the psychotherapeutic process (Brabender & Fallon, 1993).

The T-shirt project had political impact not just in the health center but also in the larger system. One immediate success of the project was its influence in generating grant funding for the violence prevention program at our health center. Four years after the adolescent group disbanded, the health center has become an important center for peace promotion in Boston with a steady budget from Children's Hospital Boston (and often from the state of Massachusetts).

Furthermore, two months after the youth group sold T-shirts to the Harvard board members, similar T-shirts (that read "Stop the Violence!") were given to state representatives at Beacon Hill (the Massachusetts state legislature), as several clinicians from our community health center testified in support of an antiviolence bill. The Harvard Medical School and the staff at the Martha Eliot Health Center heavily supported the bill. As the clinicians (including a case manager whose son had recently been the target of gunfire) concluded their testimony, state legislators stood up holding the T-shirts while the audience applauded. Thus, a group of marginalized teens was empowered through cultural psychotherapy to make a sustainable local (community based) and then more systemic (statewide) contribution to fight violence in the community.

3.10 Coping With Termination Issues

Although self- and social transformations are ongoing and never perfectible processes, psychotherapy is not endless. Psychotherapy should conclude once treatment goals are reached. Therefore, psychotherapy ends when the client is no longer pursuing a therapeutic goal. However, this process can also be intermittent: One may accomplish certain goals, decide not to meet for some time, and return if new issues arise or if a check-in is desired.

The termination process, when done correctly, provides an opportunity to review achievements as determined by treatment goals and examine the course of the therapeutic process/relationship. Within this dialogue, it is important to ask what was helpful and what could have been better; what challenges remain and what difficulties have been surpassed; and how cultural differences were addressed, how they evolved, and how they are currently understood (e.g., including difficulties).

During termination, it may be appropriate for therapists to share their experiences of their clients. For example, John Tawa told Julius how much he had learned from him and how during the early meetings of the group he had at times been fearful of him. John had been afraid of being hit. Julius laughed when he heard this. In addition to exploring individual and relational issues, it is also useful to explore how contextual understandings have evolved. Our initial understandings of the social system evolved throughout the group process, and they still continue to do so.

It is important to discuss termination not only with the client(s) but also with everyone involved in the psychotherapeutic work. For example, during the termination process of the adolescent group, John and I talked a great deal about how much this group of disenfranchised adolescents had given us. They had taught us to trust our interventions and the possibility that we can in fact have an impact on social systems. In my 16 years at the Martha Eliot Health Center, I have repeatedly seen much pain, trauma, and violence. In fact, I have often felt that the horrible tragedies are just getting worse (e.g., murders, gangs, school dropouts). This group of adolescents reminded me—or allowed me to experience although more likely the exception than the rule—that it is in fact possible to change the plot and create a different story. We are not condemned to repeat the past if we can change and improve our lives and contexts. In working with this group, my implicit and explicit systems also changed. I feel more optimistic that cultural psychotherapy is effective. Clearly, not only clients change; relationships, clinicians, and systems can improve as well.

Nevertheless, four years after this group disbanded and as I write these lines, I have just learned that a gang murdered one of my clients. This is a first for me, and the pain of this loss reminds me of how much we still need to do.

Notes

1. The Martha Eliot is the second-oldest community health center in the country. It is part of Children's Hospital Boston and affiliated with the Harvard Medical School.

2. In the last 20 years, *U.S. News & World Report* has ranked Children's Hospital Boston as the best children's hospital in the country more frequently than any other.

3. Just as in Oedipus's case, good intentions are insufficient to promote social change. Furthermore, it could be suggested that Oedipus's tragedy was not only that he was blind to his own issues (e.g., unaware of his past), but that he was also blind to the sociopolitical dynamics of his time as he did not recognize and then killed the King of Thebes (his father).

4. It is clear that Julius's rage toward his stepfather was a result of a history of physical abuse, not that he was unconsciously attracted to his mother and jealous of his father.

References

Albee, G. W. (1986). Towards a just society: Lessons from observations on the primary preventions of psychopathology. *American Psychologist, 41,* 891–898.

Andres-Hyman, R. C., Forrester, A., Achara-Abrahams, I., Lauricella, M., & Rowe, M. (2007). Oppression and empowerment: Perceptions of violence among urban youth. *Journal of Community & Applied Social Psychology, 17*(2), 147–158.

Boston Change Process Study Group (BCPSG). (2010). *Change in psychotherapy: A unifying paradigm.* New York: Norton.

Brabender, V., & Fallon, A. (1993). *Models of inpatient group psychotherapy.* Washington, DC: American Psychological Association.

Brown, L. (1994). *Subversive dialogues: Theory in feminist therapy.* New York: Basic Books.

Bulhan, H. A. (1985). *Frantz Fanon and the psychology of the oppressed.* New York: Plenum.

Christie, D. J. (2006). What is peace psychology the psychology of? *Journal of Social Issues, 62*(1), 1–17.

Christie, D. J., Tint, B. S., Wagner, R. V., & Winter, D. D. (2008). Peace psychology for a peaceful world. *American Psychologist, 63*(6), 540–552.

Cushman, P. (1995). *Constructing the self, constructing America: A cultural history of psychotherapy.* New York: Addison-Wesley.

Dovidio, J. (2009). Racial bias, unspoken but heard. *Science, 326,* 1641–1642.

Erikson, E. (1993). *Childhood and society.* New York: Norton.

Fiske, S. T., Harris, L. T., Lee, T. L., & Russell, A. M. (2009). The future of research on prejudice, stereotyping, and discrimination. In T. D. Nelson (Ed.), *Handbook of prejudice, stereotyping, and discrimination* (pp. 525–534). New York: Psychology Press.

Freire, P. (1970). *Pedagogy of the oppressed.* New York: Seabury.

Galtung, J. (1996). *Peace by peaceful means: Peace and conflict, development and civilization.* London: Sage.

Gergen, K. (1991). *The saturated self: Dilemmas of identity in contemporary life.* New York: Basic Books.

Haggis, P. (Director). (2005). *Crash* [Motion picture]. United States: Lion's Gate Films.

Helms, J. (1990). *Black and White racial identity: Theory, research, and practice.* Westport, CT: Praeger.

Herman, J. L. (1992). *Trauma and recovery: The aftermath of violence—from domestic abuse to political terror.* New York: Basic Books.

Ivey, A. (1999). Psychotherapy as liberation: Toward specific skills and strategies in multicultural counseling and therapy. In J. Ponterotto, J. M. Casas, L. A. Suzuki, & C. M. Alexander (Eds.), *Handbook of multicultural counseling.* Thousand Oaks, CA: Sage.

Kleinman, A. (1988). *Rethinking psychiatry: From cultural category to personal experience.* New York: Free Press.

La Roche, M. (2002). Psychotherapeutic considerations in treating Latinos. *Harvard Review of Psychiatry, 10,* 115–122.

La Roche, M. (2005). The psychotherapeutic process and the cultural context: Towards a cultural psychotherapy. *Journal of Behavioral Integration, 15,* 169–175.

La Roche, M., & Tawa, J. (2011). Taking back our streets: A clinical model for empowering urban youths through participation in peace promotion. *Peace and Conflict: Journal of Peace Psychology, 17*(1), 4–21.

Levant, R. (1995). *Masculinity reconstructed.* New York: Dutton.

Lind, R. L. (Ed.). (1957). *Oedipus Rex* (A. Cook, Trans.). In *Ten Greek plays in contemporary translations.* New York: Houghton Mifflin.

Pleck, J. (1995). The gender role strain paradigm: An update. In R. Levant & W. Pollack (Eds.), *Masculinity reconstructed.* New York: Dutton.

Pollack, W. (1998). *Real boys: Rescuing our sons from the myths of boyhood.* New York: Random House.

Prilleltensky, I. (1999). Values, assumption and practice: Assessing the moral implications of psychological discourse and action. *American Psychologist, 53*(2), 202–213.

Roccas, S., & Brewer, M. B. (2002). Social identity complexity. *Personality and Social Psychology Review, 6*(2), 88–106.

Sue, S., Fujino, D. C., Hu, L. T., Takeuchi, D. T., & Zane, N. W. (1991). Community mental health services for ethnic minority groups: A test of the cultural responsiveness hypothesis. *Journal of Consulting and Clinical Psychology, 59*(4), 533–540.

Wagner, R. V., de Rivera, J., & Watkins, M. (Eds.). (1988). Psychology and the promotion of peace. *Journal of Social Issues, 44*(2).

White, M., & Epston, D. (1990). *Narrative means to therapeutic ends.* New York: Norton.

Zimbardo, P. (2008). *The Lucifer effect: Understanding how good people turn evil.* New York: Random House.

CHAPTER 4

Addressing Cultural Differences in the Psychotherapeutic Process

It's time for parents to teach young people early on that in diversity there is a beauty and there is a strength.

—Maya Angelou

The United States is quickly becoming the home for individuals from all corners of the world. Throughout most of its history, the United States has experienced a vast influx of immigrants from different races, religions, and ethnicities. As a result many different generations of diverse clients are visiting our psychotherapy offices in increasing numbers. As the diversity of our clients grows, two important psychotherapeutic questions arise. First, should cultural differences be addressed in psychological treatment? And second, if cultural differences are addressed, then when and how should these differences be addressed? This chapter discusses these two questions and further elaborates my work with Aprile Maxie, entitled, "Ten Considerations in Addressing Cultural Differences in Psychotherapy" (La Roche & Maxie, 2003). In contrast to previous work, however, this chapter takes a more systematic and thorough approach to the matter. The 10 clinical recommendations are described in more detail and integrated with the three-phased cultural psychotherapeutic model. Thus, each of the 10 recommendations is introduced in relation to one of the three phases. Any of these recommendations could have been placed within any of the three treatment phases of cultural psychotherapy. That is, any one of these recommendations can be beneficial during any phase of cultural therapy. However, each is described within a particular phase for practical and theoretical reasons. Each recommendation is discussed in the phase where it is best conceptualized and/or can be of most utility.

Before describing the 10 clinical recommendations, it is important to clarify some key terms. After these terms are defined, a general description of the three prevalent clinical perspectives to address cultural differences in psychotherapy is presented, followed by the 10 clinical recommendations to address cultural differences.

UNDERSTANDING AND DEFINING KEY TERMS

Cultural Differences

When we think about cultural differences, most of us immediately imagine people who are from a different ethnic or racial background. In our culture, race and ethnicity have become the main standards to define the "we/us," and "others/them" (Sue & Sue, 2008). Our culture emphasizes an understanding of who we are and who others are based on skin color and place of birth. Unfortunately, these differences often end up separating and segregating people rather than promoting dialogue and growth. Furthermore, through explicit and implicit messages, cultural differences are consistently undervalued by the dominant culture (Dovidio, 2009; Weisbuch, Pauker, & Ambady, 2009). Cultural psychotherapy attempts to go beyond racial and ethnic stereotypes and seeks a more accurate understanding of who we are. To accomplish this goal, however, it is first necessary to define racial, ethnic, and cultural differences. These terms are distinct and are often used interchangeably in the psychotherapeutic literature, generating confusion and misunderstanding. The manner in which the concepts of race, ethnicity, and culture are understood has direct implications for the way cultural difference is defined. For this reason, I start by briefly defining each of these terms.

Race

Race is often defined in terms of selected physical characteristics, criteria, or permanent attributes (Betancourt & Lopez, 1993). Historically, skin color and facial characteristics are used to define racial groupings (e.g., Landrine & Klonoff, 1996). A racial difference occurs when people have different racial characteristics. In addition, these differences are considered permanent.

Ethnicity

Although many equate race with ethnicity, these are two distinct terms. Ethnicity is broader than race, as it relates to the shared nationality, language, common values, beliefs, and/or customs of an identifiable group of people (Betancourt & Lopez, 1993). Ethnicity includes a person's identification with their ethnic group, which may be determined by genealogical ties or geographical origins (e.g., born in the same country) or other socially related factors (Alvidrez, Azocar, & Miranda, 1996). For example, an ethnic difference would exist between individuals who are born in different geographical areas. Although these differences are permanent, they are more complex, requiring some level of flexibility. For example, a woman who has lived all her life in the United States and whose father was Filipino and mother Latino could identify herself as "Filipino American," or "Latino-Filipino" or other combinations at different times. It is also important to note that a person can identify him- or herself as Latino (ethnically), but be perceived as black because of her or his skin color (racially).

Culture

Culture has been understood in multiple ways; however, Geertz's (1973) definition of culture is particularly applicable to the discussion of cultural differences in psychotherapy. Geertz (1973) defined culture as

> a historically transmitted pattern of meanings embodied in symbols; a system of inherited conceptions expressed in symbolic forms by means of which people communicate, perpetuate, and develop their knowledge about their attitudes toward life. (p. 89)

Consequently, culture is understood as an interrelated web of meanings that are *dynamic, complex,* and *representative of a multifaceted experience,* in which a person is understood first and foremost as *homo symbolicus,* or meaning maker. This definition of culture suggests a broader and more inclusive understanding of culture, cultural variables and cultural differences not limited to ethnic or racial minorities. For this reason, when I talk about cultural variables or differences in this chapter, I am including not only racial and ethnic differences, but also sexual orientation, socioeconomic status (SES), religion, and language, just to name a few possibilities. Although in general individuals within a cultural group may share some meanings, people construe meanings in many diverse, complex, and changing manners. In addition to this conceptual reason to broaden our cultural understanding, it is suggested that addressing multiple cultural differences has significant clinical value. The first clinical recommendation proposed in this chapter, that *"cultural differences should be viewed as subjective, complex, and dynamic,"* is a direct result of this conceptualization of culture.

THEORETICAL PERSPECTIVES TO ADDRESS CULTURAL DIFFERENCES

Another result of this broad understanding of culture is that differences (e.g., skin color, religion, SES, gender orientation) are not only likely, but inevitable in the psychotherapeutic encounter (Cardemil & Battle, 2003; Davies, 2011; Gonzalez, Biever, & Gardner, 1994; Hays, 2008). However, the theoretical importance of cultural differences and the subsequent ways in which they are (or are not) considered and used in psychotherapy vary. Despite the enormous diversity of approaches, cultural differences have traditionally been understood and categorized through three distinct perspectives: universalism, particularism, and transcendism (Segall, Lonner, & Berry, 1998; Tyler, Brome, & Williams, 1991). Researchers have used different names to refer to each of these three perspectives, and although the labels may vary, the main underlying theoretical ideas are similar. There are no clinicians, however, who would label themselves using these categories; nevertheless, I have found these terms useful to identify and clarify clinicians' cultural assumptions. As clinicians become increasingly aware of their cultural assumptions, they can become more effective in designing culturally sensitive interventions. Below, each of these approaches is briefly described, as means for clinicians to further explore their cultural assumptions.

Universalist Clinicians

The common denominator of universalist clinicians is that they underscore similarities, not differences. Universalist clinicians do not believe cultural differences should be highlighted in psychotherapy. In support of this view, they argue that general factors such as the therapeutic alliance, degree of warmth, and empathy are necessary to facilitate any type of successful psychotherapy (Kaduchin, 1972). They believe that if general treatment factors are present, psychotherapy will have a favorable outcome irrespective of race, ethnicity, or context. Consequently, therapists who endorse these assumptions prioritize the need to foster these universal treatment ingredients and overlook cultural differences.

Many clinicians argue that if addressing cultural differences is an intervention that has rarely been theorized to be therapeutic or currently lacks evidence to support its usefulness, then, why should it be considered? Similarly, most clinicians would argue that it is impossible to accomplish all treatment interventions in one hour of therapy and that it is necessary to prioritize and focus on treatments theorized to be therapeutic (e.g., eradicating irrational beliefs, understanding the oedipal complex).

The emergence and development of empirically supported treatments (ESTs; Chambless, 1996; Chambless et al., 1998) is a movement highly influenced by universalist conceptualizations. In support of this statement, most EST manuals[1] do not include strategies to address cultural differences and many cultural variables are often not explored sufficiently. Many ESTs have yet to be validated with different ethnic minority samples. To be fair, most EST authors note these limitations (e.g., Chambless et al., 1996); however, only a few (although the number is growing rapidly) do in fact undertake their validation projects with culturally diverse groups. The main aim of most ESTs is the refinement of specific psychotherapeutic ingredients to ameliorate a certain constellation of symptoms as defined by the *Diagnostic and Statistical Manual of Mental Disorders* (*DSM-4;* American Psychiatric Association, 1994). These specific therapeutic ingredients are assumed to be effective independently of the therapeutic relationship or cultural context (e.g., Chambless et al., 1996; Chambless et al., 1998). It is almost suggested that these therapeutic ingredients have a universal effect. However, more recently a growing number of landmark EST studies have emphasized the importance of including both the cultural context and the therapeutic relationship (e.g., Hinton et al., 2005; Rosselló, Bernal, & Rivera-Medina, 2008) and started to develop important psychotherapeutic adaptations for different cultural groups.

Particularist Clinicians

In sharp contrast to universalists, the particularist perspective contends that ethnicity and race have a decisive and unavoidable impact on an individual's experience. Race, ethnicity, and/or culture powerfully determine the way in which people define themselves and relate to others. Given these fundamental racial and ethnic differences, it is difficult, if not impossible, for individuals from different backgrounds to understand each other (Dixon, 1976; Jackson, 1976; White, 1970). In partial support of this approach, most studies show that clients prefer therapists matched to their race, ethnicity, and native language (Coleman, Wampold, & Casali, 1995). From a particularist approach, racial/ethnic differences are insurmountable barriers that make it unlikely that clients and therapists from different backgrounds can work together successfully. Thus, the basic clinical recommendation that stems from this perspective is that clinicians of a specific background should only work with clients from that same background.

In reality, although it is possible to create some level of ethnic or racial match, it is very difficult to create multiple cultural matches. It is nearly impossible to find a clinician that shares most or even many of the cultural characteristics (e.g., sexual orientation, religion, socioeconomic status) of a client. Also, the number of clinicians from different backgrounds remains limited. For example, in a survey of psychologists, only 12% reported speaking a language other than English well enough to provide services in that language (American Psychological Association, 2010). Despite these significant practical limitations, it is important to note that partly as a result of this particularist conceptualization, many mental health associations (e.g., psychology, social work, and psychiatry) have underscored the need to train providers from a variety of racial and ethnic backgrounds.

Transcendist Clinicians

Last, the transcendist perspective affirms the importance of addressing cultural differences and designing strategies to do so. Despite the differences between individuals from different ethnic/racial backgrounds, therapists from this perspective believe these differences can be transcended. That is, clinicians can learn cultural competencies that will allow them to effectively treat clients from backgrounds different from their own.

Perhaps no one has done more to support the need to develop cultural competencies than the Sue brothers (David, Derald, and Stanley), who have worked tirelessly in developing cultural guidelines (e.g., Sue, Arredondo, & McDavis, 1992; Sue, Ivey, & Pedersen, 1996; Sue & Sue, 2008). Many of the clinical recommendations proposed in this chapter, and in this book, are influenced by their important contributions. The basic idea is that cultural competencies can be learned and that the effectiveness of psychotherapy with diverse clients increases as we develop our cultural competencies. There is an important difference between their work and mine, however. Their ideas seem to have emerged from university counseling sessions, while many of the ideas proposed in this book have originated from clinical settings. Clients seen in clinical settings have more severe mental health problems than the ones encountered in the counseling offices of universities. For this reason, I consistently talk about psychotherapy, while the Sues mostly talk about counseling.

Proponents of the common factor model (e.g., Norcross, 2002, 2010; Wampold, 2001, 2010) could be included in the transcendist group. They argue that although the therapeutic relationship is a necessary and common factor for favorable outcomes in psychotherapy, it has different meanings for each individual (Norcross, 2002, 2010; Wampold, 2001, 2010).

Segall et al. (1998) reported that most clinicians seem to subscribe to a transcendist model, thereby locating themselves theoretically somewhere between the universalist and particularistic perspectives in terms of their views on the importance of addressing cultural differences in psychotherapy. Nevertheless, the lack of mention of cultural differences in many psychotherapeutic theories indicates the prevalence of universalist assumptions. This suggestion is supported by a study conducted by Aprile Maxie and colleagues (Maxie, Arnold, & Stephenson, 2006), in which the authors found that only 43% of their sample of licensed psychologists ever had conversations with their clients about cultural differences.

Perhaps it goes without saying that cultural psychotherapy adheres to a transcendist stance and emphasizes the importance of discussing cultural differences when appropriate. Having an open conversation with diverse clients presents an opportunity to discover one's self, the client, and our contexts through the dialectic of sameness and difference. Cultural psychotherapy suggests that our desire to know and grow is fueled by both our differences and similarities (Davies, 2011). Although there is a growing and increasingly sophisticated literature that proposes various strategies to address cultural differences (e.g., Cardemil & Battle, 2003; Hays, 2008), in this chapter the goal is to integrate these recommendations with the three-phased cultural psychotherapeutic model. Unfortunately, the empirical research on the effectiveness of addressing cultural differences in psychotherapy remains limited and is supported only through clinical cases (Hays, 2008); thus, these recommendations must be viewed as tentative clinical considerations to be tested through further research and practice.

TEN CLINICAL CONSIDERATIONS IN ADDRESSING CULTURAL DIFFERENCES

The 10 clinical recommendations suggested and described in this section are designed to help determine how and under what circumstances we should discuss cultural differences in psychotherapy. The primary goal is to help clinicians intervene in a therapeutic manner when working with clients whose racial, ethnic, and/or cultural backgrounds are different from their own. Given that cultural psychotherapy defines cultural differences broadly, these recommendations should be applicable to most clinical encounters. These are guidelines only and not meant to be used in a cookbook approach. Clearly, these considerations should be adapted to the specific characteristics of each client, therapeutic relationship, and context. Under no circumstances is there an adequate substitute for good clinical judgment and an understanding of the unique requirements of the psychotherapeutic process. Moreover, it is important to appraise all 10 clinical recommendations simultaneously rather than embracing one without regard to the others. Finally, these recommendations are grouped in accordance to the clinical phase they best underscore.

Addressing Cultural Differences During Phase I

4.1   Cultural differences should be viewed as subjective, complex, and dynamic.

4.2   The most salient cultural differences should be addressed first.

4.3   Similarities should be addressed as a prelude to discussions of cultural differences.

4.4   The client's level of distress and presenting problem often determine when and if cultural differences are discussed.

4.5   Cultural differences are addressed as assets.

4.6   It is necessary to consider the client's cultural past and racial identity development.

Addressing Cultural Differences During Phase II

4.7   Meanings and cultural differences are influenced by the psychotherapeutic relationship.

4.8   The clinician's cultural competence has an impact on the way differences are addressed.

Addressing Cultural Differences During Phase III

4.9   Cultural contexts affect the therapeutic relationship.

4.10   Dialogues about cultural differences can impact the cultural context.

4.1 Cultural Differences Should Be Viewed as Subjective, Complex, and Dynamic

First, there may be some agreement in any psychotherapeutic relationship on what constitutes a cultural difference (e.g., ethnicity, religion, and race) between client and therapist. For example, there are some obvious characteristics such as skin color, accents, or socioeconomic status that are immediately categorized as a cultural difference. However, the interpretations or meanings of these differences are subjective. Clients understand these dissimilarities according to their own set of experiences, and these subjective meanings are often more relevant than the "objective" differences themselves. Therefore, therapists could benefit if they suspended their preconceptions about the meaning of cultural differences (Cardemil & Battle, 2003; Helms, Jernigan, & Macher, 2005) and allowed themselves to know their clients free from stereotypical racial/ethnic assumptions. This recommendation challenges the notion that there is one standard way to treat individuals of a specific race or ethnicity. This conceptualization dashes the belief that "one size fits all individuals" of a certain cultural group. Rather, it emphasizes the need to explore the meanings that clients ascribe to cultural differences.

Second, beyond the subjective differences that naturally exist, it is argued that cultural differences are multiple and complex (Bingham, Porché-Burke, James, Sue, & Vasquez, 2002; Hays, 2008). As previously stated, cultural differences may include multiple variables (e.g., gender, sexual orientation, socioeconomic status, age, educational level, language, and religion). It is crucial to consider all possible differences and to identify how these differences come together in defining an individual's identity and experience. For example, it might be more effective therapeutically to understand the multiple and interacting experiences of being a young second-generation Muslim Japanese American man than to focus solely on his ethnicity. Moreover, each of these characteristics is complex and includes several possible meanings within different contexts. What type of Islam does he embrace? From which town in Japan do his parents come? Furthermore, the meanings of each of these differences can vary according to contexts. For example, being a devoted Muslim may be acceptable in his family setting but a painful secret at work.

Third, the perceptions on the part of clients and therapists as to what constitutes cultural differences are dynamic, not static. At different points in the therapeutic process, what is construed as a cultural difference may shift into the background, and other factors may come to the forefront. Therefore, therapists are encouraged to engage in ongoing exploration of changing meanings rather than to assume that once cultural differences have been understood, it is no longer necessary to continue exploring. Meanings are always in flux, and it is important to explore these as well as the factors influencing them (White & Epston, 1990). For example, a dark-skinned African American female physician started to change her acquiescent attitude toward her lighter-skinned African American female therapist. The client had angrily questioned her therapist's ability to understand her. There had been no such questions during the first year of psychotherapy. In exploring this change, the client explained that she recently had been subject to discrimination at work. Her colleagues had jokingly hinted, but repeatedly, that she had obtained her medical degree because of affirmative action preferences, and she feared that her lighter-skinned therapist might also think that she had achieved her position as a physician because of something other than merit. This case also illustrates the multiple shades of "one race," which also calls into question the usefulness of classifications such as race.

4.2 The Most Salient Cultural Differences Should Be Addressed First

This consideration is based on two clinical assumptions: first, that cultural differences have varied levels of significance, and second, that it is often beneficial for clinicians to directly address cultural differences. With regard to the first assumption, cultural differences are construed in many ways and have different ascribed levels of relevance. Not all differences have the same relative value in the therapeutic relationship. Clinicians should explore these meanings and consider addressing first what is most salient. It may be possible, for example, that dissimilarities in race between client and therapist may not hold the same weight as differences in marital status. Cultural psychotherapy argues that the saliency of the difference is influenced by the histories of the therapist and client, their interpersonal history, and the cultural context in which the differences are embedded.

The second assumption of this clinical recommendation is that clinicians should directly address cultural differences. Given the power differential in the therapeutic relationship (La Roche, 1999; Pinderhughes, 1989; Sue & Sue, 2008), which may be particularly noticeable in the first phase of cultural psychotherapy, the majority of clients do not initiate discussions of cultural difference. Clients and therapists alike often feel they must tread lightly when it comes to cultural differences. Hence, the therapist may need to communicate openness and comfort in understanding the client's unique experiences, including cultural perspectives (Sue & Sue, 2008; Whaley, 2001). A therapist who directly acknowledges a difference with a client takes the first step in exploring the meaning of the difference and whether the client views the difference as important. This is particularly relevant during the second phase of cultural psychotherapy. In addition, addressing client-therapist differences opens up a dialogue about the meaning of difference within the therapeutic relationship. Although clients may choose not to immediately address these differences, having this conversation conveys the message that cultural differences are important and can be addressed at any time during the psychological process.

Many clinicians believe it is more appropriate to wait until clients bring up the issue of cultural differences. Cultural psychotherapy, however, maintains that at the very least a conversation needs to be had to let the client know it is all right to address cultural differences, if not going further and actually addressing them right away. Although in certain situations it is still recommended that the client initiate the discussion, a therapist should seriously consider that when salient differences or multiple cultural dissimilarities exist, it is important for the therapist to take the initiative. Some theorists have even suggested that the therapist routinely address differences in the first session (e.g., Gopaul-McNeil & Brice-Baker, 1998; Paniagua, 1998). Cultural psychotherapy, in contrast, argues that the decision to address differences depends on several factors. One such factor is the degree of saliency of the cultural difference between client and therapist. The clinical recommendation is that the more salient the cultural difference is, the sooner it should be addressed.

The following example illustrates this point. Eddie, an 18-year-old Puerto Rican male, was mandated to start counseling through the court system. He met with a middle-aged, White European American female therapist. From the onset of treatment, it was obvious that Eddie was reluctant to speak. He appeared very guarded, and the therapist sensed his intense anger over having to attend the counseling session. The therapist therefore stated, "It must make you angry to be forced to talk with a White female therapist." Eddie defiantly responded, "We live in different worlds." The therapist validated Eddie's point, and during the session she determined that he did not like to communicate with White people, particularly women. Therefore, she had to address the meaning of their differences. Without an explicit discussion of these differences, it would have been difficult to bridge the cultural gap that existed between them. Six months later, Eddie reported that this discussion helped him to open up slowly and talk more about his experiences. Many clinicians may believe that as they discuss differences with their clients, they are diminishing their ability to use the commonality of human experience in their therapeutic work. Nevertheless, it should be kept in mind that therapists can effectively use both client-therapist differences and similarities in their work with culturally diverse clients.

4.3 Similarities Should Be Addressed as a Prelude to Discussions of Cultural Differences

As previously noted, therapists and clients may not only differ on a number of cultural attributes; they may also share cultural characteristics (Hays, 2008; Speight & Vera, 1997). One approach that may be useful is to explicitly share commonalities before fully exploring cultural differences. A client may benefit from the therapist's acknowledgment of certain similarities between them, and addressing commonalities may serve to reduce the client's ambivalence or increase the therapist's perceived credibility (Speight & Vera, 1997). The acknowledgment of similarities may also assist therapists in establishing initial rapport, which may allow the client to experience more comfort, security, and acceptance. This strategy may also serve to reduce apprehensions about treatment, especially in the presence of significant cultural differences between therapist and client. For example, during the early stages of treatment or during stressful periods (i.e., when clients are presenting with high anxiety or depression levels), the therapist's highlighting of similarities may make clients feel more respected and accepted. As a consequence, during these times emphasizing commonalities can assist the client in engaging more successfully in psychotherapy. An initial emphasis on similarities, however, does not negate the need to address differences.

The following example illustrates a situation in which the therapist addressed similarities with a new client through self-disclosure. A Korean woman was disappointed that she was not assigned to the Asian therapist who had been recommended by her friend. The Asian therapist she wanted to see had no available openings and she disappointedly had to settle for a Latino therapist. The clinician sensed his client's ambivalence in working with someone from a different cultural background and he feared that she would drop out of treatment. Thus, the clinician decided to share in the first few sessions several commonalities: first, that they were both ethnic minorities, and second, they had both lost their fathers. After a few months of psychotherapy, the client relayed that discussing these commonalities initially had helped her to bond with the therapist and to begin to trust him. Focusing on these similarities also opened the door to examination of cultural differences in later sessions. Nevertheless, it is again important to underscore the need to use caution when and if clinicians decide to disclose personal information. Clinicians should only disclose information that furthers the therapeutic process. The decision to share personal information must be a result of careful analyses of its benefits and disadvantages, and the information disclosed must also be information that the therapist feels comfortable sharing (see recommendation 2.5: Continue to develop a culturally sensitive therapeutic relationship)..

4.4 The Client's Level of Distress and Presenting Problem Often Determine When and If Cultural Differences Are Discussed

As emphasized in Chapter 1, it is crucial to assess the degree of emotional distress and the severity of the client's chief complaint (Lopez, 1997). The more stable (optimal levels of affect regulation) a client is, the more likely it is that he or she will benefit from a discussion of cultural differences. In contrast, the frailer and less stable clients are (e.g., extremely anxious, severely depressed, delusional, or severe substance abusers), the more likely it is that they will benefit from this dialogue. Moreover, the issue of differences should not be brought up during a crisis intervention, regardless of saliency. Concerns for safety, focusing on mental status, and working toward improved functioning are paramount in working with any client. While some counseling approaches (e.g., Gopaul-McNeil & Brice-Baker, 1998; Paniagua, 1998) argue that it is beneficial to address cultural differences in the first session, cultural psychotherapy holds that this is not recommended when clients are unstable (e.g., suicidal, experiencing domestic violence).

Additionally, it is important to keep in mind that it can be detrimental to the therapeutic relationship to repeatedly address these differences when clients are pressed by other concerns. For example, many of my students, after hearing me talk about the importance of addressing cultural difference, start initiating discussions of cultural differences when clients are clearly not interested or ready to engage in such dialogues. As a result, clients may perceive therapists as not being sensitive to their concerns. This has sometimes prompted clients to drop out of treatment and underscores the risks of addressing cultural differences. Sometimes working with similarities in these circumstances may be more productive (Speight & Vera, 1997). Nevertheless, therapists should still seriously consider how cultural factors influence the severely distressed and how further treatment should incorporate addressing cultural issues.

4.5 Cultural Differences Are Addressed as Assets

Many culturally diverse clients have repeatedly experienced how the majority group construes their cultural differences as deficits (Steele & Aronson, 1995; Sue, 1998). In the United States, being a member of a nondominant group (e.g., not Caucasian, female, homosexual, non-Christian, disabled, etc.) is viewed as a deficiency, whereas persons who are White, male, Christian, and heterosexual are viewed as better. It is often helpful to suggest how these assumed "deficiencies" are fabricated by explicit and implicit messages held by mainstream culture rather than limitations that reside within clients (Zimbardo, 2008). However, efforts to discuss these differences should proceed gradually, gently, and carefully. They should always follow the client's lead. Moreover, whenever possible, clinicians should attempt to examine how differences are related to a client's strengths rather than viewing them as weaknesses. For example, one of my White psychology students stated to her Latino client, "Feel free to ask me any questions if you don't understand my English." Although the psychology intern was attempting to empower her client to ask questions, she inadvertently also assumed that it was her client's responsibility to know English rather than her own responsibility to have some fluency in Spanish. Although many of us value differences and view them as assets, this is not an easy message to convey in therapy, particularly given the large number of explicit and implicit messages suggesting that differences from the dominant groups are problematic.

Furthermore, cultural differences can make it difficult for clients and therapists to understand each other and develop an appropriate therapeutic relationship or even a good working alliance (Bordin, 1979). In the psychotherapeutic process, as in any social interaction, cultural differences can be misconstrued and lead to misunderstandings that rupture the therapeutic relationship. Nevertheless, if therapists are able to learn strategies to repair these ruptures, an opportunity for clients (and therapists) to broaden their explicit and implicit systems through cultural dialogue emerges. Through this rupture-repair process (see Chapter 2), our self-awareness is enhanced and we become more flexible in responding to our context by developing new ways to understand ourselves, our relationships, and our context.

4.6 It Is Necessary to Consider the Client's Cultural Past and Racial Identity Development

Research finds that clients' cultural history and development (e.g., racial identity and acculturation levels) can mediate the effectiveness of the ethnic/racial match between clients and therapists from different cultural backgrounds (Carter, 1995; Chun, Balls-Organista, &

Marin, 2003; Helms, 2007). Helms and Cook (1999) formulated a cognitive-developmental model in which the level of acceptance of therapists from different cultural backgrounds depends upon the client's level of racial identity and consciousness. This model proposes that ethnic matching of clients and therapists can result in "cultural mismatches" if therapists and clients from the same ethnic group show markedly different levels of racial identity. This model emphasizes cognitive and developmental characteristics of clients and implies that therapists cannot help to facilitate changes that are in conflict with their clients' cultural developmental stages. Furthermore, the racial identity literature proposes techniques or psychotherapeutic strategies for working with clients at specific stages of racial development (Helms, 2007; Helms & Cook, 1999), because clients are at different levels of readiness to explore certain issues depending on their own cultural awareness.

Similarly, within the acculturation literature (e.g., Chun et al., 2003) effective treatment recommendations are being developed. A case in point involves a therapist working with a family that had emigrated from China. The therapist noticed differences in acculturation status and racial identity among family members. The family had come to this country when the son was 8 years old. The parents had identified the son, now 17, as rebellious, and they considered his new friends from high school to be a negative influence. The father thought that limiting his contact with these friends would immediately resolve their familial issues; however, this restriction only increased his rebelliousness. After the therapist assessed the family, she found the son to be struggling with his own sociocultural development. Although he wanted to immerse himself in his friends' mainstream world, he did not want to betray his family and Chinese values. The therapist found it necessary to work individually with the son. She helped him identify his own cultural values and then develop practical strategies for bridging the cultural gap between his family and friends. As the son became more culturally aware of his own conflicted values, his rebellious behavior diminished, and he started making decisions about what was important for him (Helms, 2007; Helms & Cook, 1999). This intervention would not have been possible if the therapist had not assessed the family's level of cultural development and realized that the son was ready to confront some cultural identity issues even though his family was not. In addition, it was crucial that the therapist was knowledgeable about traditional Chinese values. Without this knowledge, she might have believed that the son's struggle was an attempt to individuate from an enmeshed family, and she might therefore have encouraged his family to give him more freedom. In turn, the family could have understood this recommendation as a threat to the family unit. Chinese families often value interdependence and harmony more than autonomy and independence (Lee, 2000; Sue & Sue, 2008); consequently, if the family had received this recommendation, they may have dropped out of psychotherapy.

4.7 Meanings and Cultural Differences Are Influenced by the Psychotherapeutic Relationship

This and the next clinical recommendation are particularly useful during the second phase of cultural psychotherapy, "understanding clients' experiences." To explain these recommendations, it is important to underscore that each psychotherapeutic relationship develops unique interpersonal dynamics that encourage some topics to be discussed and others to be overlooked. From the very first session, the way differences are examined powerfully influences what happens in treatment. Thus, the potential to discuss cultural differences is partly dependent upon this interpersonal history. Relational factors begin to play a larger role in the second phase, in which implicit systems get played out in treatment (see Chapter 2).

An illustration of this point comes from Gina, a 31-year-old single Italian American architect who realized that her White male psychotherapist was ignoring her ongoing gender issues with her boss. She repeatedly brought them up but he failed to validate them. Gina wondered if he did not comment on these differences because he did not think it was clinically important do so. As a result of this oversight, Gina stopped bringing up gender issues and then also avoided discussing cultural issues with her therapist (who had a Scottish background). She felt that if he could not understand her gender issues, he surely could not grasp the meaning of her Sicilian-Italian background. She was born into a large, close-knit, and at times loud family that was still very present in her life. Unable to share many of her important gender and cultural experiences, she considered terminating treatment. Fortunately, her therapist sensed her frustration and sought supervision in which he realized that he was dismissing Gina's gender and cultural issues. He realized that even though both were "White," they endorsed different cultural beliefs. As a result, he soon started addressing her gender (e.g., experiences with her boss) and cultural issues (e.g., how it is to grow up in a large family), which had become the elephant in the room. Once these issues were brought to the surface and thoroughly explored, Gina felt empowered to address gender issues with her male boss. This example underscores the usefulness of exploring cultural differences among members of a majority group.

Unfortunately, it is fairly common for therapists and clients alike to miss important cultural cues that could lead to beneficial discussions of cultural difference. By overlooking cues, we may misunderstand the issues that are being brought up by our clients. Consequently, cultural issues may not get the attention they require. Therefore, we should strive to listen carefully for cultural issues in all psychotherapeutic encounters. Cultural psychotherapy encourages clinicians to critically evaluate the content of psychotherapeutic dialogues and to question whether some cultural issues are overlooked or, conversely, inappropriately emphasized.

4.8 The Clinician's Cultural Competence Has an Impact on the Way Differences Are Addressed

Although the therapist's level of cultural competency is difficult to operationalize, the literature on multiculturalism has identified three common dimensions (Sue et al., 1992; Sue & Sue, 2008). First, the therapist's beliefs and attitudes toward culturally different clients play an important role in psychotherapy. Consequently, we should actively and consistently explore our feelings and thoughts (e.g., countertransference, prejudice, and ethnic biases) in providing treatment to clients from different cultural backgrounds (or any clients in general). In doing so, we will be more attuned to our own comfort levels in dealing with cultural differences. Second, although therapists and clients may be dissimilar in their cultural backgrounds, we should possess some basic knowledge of our clients' cultures

(Atkinson & Lowe, 1995; Sue & Sue, 2008). Last, the therapist's development over time of specific skills, interventions, and strategies (Sue & Zane, 1987; Sue & Sue, 2008) comes about through education and clinical experience with diverse clients.

There are many ways for clinicians to enhance their cultural competence. These include reading about culturally diverse groups, seeking consultation or supervision from culturally diverse peers, or even attending different cultural events. In addition, many of us have found that traveling to foreign countries or exposure to and participation in activities in ethnically diverse neighborhoods and communities is equally helpful in learning more about dissimilar cultures. Finally, and perhaps most important, is the understanding that the pursuit of cultural competency is a lifelong learning process that is never completed. This process may include formal cultural competency training, but what is most important is critical self-evaluation and questioning of what is taking place in cross-cultural therapeutic encounters (Sue, 1998; Sue & Sue, 2008). But perhaps even more important than this ongoing learning process is a genuine desire to learn with people of other cultural backgrounds.

4.9 Cultural Contexts Affect the Therapeutic Relationship

The final two clinical recommendations are particularly useful during the third phase of cultural psychotherapy, "fostering empowerment." These recommendations emphasize the fact that the therapeutic relationship takes place in a sociocultural, political, and historical context that is constantly producing contextual (explicit and implicit) messages (La Roche & Tawa, 2011). These contextual messages influence what takes place in psychotherapy (Ivey, 1995; La Roche, 1999, 2002). This recommendation underscores the point that psychotherapy does not occur in a historical and geographical vacuum—as seems to be assumed by many psychotherapeutic models that fail to underscore the cultural context as a source of clinical information. Although contextual messages are present even before client and therapist meet, they are often more effectively understood during the third phase of treatment. For example, it was only after a few months of treatment that some of my White clients divulged that they almost "no showed" at their first appointment with me, because they could tell by my accent on the phone that I was Latino, and that made them uncomfortable. This highlights the point that clients can sometimes be hesitant about being treated by someone from a different ethnic background, perhaps fearing that someone different from themselves may not be able to understand and therefore help them.

Furthermore, events taking place outside the therapeutic session can contribute to whether clients and therapists address cultural differences. For example, discussions of societal racism can facilitate a discussion about client-therapist differences as described in Chapters 2 and 3, where I discuss how events of discrimination and violence within the community triggered significant dialogues about differences. Alternatively, it is also conceivable that some clients are hesitant to bring up issues of difference due to negative feelings with regard to these same events taking place outside of therapy.

To avoid problems, it is often useful for a therapist to directly ask clients if important contextual events have taken place recently, or if they have any concerns about being treated by a therapist of a different background (e.g., male, heterosexual, Latino). Exploring these issues is useful in generating discussions about cultural difference or making assessments about the importance of contextual events in relation to therapist-client differences. As previously discussed in this chapter, the most salient differences should be addressed first. The client's response to the inquiry will dictate the course of the discussion. It may be that the client expresses no concern. Nevertheless, with this questioning the therapist is also conveying the message that cultural differences are important and can be addressed at any time the client feels it is important or that he or she is ready to do so. Additionally, it may be relevant to communicate the following to the client: "Please let me know if there are things that I say in our work together that do not fit with your values, beliefs, or life experiences. I would like for you to let me know about these differences because I think it will be useful in our working together."

4.10 Dialogues About Cultural Differences Can Impact the Cultural Context

There is a bidirectional relationship between the therapeutic relationship and clients' context, which means that not only can the cultural context influence the psychotherapeutic process, but changes within the psychotherapeutic relationship can potentially impact the cultural context[2] (see Chapter 3 on how a group of disfranchised adolescents had an impact on their context). As clients and therapists become increasingly aware of the multiple and complex influences of their context (e.g., systems and situations), they become more effective in responding to and transforming it (Ivey, 1995; La Roche, 2002; La Roche & Christopher, 2009).

Mainstream culture in the United States, for example, espouses values such as materialism, competition, and heterosexuality while it condones other values, such as spiritualism, collectivism, and homosexuality (Cushman, 1995; Sue & Sue, 2008). Through explicit and implicit messages, these values inadvertently exert much control over our lives by encouraging us to pursue certain objectives while minimizing others (Sue & Sue, 2008). Contextual influences seem particularly powerful among cultural minorities, who may not completely share U.S. mainstream values but feel even more pressured than people from the dominant culture to adjust to or assimilate into a more mainstream way of life. Nonetheless, as we start discussing cultural differences, identifying explicit and implicit messages and related sociopolitical issues, we become more empowered to acknowledge, choose, and speak about our important life values and goals (Ivey, 1995; La Roche, 2002). Consequently, clients are able to make better-informed decisions about their lives rather than blindly following the path that society has prescribed for them.

One way to increase this awareness is to explore how the therapeutic relationship reflects the broader sociocultural context (La Roche, 1999, 2002). Therapists often have more ascribed power than clients, and it is useful first to identify these power differentials and second to examine their consequences and meanings. As clients become aware of these power inequities and other cultural assumptions, they are encouraged to question the impact that these assumptions have on their own lives in both positive and negative ways. If clients are aware of the multiplicity and complexity of cultural influences both within the psychotherapeutic relationship and in society, they may decide to embrace certain cultural values and reject others.

This enhanced awareness of cultural assumptions often leads clients to question their therapists' privileged position (e.g., power, education, religion, ethnicity). Unfortunately, at times, this questioning is experienced as a confrontation, or resistance, by clinicians who may feel clients are attacking what is most precious to them. As a result, clinicians may develop a strong negative response, which can create a psychotherapeutic impasse (La Roche, 1999). However, if clinicians are able to keep providing clients with sufficient support and validation through the therapeutic relationship, then clients will explore and learn alternative ways to cope with cultural differences rather than the standard and ascribed means assigned by society (e.g., avoidance, silent discrimination, acquiescence). Cultural dialogues are a unique opportunity to grow and develop beyond prescribed cultural expectations.

Conclusion

As we become an increasingly diverse society, it is more pressing to design psychotherapeutic interventions that consider and benefit from cultural differences. Culture plays a crucial role in our lives, and if we do not acknowledge its powerful influence, it will restrict our growth. We will blindly succumb to its influence, and we will follow prescribed cultural standards rather than creating our preferred lifestyles. Unfortunately, many universalist psychotherapeutic models have yet not incorporated elements of cultural understanding and as a result have not developed strategies that could benefit from cultural dialogues. Universalist models have often ended up reinforcing the conceptions of the dominant group. In contrast, cultural psychotherapy argues that as we explore cultural differences, we become more aware of different cultural forces (e.g., explicit and implicit messages). This enhanced understanding can lead us to improve both our communities and ourselves. However, if differences are not appropriately addressed, this can discourage our efforts to examine these differences and lead us to avoid the "others." The 10 clinical recommendations described in this chapter are an attempt to reduce these risks and promote a better understanding of cultural differences in the clinical encounter.

There are, however, no simple answers to the questions of when and how to address cultural differences in psychotherapy. Instead, these 10 clinical recommendations should be understood as general guidelines framed within the three-phased cultural psychotherapeutic model and are provided as a means to more systematically guide clinicians in these efforts. Clinicians are encouraged to explore the meanings of cultural differences and similarities rather than to assume that clients will bring a particular experience or perspective to therapy because of their religion, ethnicity, or race. Cultural discussions may actually make the difference in whether clients remain in therapy or drop out prematurely. Since cultural differences are defined broadly, it is argued that they are present to some degree in all clinical encounters.

Finally, the sociopolitical importance of developing a culturally sensitive model to address differences cannot be understated. As the diversity in the U.S. population grows, so does the potential for cultural misunderstandings and injustice. Both misunderstandings and injustices can exacerbate acts of discrimination, microaggressions, terrorism, and even ethnic cleansing or genocide (see Chapter 8). Not exploring cultural differences can make the barriers between cultural groups seem even more insurmountable. As the United States becomes ever more multicultural and a place in which diverse ethnic groups coexist, it is essential to develop effective psychological strategies that respect and validate our individual and group differences.

The psychotherapeutic relationship is a unique opportunity for both clients and therapists to further develop their cultural awareness. That type of growth, however, is not enough for social and cultural transformation. To accomplish that, it is necessary to develop and promote systematic community efforts that allow individuals from a very young age to interact with and learn from people of diverse backgrounds. It is important that we know, as well as experience, how cultural differences are assets that enrich our lives and possibilities. Nevertheless, empirical research is clearly needed to confirm and refine the validity of these approaches and also to elaborate on the strengths and limitations of what has been proposed. This research could benefit by not being limited to psychotherapy, but extended also into communities, schools, and even international relations.

Notes

1. I have read many EST manuals and do not remember reading any explicit strategies for therapists to explore cultural differences. Nevertheless, this is just an observation that is not based on a systematic and representative review of the literature; it is an observation that requires significantly more rigorous study to be confirmed.

2. Unfortunately, the impact of the psychotherapeutic relationship on the context is often more restricted than that of the context on the psychotherapeutic relationship.

References

Alvidrez, J., Azocar, F., & Miranda, J. (1996). Demystifying the concept of ethnicity for psychotherapy research. *Journal of Consulting and Clinical Psychology, 64,* 903–908.

American Psychiatric Association. (1994). *Diagnostic and statistical manual of mental disorders* (4th ed.). Washington, DC: Author.

American Psychological Association. (2010). *2008 APA survey of psychology health service providers: Special analysis.* Washington, DC: Author.

Atkinson, D. R., & Lowe, S. M. (1995). The role of ethnicity, cultural knowledge, and conventional techniques in counseling and psychotherapy. In J. G. Ponterotto, J. M. Casas, L. A. Suzuki, & C. M. Alexander (Eds.), *Handbook of multicultural counseling* (pp. 387–414). Thousand Oaks, CA: Sage.

Betancourt, H., & Lopez, S. (1993). The study of culture, ethnicity, and race in American psychology. *American Psychologist, 48,* 629–637.

Bingham, R. P., Porché-Burke, L., James, S., Sue, D. W., & Vasquez, M. J. T. (2002). Introduction: A report on the National Multicultural Conference and Summit II. *Cultural Diversity and Ethnic Minority Psychology, 8*(2), 75–87.

Bordin, E. S. (1979). The generalizability of the psychoanalytical concept of the working alliance. *Psychotherapy: Theory, Research, and Practice, 16,* 252–260.

Cardemil, E., & Battle, C. (2003). Guess who's coming to therapy? Getting comfortable with conversations about race and ethnicity in psychotherapy. *Professional Psychology: Research and Practice, 34,* 278–286.

Carter, R. T. (1995). *The influence of race and racial identity in psychotherapy: Toward a racially inclusive model.* Hoboken, NJ: John Wiley.

Chambless, D. L. (1996). In defense of dissemination of empirically supported psychological interventions. *Clinical Psychology: Science and Practice, 3,* 230–235.

Chambless, D. L., Baker, M. J., Baucom, D. H., Beutler, L. E., Calhoun, K. S., Crits-Christoph, P., et al. (1998). An update on empirically validated therapies II. *The Clinical Psychologist, 51,* 3–16.

Chambless, D. L., Sanderson, W. C., Shoham, V., Bennet, B. E., Johnson, S., Pope, K. S., et al. (1996). An update on empirically validated therapies. *The Clinical Psychologist, 49,* 5–18.

Chun, K., Balls-Organista, P., & Marin, G. (2003). *Acculturation: Advances in theory, measurement, and applied research.* Washington, DC: American Psychological Association.

Coleman, H. L. K., Wampold, B. E., & Casali, S. L. (1995). Ethnic minorities' ratings of ethnically similar and European American counselors: A meta-analysis. *Journal of Counseling Psychology, 42*(1), 55–64.

Cushman, P. (1995). *Constructing the self, constructing America: A cultural history of psychotherapy.* New York: Addison-Wesley.

Davies, J. (2011). Cultural dimensions of intersubjectivity: Negotiating "sameness" and "otherness" in the analytic relationship. *Psychoanalytic Psychology, 28,* 549–559.

Dixon, Y. (1976). Worldviews and research methodology. In L. King, V. Dixon, & W. Nobles (Eds.), *African philosophy: Assumptions and paradigms for research on Black persons.* Los Angeles, CA: Fannon Research & Development Center.

Dovidio, J. (2009). Racial bias, unspoken but heard. *Science, 326,* 1641–1642.

Geertz, C. (1973). *Interpretation of cultures.* New York: Basic Books.

Gonzalez, R. C., Biever, J. L., & Gardner, G. T. (1994). The multicultural perspective in therapy: A social constructivist approach. *Psychotherapy, 31,* 515–524.

Gopaul-McNeil, S., & Brice-Baker, J. (1998). *Cross-cultural practice.* Hoboken, NJ: John Wiley.

Hays, P. A. (2008). *Addressing cultural complexities in practice: Assessment, diagnosis, and therapy* (2nd ed.). Washington, DC: American Psychological Association.

Helms, J. (2007). Some better practices for measuring racial and ethnic identity constructs. *Journal of Counseling Psychology, 54,* 235–246.

Helms, J., & Cook, D. (1999). *Using race and culture in counseling and psychotherapy: Theory and processes.* Boston: Allyn & Bacon.

Helms, J. E., Jernigan, M., & Macher, J. (2005). The meaning of race in psychology and how to change it: A methodological perspective. *American Psychologist, 60,* 27–36.

Hinton, D. E., Chhean, D., Pich, V., Safren, S. A., Hofmann, S. G., & Pollack, M. H. (2005). A randomized controlled trial of cognitive-behavior therapy for Cambodian refugees with treatment-resistant PTSD and panic attacks: A cross-over design. *Journal of Traumatic Stress, 18*(6), 617–629.

Ivey, A. (1995). Psychotherapy as liberation: Toward specific skills and strategies in multicultural counseling and therapy. In J. G. Ponterotto, J. M. Casas, L. A. Suzuki, & C. M. Alexander (Eds.), *Handbook of multicultural counseling* (pp. 53–72). Thousand Oaks, CA: Sage.

Jackson, G. (1976). Cultural seedbeds of the Black backlash in mental health. *Journal of Afro-American Issues, 4,* 70–91.

Kaduchin, A. (1972). The racial factor in the interview. *Social Work, 17,* 88–98.

Landrine, H., & Klonoff, E. A. (1996). *African American acculturation.* Thousand Oaks, CA: Sage.

La Roche, M. (1999). Culture, transference, and countertransference among Latinos. *Psychotherapy: Theory, Research, Practice, Training, 36,* 389–397.

La Roche, M. (2002). Psychotherapeutic considerations in treating Latinos. *Harvard Review of Psychiatry, 10,* 115–122.

La Roche, M., & Christopher, M. (2009). Changing paradigms from empirically supported treatment to evidence-based practice: A cultural perspective. *Professional Psychology: Research and Practice, 40*(4), 396–402.

La Roche, M., & Maxie, A. (2003). Ten considerations in addressing cultural differences in psychotherapy. *Professional Psychology: Research and Practice, 34*(2), 180–186.

La Roche, M., & Tawa, J. (2011). Taking back our streets: A clinical model for empowering urban youths through participation in peace promotion. *Peace and Conflict: Journal of Peace Psychology, 17*(1), 4–21.

Lee, E. (2000). Chinese families. In M. McGoldrick, J. Giordano, & J. K. Pearce (Eds.), *Ethnicity and family therapy* (pp. 249–268). New York: Guilford.

Lopez, S. (1997). Cultural competence in psychotherapy: A guide for clinicians and their supervisors. In J. Watkins (Ed.), *Handbook of psychotherapy* (pp. 570–588). Hoboken, NJ: John Wiley.

Maxie, A., Arnold, D., & Stephenson, M. (2006). Do therapists address ethnic and racial differences in cross-cultural psychotherapy? *Psychotherapy: Theory, Research, Practice, Training, 43,* 85–98.

Norcross, J. C. (2002). *Psychotherapy relationships that work: Therapist contributions and responsiveness to client needs.* New York: Oxford University Press.

Norcross, J. C. (2010). The therapeutic relationship. In B. Duncan, S. Miller, B. Wampold, & M. Hubble (Eds.), *The heart and soul of change: Delivering what works in therapy* (pp. 113–141). Washington, DC: American Psychological Association.

Paniagua, F. (1998). *Assessing and treating culturally diverse clients: A practical guide.* Thousand Oaks, CA: Sage.

Pinderhughes, E. (1989). *Understanding race, ethnicity, and power: The key to efficacy in clinical practice.* New York: Free Press.

Rosselló, J., Bernal, G., & Rivera-Medina, C. (2008). Individual and group CBT and IPT for Puerto Rican adolescents with depressive symptoms. *Cultural Diversity and Ethnic Minority Psychology, 14,* 234–245.

Segall, M., Lonner, W., & Berry, J. (1998). Cross-cultural psychology as a scholarly discipline: On the flowering of culture in behavioral research. *American Psychologist, 53,* 1101–1110.

Speight, S., & Vera, E. (1997). Similarity and differences in multicultural counseling: Considering the attraction and repulsion hypotheses. *The Counseling Psychologist, 25,* 280–298.

Steele, C., & Aronson, J. (1995). Stereotype threat and the intellectual test performance of African Americans. *Journal of Personality and Social Psychology, 69,* 797–811.

Sue, D. W., Arredondo, P., & McDavis, R. J. (1992). Multicultural counseling competencies and standards: A call to the profession. *Journal of Counseling & Development, 70,* 477–486.

Sue, D. W., Ivey, A. E., & Pedersen, P. B. (1996). *A theory of multicultural therapy and therapy.* Pacific Grove, CA: Brooks/Cole.

Sue, S. (1998). In search of cultural competence in psychotherapy and counseling. *American Psychologist, 53,* 440–448.

Sue, S., & Zane, N. (1987). The role of culture and cultural techniques in psychotherapy. *American Psychologist, 42,* 37–45.

Sue, W. S., & Sue, D. (2008). *Counseling the culturally diverse: Theory and practice* (5th ed.). Hoboken, NJ: John Wiley.

Tyler, F., Brome, D., & Williams, J. (1991). *Ethnic validity, ecology, and psychotherapy: A psychosocial competence model.* New York: Plenum.

Wampold, B. E. (2001). *The great psychotherapy debate: Models, methods, and findings.* Mahwah, NJ: Erlbaum.

Wampold, B. E. (2010). The research evidence for the common factors models: A historically situated perspective. In B. Duncan, S. Miller, B. Wampold, & M. Hubble (Eds.), *The heart and soul of change: Delivering what works in therapy.* Washington, DC: American Psychological Association.

Weisbuch, M., Pauker, K., & Ambady, N. (2009). The subtle transmission of race bias via televised nonverbal behavior. *Science, 326,* 1711–1714.

Whaley, A. L. (2001). Cultural mistrust: An important psychological construct for diagnosis and treatment of African Americans. *Professional Psychology: Research and Practice, 32,* 555–562.

White, J. (1970). Guidelines for Black psychologists. *Black Scholar, 1,* 52–57.

White, M., & Epston, D. (1990). *Narrative means to therapeutic ends.* New York: Norton.

Wilkinson, C. B., & Spurlock, J. (1986). The mental health of Black Americans: Psychiatric diagnosis and treatment. In C. B. Wilkerson (Ed.), *Ethnic psychiatry* (pp. 13–59). New York: Plenum.

Zimbardo, P. (2008). *The Lucifer effect: Understanding how good people turn evil.* New York: Random House.

CHAPTER 5

The Cultural Formulation and Conceptual Foundations of Cultural Psychotherapy

*It was six men from Hindustan who went to see the Elephant, though all of them
were blind. . . . The first approached the Elephant and happening to fall against his
broad and sturdy side at once began to bawl: "God bless me! But the Elephant is very
much like a wall." . . . The second man feeling the tusk thought it was a spear. . . . The
sixth blind man touched the tail and thought it was a snake. And so these men of
Hindustan disputed loud and long. Each in his opinion exceeding stiff and strong.
Though each was partly in the right and all were in the wrong.*

—John Godfrey Saxe, *Poems,* "The Blind Men and the Elephant," 1852

The Blind Men and Elephant tale is often used as a metaphor to describe the coexistence of disparate theories that explain one phenomenon. Similarly, in the psychotherapeutic process more than one clinical explanation is possible. The clinical formulation is often defined as the processes by which hypotheses are generated about the etiology of a client's symptoms or problems (Winters, Hanson, & Stoyanova, 2007). Even if not articulated explicitly, the case formulation guides all clinical activity (Winters et al., 2007). Through our clinical formulations, we make sense of our clients' problems as well as prioritize which interventions are used. Our theoretical views are critical to explaining and understanding our clients' issues. The theories we endorse lead us to underscore some elephant parts (e.g., genes, behavior, cognitions, or unconscious processes) but not others. Theories allow us to organize, simplify, and prioritize information that guides us to choose certain interventions over others.

In contrast to traditional formulations, the cultural psychotherapeutic model emphasizes the need to develop multiple and complex explanations of clients' issues. Although consistency is sought, explanations do not necessarily have to fit neatly together. Just as we can endorse multiple stories (clinical recommendation 3.6: *Embrace multiple stories*), the psychotherapeutic cultural formulation can benefit from many disparate and independent understandings. The primary aim of this chapter is to demonstrate the generation of a cultural psychotherapeutic formulation by way of a clinical case illustration. A secondary aim is to describe some of the conceptual foundations of cultural psychotherapy.

The number of psychotherapeutic models and theories has grown exponentially, and some authors have counted over 500 (e.g., Gold, 1993; Luborsky et al., 2002). In contrast to psychotherapy, Western medicine has parsimoniously refined myriad theories into a few specific explanations that make up the biomedical model. Some in other scientific fields may view our lack of one unitary theory as a discredit to the stature of the field and its interventions. If so many psychotherapeutic theories exist, which one is the correct one? Which is the best? How do we know if a theory is right or wrong? Furthermore, having a plethora of theories can confuse even the most knowledgeable clinician as to what is the best way to intervene.

Cultural psychotherapy attempts to clarify these issues by arguing that currently there are three prevalent types of psychotherapeutic explanations or paradigms, namely, the individualistic, relational, and contextual/ecological (La Roche, 2005). Although there is much diversity within each of these broadly defined paradigms, there is also some overlap (see Figure I.1). In this chapter, these three paradigms are described in some detail and defined by their ontological, epistemological, and ethical characteristics. But first, however, it is necessary to describe the term *paradigm* and how it relates to the concepts of ontology, epistemology, and ethics in a clinical chapter that aims to describe the psychotherapeutic cultural formulation.

WHAT ARE PARADIGMS AND WHY ARE THEY IMPORTANT IN THE PSYCHOTHERAPEUTIC PROCESS?

Paradigms are basic assumptions of what knowledge is. They contain ontological, epistemological, and ethical assumptions that set unspoken limits on the questions, methods, and goals that are deemed legitimate for each science. Ontology is often defined as a response to questions of what is being or what exists (e.g., what parts of the elephant are important). Epistemology is often described as the methods or research strategies that are acceptable to glean valid data to explore or validate clinical interventions (e.g., touch is the only way to know). Ethics refers to principles or guidelines that dictate what is right or wrong. Scientists do not merely describe human nature as it exists; rather, we organize through paradigms the limitless number of observations that are conducted toward the end of understanding, predicting, and controlling (Kuhn, 1970). The dominant conceptions of each paradigm provide a framework for such perceptions and a coherent structure for scientific inquiry.

Similarly, psychotherapeutic models are highly influenced not only by our observations but also by the prevalent cultural assumptions (e.g., materialism, individualism) of our sociocultural and economic context. Cultural psychotherapy asserts that an enhanced awareness of these sociocultural and economic forces allows clinicians to take these influences into account when developing and implementing interventions rather than being limited by them. This is particularly true during the process of developing a psychotherapeutic cultural formulation.

All psychotherapeutic models emphasize ontological, epistemological, and ethical assumptions (Martin & Sugarman, 1999, 2009; Messer, Sass, & Woolfolk, 1988) that lead clinicians or researchers to prioritize some questions and interventions while minimizing or even ignoring others. These ontological, epistemological, and ethical assumptions are not unlike cultural assumptions that influence and organize our understandings. Unfortunately, like the blind men, we are often unaware of the assumptions we endorse. Further, we may also be blind to the implications of our lack of awareness, which may hinder our ability to understand different clinical hypotheses and seek additional sources of knowledge. If this occurs, the psychotherapeutic process can become stagnant. Thus, it is important that clinicians and clients continuously and actively search for alternative ideas to enrich our understandings of the psychotherapeutic process.

Although I underscore the unique characteristics of each paradigm, it is important to note that other ways to organize psychotherapeutic systems are possible. Even more, within each paradigm there are countless models that limit our ability to find generalities. All psychotherapeutic paradigms emphasize different interactions between individualistic, relational, and/or contextual variables but give ontological, epistemological, or ethical priority to one or a combination of these factors. Virtually all psychotherapies attempt to explain individual, relational, and contextual variables, but they do so by underscoring, reconceptualizing, or reducing all three (i.e., individual, relational, and contextual) into one or two of these dimensions. The broad, common, and at times overlapping denominators underscored in each paradigm should, however, be viewed as heuristics that aim to clarify clinicians' psychotherapeutic cultural formulations rather than as absolute characteristics that define paradigms. The goal of these constructs is to help clinicians develop more thorough and clinically useful formulations, not to develop a classification system to organize all psychotherapeutic models.

Each paradigm thus is described using three philosophical constructs: (1) *ontological characteristics,* (2) *epistemological and research assumptions,* and (3) *ethical assumptions.* In this chapter, I frequently use the elephant and blind men tale to illustrate the characteristics of the individualistic, relational, contextual, and cultural paradigms. Unfortunately, the elephant and blind men tale has been used, or even overused, so frequently that it may now be a cultural cliché. Despite its popularity, or perhaps because of it (given that it is well-known), I will use it to sketch the basic conceptual ideas of cultural psychotherapy.

Individualistic Paradigm

Ontologically, individualistic formulations are characterized by an understanding where the client is conceptualized as an independent, separate, and autonomous "individual" with well-defined boundaries between observers, social contexts, and themselves. Clients are the focus, while therapists and their sociocultural contexts fade into the background. This emphasis on the individual is grossly present within much of the psychotherapeutic literature and also seems to be a reflection of dominant Western values (e.g., Cushman, 1995; Gergen, 1991; La Roche, Batista, & D'Angelo, 2010; Taylor, 1989). This emphasis can be noted by the importance given to individualistic psychotherapeutic constructs and goals (e.g., ego, cognitive schemes, constructs, rational or irrational beliefs, information-processing styles, self, self-esteem, self-cohesiveness, wiring of the brain, identity, self-actualization, and self-efficacy) predominant in the literature and most interventions. Although most individualistic models differ in the parts they emphasize (e.g., consciousness, cognitions, behaviors, genes, or neurological functions), they all emphasize elements that reside within the individual and use each individual as the basic unit of analysis. An important subcategory that should almost always be underscored within the individualistic category is the biological one, necessarily if treatment includes psychopharmacological treatment. The need to understand if there is mental health history in the family or, for example, a deficiency in serotonin levels cannot be emphasized sufficiently.

However, it is important to reiterate that these individualistic models do not disregard relationships or contexts, only that their relational or contextual constructs are not as central. In all fairness, individualistic psychotherapies include and underscore relational and contextual variables, but these variables are derivatives of more prominent or central individualistic attributes. Much like the men in the elephant tale, it is not that they do not accept that there are other parts of the elephant; it is just that they emphasize what they touch (the prominent ontological features).

Epistemologically speaking, individualistic psychotherapies emphasize the importance of obtaining data through objective methods, the aims of which are to accurately reflect the characteristics of an object (one client) free from contextual or personal (clinician/researcher) distortions. Objective research methods are derived from the naturalistic/positivistic tradition that treats nature as objects that are best known through the scientific method. Objective methods are more effective when they focus on the individual, or parts of the individual (e.g., depressive levels). With the elephant and the blind men, the elephant is described independently of the characteristics of the blind men (who are anonymous and homogeneous) and sterilized (just like a laboratory) from the sounds, smells, and actions of the surrounding jungle. Although, alone, none of the blind men arrives at a thorough understanding of an elephant, together they are eventually able to do so. This is much the way clinicians try to piece multiple symptoms, behaviors, and/or cognitions into a formulation that makes sense of their clients' issues.

Intrapersonal perspectives can also be considered a type of individualistic epistemology as they seek to understand a client's experience minimizing the influence of the context and therapist's experience, even though they do not emphasize objectivity. Intrapersonal strategies emphasize the need for an observer/therapist to direct all his or her efforts at understanding a client's experience, motives, and meanings. Empathy is a crucial tool to understand the contents of another person's experience, leading to an understanding of how a client feels, thinks, and perceives reality. In this process, therapists are to focus on clients' experiences, and although they may resonate affectively with their experiences, what really matters is the client's experience, not therapists' experiences or the context in which the therapeutic relationship occurs. Intrapersonal strategies are currently one of the most frequently used types of psychotherapeutic tools to understand others.

Ethics often refers to what is considered right or wrong and what is worthwhile to pursue. In psychotherapy, this can be translated into what is pursued in treatment or the nature of the treatment goals. It can be argued that individualistic psychotherapies focus on improving clients first, although it is also necessary to improve relationships or contexts, as these are derivative of changes within the client. Individualistic approaches are exemplified by classic psychoanalytic models that emphasize the need to treat by making clients aware of their unconscious dynamics, while therapists act as neutral blank screens onto which clients transfer their subjective experiences (Freud, 1933). Similarly, most psychotherapeutic models emphasize individualistic goals such as "strengthening the ego," "exploring the self," "enhancing self-esteem," "fostering self-actualization," "developing self-efficacy," "promoting autonomy, separateness, and independence," or seeking individuation, just to mention a few current and prominent therapeutic aims.

Relational Paradigms

In contrast to individualistic formulations, relational formulations emphasize an understanding in which the human mind is interactive rather than monadic and that psychotherapy should be understood as occurring between subjects rather than within individuals. The main object of study, therefore, is the interaction and relationship of the client and therapist. If the tale of the blind men is used as a metaphor to illustrate relational ideas, it is the elephant's interactions with other elephants (or herd) and with the blind men at the core of the psychotherapeutic process rather than each elephant or its parts (tusk, back, leg). Relational models have grown out of approaches that underscore the interpersonal nature of psychotherapy, such as object relations, interpersonal psychiatry (e.g., Sullivan, 1953), modern intersubjective psychoanalysis (Stolorow & Atwood, 2002), feminism (Jordan, 2010), and attachment theory (Bowlby, 1988), among others. Such approaches are more focused on the immediate affective or experiential interchange that has been variously called corrective experience (Alexander & French, 1946), moment of meeting (Stern et al., 1998), and repairing the ruptures in the therapeutic relationship (Safran & Muran, 2000). Similarly, cross-cultural researchers have found that many cultural groups have a "collective" or a relational self-orientation in contrast to an individualistic self-orientation (Oyserman, Coon, & Kemmelmeier, 2002; Triandis, 1994). Furthermore, an increasing amount of systematic research indicates that the therapeutic relationship is one of, if not the most important source for therapeutic change (Lambert & Ogles, 2004; Norcross, 2002, 2010; Wampold, 2001, 2010).

In contrast to individualistic research methods that focus on clients, proponents of relational psychotherapies include clinicians' influence as an essential part of the research process. Clinicians are construed as instruments of research and psychotherapy, and their subjectivity is not just acknowledged; it is embraced (see Figure 5.1).

This relational stance may have grown from Heisenberg's uncertainty principle, which posits that measurements do not exist independently of the measurement process (Greene, 1999). Quantum mechanics and string theory have advanced exponentially by employing this principle. In psychology, this conceptualization has fostered the development of sophisticated qualitative methods and many variants (e.g., ethnographic research) that consider clinicians as a source of knowledge, particularly within the cross-cultural literature (Morrow, Rakhsha, & Castaneda, 1999). Nevertheless, even within the social sciences, qualitative and relational methods are often considered less helpful and lack the credibility that more rigorous or traditional research strategies garner.

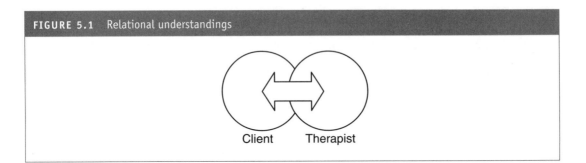

FIGURE 5.1   Relational understandings

Client   Therapist

For relational psychotherapists, "goodness" resides within the psychotherapeutic relationship, which is a result of the exchanges between clients and therapists. Thus, the main aim of relational psychotherapies is to enhance clients' relationships through the use of the psychotherapeutic relationship. Relational therapists are often concerned about developing relationships in which a mutual and reciprocal influence is accepted and promoted (Jordan, Surrey, & Kaplan, 1983; Kohut, 1984; Slife & Wiggins, 2009). This type of therapeutic relationship is crucial for psychotherapeutic change, as it is often assumed that interpersonal dynamics are key to propelling significant psychotherapeutic change. Furthermore, many relational approaches espouse a view in which therapists' objective and privileged standpoint is questioned, thereby encouraging a more egalitarian relationship between clients and therapists (Jordan, 2010; Jordan et al., 1983).

Contextual/Ecological Paradigms

The decisive ontological assumption of contextual/ecological formulations is the importance of cultural and social contexts that influence what we know. Models such as socio-constructivism, ecological psychology, critical psychology, hermeneutics, community psychology, social psychology, deconstructive approaches, and most cross-cultural approaches posit that individuals are unknowable without an understanding that locates them within a cultural and historical context (Bronfenbrenner, 1979; Cushman, 1995; Gergen, 1991). In psychotherapy, this would mean that clients are unknowable without understanding the contexts in which they are embedded. Again using the blind men to illustrate, it could be argued that if the blind men were Americans, they may have construed the elephant's back and tail as a plasma TV and its cord, a computer, or a car.

An increasing number of authors have emphasized the differences between individualistic and relational paradigms (e.g., Slife & Wiggins, 2009) but have neglected the contextual paradigm. Some relational psychotherapies seem to construe the context as an extension of the relational world (as residing within a relationship), minimizing and at times distorting the influence of social, economic, and historic forces. However, the context affects not just the therapeutic relationship; it influences us all. Ecological authors explain that minimizing contextual influences undermines our ability to effectively understand, cope with, and then transform these influences.

Proponents of contextual/ecological paradigms believe that knowledge is not refined through empirical tests, but rather is the result of what emerges from social processes within science and society (Gergen, 1991). For example, Cushman (1995) understands the popularity of certain psychotherapeutic models as expressions of complex sociopolitical, historical, and economic interests. Similarly, Hacking (2002) explains the emergence of certain diagnoses (e.g., multiple personality disorder) as a result of sociocultural influences. Alternatively, the disappearance of some disorders in the fifth edition of the *Diagnostic and Statistical Manual of Mental Disorders* (*DSM-5;* American Psychiatric Association, forthcoming), for example, the likely disappearance of narcissistic personality disorder, could also be explained as the normalization of some features (e.g., excessive self-regard) that were uncommon in the past. Contextual/ecological epistemologies emphasize the need to value methods according to the purposes for which the information is used or not. For example, clinicians who emphasize a contextual paradigm often seek a knowledge that is sensitive to the political and socioeconomic needs of oppressed and underprivileged groups, not only the client (individualistic approaches) or the psychotherapeutic relationship (relational approaches). Contextual/ecological approaches attempt to identify the benefactors of different understandings. For example, many contextual researchers have noted how the psychopharmacological companies have benefited from the biological emphasis in the *DSM-IV* and *-5.*

Ethics in contextual/ecological models are expressed in the need to articulate a political agenda that aims to combat a social order in which minority groups (e.g., ethnic minorities, disabled, Muslims, and homosexuals) are oppressed by the norms of one segment of the majority (e.g., White, Protestant, and heterosexual males). Consequently, contextual models have encouraged the development of the liberation psychotherapy movement, which promotes therapeutic goals such as "empowerment" (Ivey, 1999; Martín-Baró, 1994; Ramirez, 1999) and "*conscientizacao*/social awakening" (Freire, 1972), and emphasizes social transformation rather than individual or relational change alone. The overarching goal of these orientations is to increase the personal and collective power of the people who are powerless and subject to oppressive forces such as colonialism (Sanchez & Garriga, 1996), alienation (Fromm, 1955), poverty (Freire, 1972), gender discrimination (Ballou, Matsumuto, & Wagner, 2002), and racism (Sue & Sue, 2008). Therefore, contextual authors could be troubled by the lack of mention in the blind men tale of a social purpose for which knowledge of the elephant is needed. Furthermore, they may promote the development of additional tales in which the elephant(s) rebels against the hegemony of the blind men. Others may wonder why women or homosexuals are not included. Clinicians and clients are thus encouraged to explore how their own questions, interactions, and feelings may reflect larger sociopolitical, cultural, and economic issues. Nevertheless, it is always important to wonder whose agenda is enacted. Has clinicians' "noble agenda" been imposed on clients' lives?

THE PSYCHOTHERAPEUTIC CULTURAL FORMULATION

The main characteristic of the psychotherapeutic cultural formulation is that it emphasizes the interaction of three sets of understandings: the individualistic, relational, and contextual. Multiple understandings enrich our clinical formulations, which in turn allow us to have a more thorough, effective, and dynamic understanding of the psychotherapeutic process. The aim is not to discredit any of these paradigms but to benefit from their strengths. An adaptation of cultural psychotherapy's main equation illustrates this need:

$$\text{psychotherapeutic cultural formulation} = \text{individual explanations} \times \text{relational explanations} \times \text{contextual explanations.}$$

Each of these three broadly defined paradigms offers an essential, at times overlapping, or disparate understanding of the psychotherapeutic process. But alone or summed together, they do not add up; they are insufficient. This leads to the following corollary:

$$\text{psychotherapeutic cultural formulation} > \text{individual explanations} + \text{relational explanations} + \text{contextual explanations.}$$

Drawing again on the elephant and the blind men, cultural psychotherapy studies the elephant and its parts, the herd and relationship with the blind men (and women) embedded in the jungle, and other contexts (e.g., Indostan's history, geography, economy). Each of these explanations is central at different times during the psychotherapeutic process. The three-phased psychotherapeutic model is an attempt to take advantage of the centrality of each of these explanations during different psychotherapeutic phases in a coherent and systematic manner. Each of these three paradigms receives more emphasis than others during different phases of the psychotherapeutic process; however, taking away any of these understandings during any phase would render the formulation incomplete.

$$\text{Phase I} = \text{individual explanations}^2 \times \text{relational explanations} \times \text{contextual explanations}$$

$$\text{Phase II} = \text{individual explanations} \times \text{relational explanations}^2 \times \text{contextual explanations}$$

$$\text{Phase III} = \text{individual explanations} \times \text{relational explanations} \times \text{contextual explanations}^2$$

Nevertheless, in each of these phases all formulations are possible. Cultural psychotherapy argues that psychotherapy is more effective when different explanations are acknowledged and utilized coherently rather than independently. The three-phased psychotherapeutic model is an attempt to prioritize in a systematic manner these different sets of explanations.

As clinicians increase their awareness of the ontological assumptions underlying different psychotherapeutic theories, they are more effective in adapting these interventions to the characteristics of each client. For example, if clinicians ignore contextual variables, they make assumptions that an intervention is universally effective or moreover, if an intervention fails, they may further psychopathologize the client when it was really adverse contextual variables at play. Additionally, clinicians may end up imposing their ontological understanding on clients who endorse alternative ontological understandings.

Cultural psychotherapy emphasizes the need to increase practitioners' awareness of ontological, epistemological, and ethical assumptions. For that purpose, it is useful to continually ask critical questions, such as which variables are consistently emphasized during sessions/research and which ones are overlooked or rarely discussed? Which narratives and/or meanings are underscored? Do the narratives focus on the individualistic, relational, or contextual? How would understandings vary if other researchers/clinicians assessed the same issues? How do clinicians' personal issues or beliefs affect the psychotherapeutic relationship? How would clients' issues be constructed in a different context? How might the current psychotherapeutic relationship be understood in a different time or place? Do the formulations used emphasize or overlook any of these questions? If so, which areas and why? What types of assessment tools or diagnostic criteria are used to evaluate clinical hypotheses? Are clinicians using standardized questionnaires or structured clinical interviews, or following clients' lead? Have assessment tools or diagnostic categories been validated with diverse clients? Are clinical hypotheses discussed and checked with clients? Do clinicians consider their own personal and cultural biases in the process of diagnosing and understanding clients? Moreover, are clients' cultural and socioeconomic contexts considered in the process of understanding them? Do clinicians explore explicit and implicit messages/systems? How do clinicians make sense of discrepancies? What goals are pursued? From which cultural values do these goals arise? Are these goals prescribed by our society?

These questions and many more aim to widen the space for alternative or more complex formulations to emerge. An emphasis on any given paradigm often curtails the emergence of additional ones. To prevent this from limiting us, it is important for clinicians to continuously question multiple and emerging understandings. The aim is to develop multiple hypotheses for specific issues. Furthermore, this continuous questioning encourages flexibility so that these formulations and narratives change and evolve as they are developed and tested. By exploring individual, relational, and contextual issues, clients and therapists can more fully understand and effectively address complex issues. Through cultural formulations, therapists and clients develop a more thorough understanding of the psychotherapeutic process and generate more possibilities, which will allow them to choose the most appropriate treatment goal, meaning, or intervention at a specific time and place and not being blinded by prevalent cultural assumptions.

The complex nature of the therapeutic endeavor makes diagnosis and treatment extremely challenging. For most clinicians, this complexity is confusing and anxiety provoking. It would be much easier if there were a simple universal algorithm to generate one clinical formulation that translated into clear-cut interventions. Although cultural psychotherapy argues that this complexity is reflective of our nature, it does not justify the many practical disadvantages it entails. Therefore, strategies to effectively organize ideas are necessary. Although many organizational systems have been proposed below, I will highlight three possible strategies.

First, cultural psychotherapy argues that when appropriate it is important that therapists discuss the advantages and disadvantages of each formulation, hypothesis, and intervention and consider the context in which these decisions are embedded with their clients. Together, clients and clinicians evaluate problems and goals and select the means to address each. However, depending on the situation or phase of treatment, this technique may not always be appropriate. For example, consider clinical recommendation

1.3: *Safety and basic needs are always a priority.* If a client is in crisis (e.g., suicidal), then the clinician may need to be directive and encourage some plan of action, intervention, or precaution (e.g., safety plan or hospitalization). In contrast, if the client is in the third phase and the aim is to foster empowerment, then a clinician's voice may become less relevant.

Second, it is important that clinicians understand both the strengths and limitations of a clinical intervention before it is implemented (American Psychological Association [APA], 2006). Most clinical guidelines (e.g., APA, 2006) recommend that empirically validated interventions be prioritized over interventions that have not been tested empirically. However, cultural psychotherapy also emphasizes the need to include clients' views/ideas (clinical recommendation 1.7: *Understand clients' formulations of problems in a culturally sensitive manner,* and 1.8: *Use indigenous healing practices to address symptoms*) in this decision-making process and, consistent with most clinical guidelines, also check if the recommended clinical strategies have been validated with samples of the clients' cultural background (e.g., race, religion, socioeconomic status, gender orientation).

Third, it is helpful to understand how our cultural assumptions are influencing our hypotheses and it is helpful for clinicians to analyze how the sources or methods (quantitative vs. qualitative) by which clinical knowledge is obtained influence a formulation (APA, 2006). It is often useful to understand the specific contribution each method has in influencing our hypotheses. Although most evidenced-based practices (Chambless et al., 1996) and evidenced-based psychological practices (e.g., APA, 2006) recommend that information gleaned from objective rigorous approaches (e.g., randomized control trials) be prioritized and be considered more credible, cultural psychotherapy argues, in contrast, that when information differs it is also useful to understand the meaning of each set of evidence within their specific contexts before prioritizing the credibility of data. By exploring the context in which the findings are extracted, cultural researchers aim to develop more refined hypotheses that are specific to contexts.

Not considering one source of knowledge can undermine the psychotherapeutic process. Within the psychotherapeutic process, it is useful for therapists and clients to discuss multiple individual, relational, and contextual issues and explore/decide together which are more helpful. During different times and contexts, some psychotherapeutic sources (i.e., individualistic, relational, or contextual) may be more prominent and useful than others. I illustrate ways to conceptualize cultural psychotherapy in the following case.

Case Illustration: Robert

Robert, a muscular 32-year-old man of Irish descent, was recently married and sought treatment for the first time because of the sudden apparition of crying spells that were impairing his ability to work. Robert was the youngest of six siblings from a military family. He went into the Marines, much like his father, but with one important difference. His father had fought during the Vietnam War, whereas Robert had never experienced combat. Similarly, several of his uncles and siblings were also combat veterans from different wars ranging from Vietnam to the Gulf War, and one of his relatives had even received a purple heart. Robert grew up among tales of raging battles, bravery, and courage. It was instilled in him from a very young age that it was important to be tough and fearless.

Recently, however, he felt far from fearless, and instead of being tough, he "cried like a baby." Suddenly and unexpectedly, he would feel a sob rise up in his throat and he would be unable to choke it down. Further, he worked in construction and he feared that if one of these episodes should erupt on the job, he would have to hide his tears as if there was some unspoken rule forbidding crying or other demonstrations of emotion. This was also true of his family, where he had been teased for his lack of combat experience, and he could only imagine what they would say if they knew of his crying spells. Robert often worried that he was losing his mind.

In thinking about a cultural psychotherapeutic formulation, my first hypothesis emphasized the toll that explicit and implicit contextual messages about masculinity were having on Robert. I thought that his gender roles were restricting the range of affects that he allowed himself to experience. However, it was not the right time to bring up this ecological/contextual formulation. Instead of focusing on my understandings (clinical guideline 1.5: *Stay in the experiential level*), I pursued Robert's treatment goal (clinical guideline 1.1: *Chief complaints need to be understood in a culturally sensitive manner*), which was not to explore his cultural values, but to get rid of his crying spells.

To address his treatment goal, we explored when the crying spells began and the conditions that surrounded their apparition. The spells had first appeared a year earlier. He reported that nothing bad had happened during that time and added that, in fact, it was a time when he actually felt happy. He had just been promoted at his job and he had also gotten engaged. Robert explained that he had had numerous girlfriends, but none like Catherine. He had never loved a woman as much as he loved her. They had been together for more than three years and she listened to him, tolerated his outbursts and silences, and even liked his electric guitar playing. He felt understood and close to her. In describing his love for Catherine, he suddenly recalled his deceased mother. His blue eyes welled up as he remembered how much she loved him and he her. To my surprise, he allowed himself to be tearful and sad. Robert soon started sharing stories about his mother. For example, he recalled that sometimes when she argued with his father, she would leave home and take him with her. They would stay with his grandmother, who would "spoil him rotten" and make him feel very special. When his grandmother passed away, he was proud that he was able to keep a straight face, just like his father. He was again proud to do the same when his mother passed away a few years later.

In treatment, he quickly realized that vivid memories of his mother would follow when he felt close to Catherine, who shared many similarities with his mother. His feelings of closeness with Catherine would inevitably lead him to remember the closeness he experienced with his mother and grandmother and then he would feel like crying. In treatment, he confessed that he missed his mother and grandmother, and he was sometimes afraid that Catherine would also leave him. An enhanced understanding of his grief allowed Robert to more effectively handle it and develop coping strategies to manage his feelings, rather than avoid them.

(Continued)

(Continued)

Throughout treatment, I constantly asked myself which issues I was or should be emphasizing with Robert. Clearly, I was underscoring individualistic issues (e.g., exploring triggers for his crying spells) at the expense of relational and contextual ones. However, when I asked Robert about matters relating to the therapeutic relationship or his context, he seemed unmoved and uninterested. I wondered how the therapeutic relationship was influencing him? More specifically, for example, was it hard to discuss his grief with a Latino male? I also explored my feelings about the psychotherapeutic process. Why did I not feel much for him? In fact, why did I so often feel annoyed with him? How were these feelings influencing treatment? Where were they coming from?

In exploring such questions, I began to understand that some of my feelings arose from my biased belief that soldiers are trained to repress emotions. I am a pacifist and have repeatedly protested against war. I am also a progressive liberal and I thought that Robert was a traditional, conservative Republican.[1] I wondered if my beliefs limited the range of options or interventions I offered him. Was Robert being shortchanged because of my prejudices? Furthermore, was I following my own clinical recommendations (e.g., clinical recommendation 4.5: *Cultural differences are addressed as assets*)? Clearly, these recommendations are more easily said than practiced, as I experienced with Robert.

I also realized that I had not explored contextual influences with Robert and that now it could be too late. In an attempt to unearth a possible contextual issue, I gently explored with Robert the notion that men can express feelings and even cry; but much like when I had explored relational issues within the therapeutic relationship, he seemed uninterested. Thus, I did not bring them up again. I wanted Robert to direct his treatment (clinical recommendation 3.2: *Clients lead the way*) and I needed to avoid imposing my own values.

After a few sessions, Robert decided he was ready to terminate treatment because his crying spells had completely vanished. His treatment goal had been met and there was no need for further treatment. Consistent with individualistic explanations, he had learned that current events (closeness with Catherine) triggered memories of loss that made him prone to crying. In addition, he had learned alternative ways to cope with his grief. He would sometimes allow himself to experience sadness and remember his mother and grandmother. He realized that he could feel sad, and it did not necessarily mean that he would have an uncontrollable crying spell. He could accept his sadness, rather than avoid it. Instead of fighting against his grief and memories of loss he could open himself to these feelings and more effectively cope with them (Hayes, 2011). As a result, Robert was better able to regulate his affect and respond flexibly to it (clinical recommendation 1.14: *Enhance affect regulation and psychological flexibility*), and although I said it might be better to stay in treatment a bit longer to ensure that he would not relapse, he categorically refused.

A few months after termination, Robert called to schedule an emergency appointment because he said he was fearful that Catherine was going to leave him. He explained that everyone who had loved him had in fact left him, so why would Catherine be different? During this time, we focused on his relationship with Catherine, his mother, and, increasingly, me. After a few sessions in which we explored his abandonment fears and his relationship with his mother, he revealed to my surprise that he was in fact angry with me because I had suggested he was a wimp. How could I have suggested that men cry? Where did I come from? Maybe Hispanics can do that, but not men, not real men! *"Are you saying that I am not a man?"* he asked angrily.

It was an impasse (clinical recommendation 2.8: *Understand that ruptures are inevitable*). He had taken my exploration of masculine beliefs as a challenge to his masculinity, and ultimately his identity. Even though I attempted to be very careful and respectful while I explored his gender expectations, he experienced it as an affront. His reaction underscores the need to address cultural differences in a supportive and respectful manner. There is often a risk when exploring cultural differences of a rupture or an impasse.

Only after I assured him that I did not think he was a wimp could we proceed to examine his experience. He explained that the reason he left treatment was that he felt insulted by my comment. Throughout his life, he had repeatedly heard his father, uncles, and brothers talk about men's need to be strong, and then in therapy I had questioned this belief. *"What is your problem?"* Robert asked. I again explained that I believed it was important to first see and experience a problem before moving on. He understood this idea and in fact had benefited from it. His crying spells were gone because of this approach. But only after I validated his experience—not ever being in combat and being spoiled by his mother and grandmother—was he able to share his fears that he was not man enough.

However, I realized that I too was angered by his tone and comments (particularly about Hispanics) and wanted to ensure that my interactions and recommendations were not a response to my frustration. Aware of my own anger, I continued to carefully encourage relational issues to unfold. After a few more sessions, Robert said it was hard to accept help from a Hispanic, who very likely held different political views than he did. I asked him about his political beliefs and thoughts about Hispanics. As expected, he described himself as a conservative Republican, but, to my surprise, his feelings about Hispanics were not as negative as I had feared. He then asked me directly about my political beliefs. After we discussed his expectations about my political beliefs and the importance of this understanding consistent with clinical recommendation 1.12: *Address cultural and demographic differences,* I validated some of his views of me as a progressive liberal and, as he feared, a pacifist. Robert responded by stating that he did not understand how anybody could be a pacifist. He said his family always despised people like me who did not have the courage to fight for their beliefs. It is very easy to oppose something, he argued, but *"what really counts is what you fight for."* Despite his views, he still wanted to know why I thought the way I did. Although Robert was in complete disagreement with me, he seemed to make an effort to understand my views, just as he was making an effort to understand the growing number of feelings that did not fit his assumptions. After this discussion, I felt surprised again. It seemed I was making contact with Robert (clinical recommendation 2.9: *Make contact*). Pacifism is an important and signature part of my identity that I had not ever

(Continued)

(Continued)

disclosed to a client before. But Robert's interest drew me out. Sharing this had a powerful impact on my feelings about treating Robert. From this point on, consistent with the second phase, I thought about treatment more in terms of "we" (clinical recommendation 2.1: *Understand the therapeutic relationship as more than the sum of the characteristics of clients and therapists*). Paradoxically, in exploring our political differences, we actually started to connect. If we had not discussed our political views, we may not have been able to "make contact." However, for a connection to be made after an impasse, more important than the content of the difference and/or rupture is often the manner in which ruptures are repaired.

Soon, we were able to discuss the meaning of masculinity (clinical recommendation 2.4: *Address the cultural influences of explicit and implicit systems*) in our culture. He explained that his suppression of his feelings often irritated Catherine. He said many of their recent arguments arose from misunderstandings. Catherine would get annoyed with him because she could not read him. In fact, he (himself) could not read many of his feelings. But he did finally understand how his father had emphasized strong-warrior values (clinical recommendation 3.1: *Link contextual influences to clients' lives*), which were effective in the military and at his job, but not so effective with Robert's mother. This sparked new memories of problems his father had had with his mother. He understood that in certain situations (e.g., on the job), it was useful to compartmentalize feelings. However, he also learned that sometimes in relationships (e.g., with Catherine) it was more effective to express emotions as a means to feel close (clinical recommendation 1.11: *Learn and use clients' cultural context*).

A few months into the second round of treatment, I disclosed my irritation with his put-downs of my political views. He listened but did not apologize. It appeared Robert had learned not only to accept disparate feelings (sadness, love) from within, but also from others (e.g., Hispanics, pacifists). I must also admit that consistent with contextual ethics, I fantasized about the possibility that Robert would share his feelings with his buddies and start to change his social landscape at work. However, this is not what Robert wanted or what happened.

This clinical example illustrates how both therapist and client can benefit from individualistic, relational, and contextual conceptualizations. From the onset, I assumed that Robert's crying spells were related to his gender role expectations (explicit and implicit social messages), the grief of losing his mother and grandmother (implicit systems), and feelings that were retriggered by his love for Catherine and were difficult to express with another male, particularly because of our ethnic and political differences. Initially, he was not interested in delving into contextual conceptualizations; instead, he just wanted to address his presenting problems. Only after his initial symptoms were assuaged (e.g., crying spells) was it useful for his treatment to delve into our differences. It was important for

Robert to understand that our cultural context fosters an environment in which men are encouraged to be strong, independent, and emotionally distant. Culture prescribes many of the roles we enact, and it was beneficial for him to understand the influence of social forces. This allowed him to make decisions about which values he wanted to endorse, rather than blindly following what had been pronounced by society (or his family). It also allowed him to endorse certain values at some times (e.g., his job) but not others (with Catherine).

Conclusions

1. Cultural psychotherapy complements psychotherapeutic interventions by providing an integrative framework that incorporates individualistic, relational, and contextual conceptualizations. Cultural psychotherapy views all psychotherapeutic processes (e.g., assessments, narratives, formulations, interventions) in relation to these explanations.

2. Multiple explanations enrich the psychotherapeutic cultural formulation. Furthermore, within each of these three formulations, multiple, interacting, and overlapping understandings exist (e.g., biological, cognitive).

3. An enhanced awareness of the individual, relational, and contextual psychotherapeutic implications of each psychotherapeutic paradigm informs our clinical formulations and consequently improves the effectiveness of psychotherapy.

4. Meanings and cultural formulations are constantly evolving. As clients and therapists interact, alternative or more complex formulations are developed. This continuous refinement of clinical formulations emphasizes the dynamic nature of our clinical hypotheses. Rather than understanding this constant approximation to "truth" as an insurmountable deficiency, we can also view it as an asset that enriches our interventions as it reflects the countless and changing possibilities of our complex nature.

5. Not all paradigms are equally therapeutic at all times and places. Clients and therapists are encouraged to test which are more amenable to their needs, goals, and contexts. Overall, clinicians may suggest alternative views, but clients often decide which are more meaningful and beneficial for them at specific times and places.

6. Ethnic minority populations are not the only ones influenced by the cultural context; thus, cultural psychotherapy is applicable not only to ethnic minorities but to all.

7. In contrast to the majority of psychotherapeutic models, in cultural psychotherapy clinicians acknowledge that they are not neutral. Their ethics and beliefs constantly influence clinical decisions affecting what they do or choose not to do. It is important to explore the ethical implications of our clinical formulations to keep them from inadvertently diminishing the efficacy of our interventions.

Note

1. At times, particularly during electoral periods, the United States seems to become a politically polarized country in which Democrats and Republicans live in diametrically opposed camps. It is important to further explore these political differences and contextual conditions within cultural psychotherapy.

References

Alexander, F., & French, T. M. (1946). *Psychoanalytic therapy: Principles and application*. New York: Ronald Press.

American Psychiatric Association. (forthcoming). *Diagnostic and statistical manual of mental disorders* (5th ed.). Washington, DC: Author.

American Psychological Association. (2006). Evidence-based practice in psychology: APA presidential task force on evidence-based practice. *American Psychologist, 61,* 271–285.

Ballou, M., Matsumuto, A., & Wagner, M. (2002). Feminist ecological theory. In M. Ballou & L. L. Brown (Eds.), *Rethinking mental health disorders: Feminist perspectives* (pp. 99–141). New York: Guilford.

Bowlby, J. (1988). *A secure base: Parent-child attachment and healthy human development*. New York: Basic Books.

Bronfenbrenner, U. (1979). *The ecology of human development*. Cambridge, MA: Harvard University Press.

Chambless, D. L., Sanderson, W. C., Shoham, V., Johnson, S. B., Pope, K. K. S., Critis-Cristoph, P., et al. (1996). An update on empirically validated therapies. *The Clinical Psychologist, 49,* 5–18.

Cushman, P. (1995). *Constructing the self, constructing America: Studies in the cultural history of psychotherapy*. New York: Addison-Wesley.

Freire, P. (1972). *Pedagogy of the oppressed*. New York: Herder & Herder.

Freud, S. (1933). *New introductory lectures on psychoanalysis*. New York: Norton.

Fromm, E. (1955). *The sane society*. New York: Rinehart.

Gergen, K. (1991). *The saturated self: Dilemmas of identity in contemporary life*. New York: Basic Books.

Gold, J. (1993). The sociohistorical context of psychotherapy integration. In G. Stricker & J. Gold (Eds.), *Comprehensive handbook of psychotherapy integration*. New York: Plenum.

Greene, B. (1999). *The elegant universe: Superstrings, hidden dimensions, and the quest for the ultimate theory*. New York: Vintage.

Hacking, I. (2002). *Historical ontology*. Cambridge, MA: Harvard University Press.

Hayes, S. (2011). Acceptance and commitment therapy and the new behavior therapies: Mindfulness, acceptance and relationship. In S. Hayes, V. Follette, & M. Linehan (Eds.), *Mindfulness and acceptance: Expanding the cognitive-behavioral tradition*. New York: Guilford.

Ivey, A. (1999). Psychotherapy as liberation: Toward specific skills and strategies in multicultural counseling and therapy. In J. Ponterotto, J. M. Casas, L. A. Suzuki, & C. M. Alexander (Eds.), *Handbook of multicultural counseling*. Thousand Oaks, CA: Sage.

Jordan, J. V. (2010). *Relational–cultural therapy*. Washington, DC: American Psychological Association.

Jordan, J. V., Surrey, J. L., & Kaplan, A. G. (1983). *Women and empathy: Implications for psychological development and psychotherapy*. Wellesley, MA: Stone Center for Developmental Services and Studies.

Kohut, H. (1984). *How does analysis cure?* Chicago: University of Chicago Press.

Kuhn, T. S. (1970). *The structure of scientific revolutions.* Chicago: University of Chicago Press.

Lambert, M., & Ogles, B. M. (2004). *The efficacy and effectiveness of psychotherapy.* In M. J. Lambert (Ed.), *Bergin and Garfield's handbook of psychotherapy and behavior change* (5th ed., pp. 139–193). New York: John Wiley.

La Roche, M. (2005). The psychotherapeutic process and the cultural context: Towards a cultural psychotherapy. *Journal of Behavioral Integration, 15,* 169–175.

La Roche, M., Batista, C., & D'Angelo, E. (2010). A content analysis of guided imagery scripts: A strategy for the development of cultural adaptations. *Journal of Clinical Psychology, 67*(1), 45–57.

Luborsky, L., Rosenthal, R., Diguer, L., Andrusyna, T. P., Berman, J. S., Levitt, J. T., et al. (2002). The Dodo bird verdict is alive and well—mostly. *Clinical Psychology: Science and Practice, 9,* 2–12.

Martin, J., & Sugarman, J. (1999). *The psychology of possibility and constraint.* Albany: SUNY Press.

Martin, J., & Sugarman, J. (2009). Does interpretation in psychology differ from interpretation in natural science? *Journal for the Theory of Social Behavior, 39,* 19–37.

Martín-Baró, I. (1994). *Writing for a liberation psychology.* Cambridge, MA: Harvard University Press.

Messer, S., Sass, L., & Woolfolk, R. (1988). *Hermeneutics and psychological theory: Interpretive perspectives on personality, psychotherapy, and psychopathology.* New Brunswick, NJ: Rutgers University Press.

Morrow, S. L., Rakhsha, G., & Castaneda, C. (1999). Qualitative research methods for multicultural counseling. In J. Ponterotto, J. M. Casas, L. A. Suzuki, & C. M. Alexander (Eds.), *Handbook of multicultural counseling.* Thousand Oaks, CA: Sage.

Norcross, J. C. (Ed.). (2002). *Psychotherapy relationships that work: Therapist contributions and responsiveness to patients.* New York: Oxford University Press.

Norcross, J. C. (2010). The therapeutic relationship. In B. Duncan, S. Miller, B. Wampold, & M. Hubble (Eds.), *The heart and soul of change: Delivering what works in therapy* (pp. 113–141). Washington, DC: American Psychological Association.

Oyserman, D., Coon, H., & Kemmelmeier, M. (2002). Rethinking individualism and collectivism: Evaluation of theoretical assumptions and meta-analyses. *Psychological Bulletin, 128,* 3–72.

Ramirez, M. (1999). *Multicultural psychotherapy: An approach to individual and cultural differences* (2nd ed.). Boston: Allyn & Bacon.

Safran, J. D., & Muran, J. C. (2000). *Negotiating the therapeutic alliance: A relational treatment guide.* New York: Guilford.

Sanchez, W., & Garriga, O. (1996). Psychotherapy, Puerto Ricans and colonialism: The issue of awareness. *Latino Studies Journal, 7,* 29–50.

Slife, B., & Wiggins, B. (2009). Taking relationship seriously in psychotherapy: Radical relationality. *Journal of Contemporary Psychotherapy, 39,* 17–24.

Stern, D. N., Sander, L. W., Nahum, J. P., Harrison, A. M., Lyosn-Ruth, K., Morgan, A. C., et al. (1998). Non-interpretative mechanisms in psychoanalytic therapy: The "something more" than interpretation. *International Journal of Psychoanalysis, 79,* 903–921.

Stolorow, R. D., & Atwood, G. E. (2002). *Contexts of being: The intersubjective foundations of psychological life.* New York: Analytical Press.

Sue, W. S., & Sue, D. (2008). *Counseling the culturally diverse: Theory and practice* (5th ed.). Hoboken, NJ: John Wiley.

Sullivan, H. S. (1953). *The interpersonal theory of psychiatry.* New York: Norton.

Taylor, C. (1989). *Sources of the self: The making of the modern identity.* Cambridge, MA: Harvard University Press.

Triandis, H. (1994). Theoretical and methodological approaches to the study of collectivism and individualism. In U. Kim, H. Triandis, C. Kagitcibasi, S. Choi, & G. Yoon (Eds.), *Individualism and collectivism* (pp. 41–51). Thousand Oaks, CA: Sage.

Wampold, B. E. (2001). *The great debate: Models, methods, and findings.* Mahwah, NJ: Erlbaum.

Wampold, B. E. (2010). The research evidence for the common factors models: A historically situated perspective. In B. Duncan, S. Miller, B. Wampold, and M. Hubble (Eds.), *The heart and soul of change: Delivering what works in therapy.* Washington, DC: American Psychological Association.

Winters, N. C., Hanson, G., & Stoyanova, V. (2007). The case formulation in child and adolescent psychiatry. *Child and Adolescent Psychiatric Clinics of North America, 16,* 111–132.

CHAPTER 6

Developing Culturally Competent Interventions

All healing practices are social artifacts, producers (and reproducers) of their cultural landscape, and as such are embedded in an inescapable web of moral agreements and political activities.

—Philip Cushman, *Constructing the Self, Constructing America,* 1995

Research strategies to validate psychotherapeutic interventions are evolving and becoming increasingly sophisticated. In the process, however, different sets of standards to assess the efficacy and effectiveness of psychological interventions have been developed. In this chapter, I underscore three different research approaches based on their conceptualization of race, ethnicity, and/or culture. I call these three approaches universalist, race and ethnic models (REMs), and cultural psychotherapy. Finally, I use my own, ongoing research of a culturally competent relaxation intervention (CCRI; La Roche, Batista, & D'Angelo, 2011; La Roche, D'Angelo, Gualdron, & Leavell, 2006) to illustrate some of cultural psychotherapy's research strategies.

Each of the three identified research approaches has specific methodological requirements that define acceptable types of "scientific evidence," "truth," or "data." The three categories highlighted here, however, are not exhaustive of all research strategies; instead, they are designed to underscore the influence of race, ethnicity, or culture on the psychotherapeutic literature. The accepted types of scientific evidence are the building blocks that define psychotherapeutic interventions that in turn influence what unfolds during the psychotherapeutic session. Our research standards play a pivotal role in defining what is therapeutic or not. These research standards are highly influenced by our cultural landscape (Cushman, 1995). Furthermore, the ways in which race, ethnicity, and culture are conceptualized and measured influence the manner in which they are addressed during the psychotherapeutic process. I will illustrate these three research approaches with one of my first clinical cases as a student at a mental health hospital in Boston.

Case Illustration: Megumi

Megumi, a 32-year-old lesbian attorney of Japanese descent, had arrived in the United States when she was 5 years old. She now worked at a prestigious, predominantly White law firm. She initially came to psychological treatment because of frequent and intense anxiety symptoms that included insomnia, loss of appetite, and fatigue. Sometimes when she got nervous, she would become "paralyzed" and unable to respond quickly to people's comments—particularly their criticisms.

I started treating her anxiety symptoms with a standard relaxation and guided imagery protocol that included diaphragmatic breathing. As she rehearsed the breathing exercise, I asked her to visualize herself alone on a beautiful beach. Megumi immediately and very politely objected to this image and stated, *"I don't find this relaxation exercise useful. . . . It is only getting me more nervous. . . . I don't like to be alone. . . . I prefer to be with my family, or Susan (her partner)."*

I was aware that many people from the Japanese culture understand themselves in collectivistic or allocentric terms, or in other words, through relationships. Upon receiving this feedback and combining it with my knowledge of her culture, I immediately modified the individualistic guided imagery script—I was encouraging her to be alone—to include images of significant positive people in her life, particularly her partner, Susan. Further, I asked her when she liked to be with her family and she said that the holidays were always good. As Megumi visualized herself with her family or Susan during the holidays, she began to relax. Through continued practice of this culturally tailored imagery, Megumi gradually learned to control her anxiety symptoms.

Once she had learned how to control these symptoms, she turned to a new challenge: to become a partner in her law firm. She had worked hard for the past five years and had one of the highest success rates at the firm. However, some of the partners expressed doubts about her ability to engage with high-paying clients, given her—as they put it— "nontraditional background," meaning her sexual orientation. Additionally, some of the partners also hinted that rich clients would prefer having a more assertive attorney (not Japanese or female). Given her cultural background, she was assumed to be submissive, even though she was actually quite articulate and assertive.

Megumi confronted these microaggressions[1] head-on by reminding the partners of her high success rate, but as she did she started to reexperience the anxiety symptoms that had been in remission. Feelings of paralysis reappeared. She soon realized that she tended to freeze when she felt helpless and discriminated against (for being Japanese, a lesbian, or a woman). She said this immobilization occurred in part because she was so enraged and did not know what to do with her anger.

As her anger and frustration were validated in treatment, coupled with the continued practice of the culturally adapted relaxation exercises, she learned to control and channel her frustration more effectively. Six months later, Megumi was finally promoted. She argued that her differences were a unique asset to attract a more diverse and growing number of clients to the firm.

UNIVERSALIST PSYCHOTHERAPY

My initial response was to treat Megumi's anxiety symptoms with a standard relaxation intervention that is often considered a universal psychotherapeutic strategy (La Roche, Batista, & D'Angelo, 2010; Leavell, 2004). I define universalist psychotherapies as those interventions that view all individuals as sharing similar core characteristics. An effective way to identify universalist approaches is by determining if they omit racial, ethnic, and cultural variables (see Chapter 4). For example, if studies to assess difference in therapeutic outcomes by ethnicity or race have not been conducted—or suggested—or if cultural variables (e.g., self-orientation, levels of discrimination, gender roles) have not been considered, it is very likely that the psychotherapeutic model is emphasizing universalist assumptions. Unfortunately, most psychotherapy models do not consider race, ethnicity, or culture. For universalist interventions, cultural variables are secondary; it is not essential to measure them or theorize about their effects. If universalists do measure cultural variables, they are treated as noise or error and no significant effort is made to understand their influence. In fact, statistically, this noise is often factored out (La Roche & Christopher, 2008).

Instead of considering racial, ethnic, or cultural variables, universalist psychotherapies emphasize the need to refine strategies to treat specific dysfunctions, deficits, or disorders within certain invariable characteristics (e.g., unconscious issues, serotonin deficiencies, lack of self-efficacy or self-esteem, etc.). Because we all share these characteristics, psychotherapeutic strategies to fix our deficits/problems are applicable to all. Consequently, psychotherapeutic strategies developed in one group are easily transferred to another cultural group, just as I assumed that a standard relaxation strategy would work well for Megumi.

Many researchers who take a universalist stance assume that psychotherapeutic interventions are more credible if they are tested through rigorous methodological procedures (e.g., randomized controlled trials, laboratory experiments). Psychotherapeutic research guidelines (e.g., empirically supported treatments, or ESTs) assume that randomized controlled trials (RCTs) are the most valid method to obtain efficacy data (Chambless et al., 1998). In this research process, objective data that is both reliable and valid is collected (e.g., standardized diagnostic interviews). In doing so, practitioners' personal influence is minimized to avoid tainting the objectivity of the data. Data collected through the scientific method allows researchers to systematically test their hypotheses, isolate variables of causation, and demonstrate that therapeutic change can be generalized.

Millions of clients who would otherwise have continued to suffer from severe and debilitating mental health problems have benefited from the interventions generated by these scientific advances. These efforts have generated a vast psychotherapeutic literature that is followed by independent clinicians and replicated by different research teams. However, it is also the case that a large number of ethnic minorities are not accessing mental health services or are not benefiting sufficiently from these interventions, compared with their White counterparts (Alegria et al., 2008; Cook, McGuire, & Miranda, 2007; U.S. Department of Health and Human Services [DHHS], 2001). Many ethnic minorities in the United States not only present with more severe and enduring mental health problems, but also receive less effective services to ameliorate these problems (Alegria et al., 2008; Cook et al., 2007;

DHHS, 2001). Many universalist interventions may not match clients' cultural characteristics, as we saw with Megumi when the individualistic relaxation intervention made her more rather than less nervous.

RACIAL AND ETHNIC MODELS

New research and treatment approaches (e.g., culturally competent psychotherapy) are emerging that include the effects of race and ethnicity in their formulations and do address the growing ethnic minority health disparities in our country. I call these approaches the racial and ethnic models (REMs) and start by illustrating them through my work with Megumi. Consistent with my understanding of REMs, I quickly "adapted" my intervention to her presumed cultural characteristics. I had repeatedly read that people from Asian cultures have a collectivistic self-orientation and thus modified the individualistic relaxation intervention (i.e., imagine yourself alone . . .) into a relational one that seemed to more clearly match her characteristics. Similar to what I did with Megumi, REMs encourage the development of intervention strategies that are more effective with different racial and ethnic groups.

As a result of the cultural modifications being promoted by REMs, the assumption that certain interventions are universally effective is being challenged. This has fostered the emergence of the culturally competent movement, which promotes the development of treatment strategies for each ethnic or racial group. REMs are playing a crucial role in the growth of the culturally competent movement. The ultimate goal of culturally competent interventions is to ameliorate ethnic minority health disparities. In contrast to universalist psychotherapies, REMs argue that all outcome studies need to include race and ethnicity. Not including these variables is missing an essential part of clients' or research participants' identity. Similarly, an understanding of race and/or ethnicity influences the manner in which findings are conceptualized. REMS assume that we are not all the same—significant racial and ethnic differences exist.

Unfortunately, before 1995 most studies did not ask about race or ethnicity, and when they did, the majority (92%) of participants were White (e.g., DHHS, 2001; Doyle, 1998). More recently, researchers have recognized the need to take these variables into account. Starting in 1993, the National Institutes of Health (NIH) mandated that the race and ethnicity of subjects participating in any research project be documented. Similarly, APA's empirically supported treatment (EST) task force strongly recommended specifying the race and ethnicity of subjects in all psychotherapy research studies (Chambless et al., 1998). Nevertheless, ethnic minority participation in research studies and documentation of this participation remains low (Gonzalez et al., 2010).

Rosselló and Bernal's (1999) landmark study among depressed Puerto Rican adolescents is an illustration of a good REM. They found that although both cognitive behavioral therapy (CBT) and interpersonal therapy (IPT) resulted in a greater reduction in depression over a wait-listed control group, IPT was associated with improvements in self-concept and social adaptation whereas CBT was not. Rosselló and Bernal (1999) suggested that IPT might be more compatible with the Puerto Rican values of *personalismo* (the preference for personal contacts in social situations) and *familismo* (the tendency to place the interest of the family over the interests of the individual) than CBT, which may make IPT more effective in other areas for Puerto Rican adolescents. Rosselló and Bernal (1999) concluded that IPT was more effective in alleviating depressive symptoms among Puerto Rican adolescents than CBT. The Rosselló and Bernal (1999) study exemplifies an REM as it clearly measured ethnicity and integrated an ethnic understanding into their conclusions.

Rosselló and Bernal's (1999) study demonstrates that some interventions are more effective with different ethnic minorities. However, many of these studies do not define clearly what is meant by a cultural adaptation (Bernal, Jiménez-Chafey, & Domenech Rodrıguez, 2009; Cardemil, 2010; Huey & Polo, 2008). Frequently, cultural adaptations only include minor, superficial modifications to the intervention (e.g., matching clients' ethnic background or language dominance with similar therapists) (Huey & Polo, 2008).

CULTURAL PSYCHOTHERAPY

Cultural psychotherapy research strategies emphasize the need to measure cultural variables. In contrast, REMs emphasize the influence of ethnicity and race, but do not directly measure cultural variables (e.g., levels of perceived discrimination, gender roles, self-orientation). As a result of this lack, REMs seem to assume that people from the same ethnic or racial group are similar. Consistent with REMs, my work with Megumi illustrated how someone could benefit from culturally tailored guided imagery. However, my success was partly due to an informed guess or even a cultural stereotype. I had assumed that Megumi would benefit from relational strategies because she was of Japanese descent and she was not benefiting from a standard relaxation exercise. Cultural psychotherapy's validation strategies attempt to avoid this guessing by actually measuring cultural variables. Cultural psychotherapy would assess Megumi's self-orientation level and would explore other variables. For example, how was discrimination affecting Megumi's anxiety symptoms? Was religion or age an issue? Cultural psychotherapy considers not only the influence of race and ethnicity, but also of multiple cultural (e.g., gender orientation, ethnic identity, acculturation), relational, and contextual variables that could affect psychotherapeutic treatments.

To further contrast REMs with cultural psychotherapy, I again use Rosselló and Bernal's (1999) landmark study. Rosselló, Bernal, & Rivera-Medina (2008) replicated their study almost a decade later and this time found CBT to be significantly superior to IPT for most outcome variables, even those variables assumed in the earlier study to be more compatible with Puerto Rican culture. Rosselló et al. (2008) explained the discrepant findings by suggesting that the outcome measures of their second study (2008) were biased, and/or that CBT was in fact superior to IPT, and/or that IPT treatment fidelity measures were flawed. However, a cultural psychotherapy view would also suggest that these divergent findings could be explained by samples differing in levels of *familismo* and *personalismo*. The effectiveness of IPT may have diminished because of a lower rate of cultural match on their last sample compared with the first one. To assess this possibility, however, their study would have needed to determine the presence of these cultural variables, instead of inferring them based on ethnicity or race. A central tenet underlying many of cultural psychotherapy's treatment strategies is the cultural match theory (CMT). For this reason I briefly describe CMT.

Cultural Match Theory

An increasing number of researchers find that psychological interventions are more effective when they are consistent with clients' characteristics and needs (e.g., Barlow, 2004; Blatt & Felsen, 1993). This match idea is becoming more important to the development of empirically based treatments. David Barlow's (2004) pioneering formulation of psychological treatment has underscored the importance of assessing the level of match between clients and treatment characteristics. We have argued in turn that CMT is an extension of this treatment match model that suggests some treatments are more effective with the prevalent cultural characteristics of certain racial, ethnic, or cultural groups (La Roche & Christopher, 2008, 2009). More specifically, CMT explains that cultural similarities between clients and interventions increase psychotherapy's effectiveness (Bernal et al., 2009; Kleinman, 1988; La Roche, D'Angelo, et al., 2006; Sue, 1998; Tharp, 1991). CMT is a central assumption to validate any intervention with a different group. Unfortunately, to the best of my knowledge, CMT has not been systematically assessed.

I have argued that it is difficult to examine CMT and validate interventions for different groups because most studies conceptualize cultural differences in terms of ethnicity or race (La Roche & Christopher, 2009; La Roche & Lustig, 2010, 2012). REMs are designed to treat groups categorized in ethnic terms (e.g., Latinos, African Americans). Just as I guessed that Megumi would benefit from relational approaches because she was of Japanese ancestry, REMs assume that individuals of the same race or ethnicity share similar characteristics (e.g., personality attributes, intelligence levels) by virtue of their skin color or place of birth (underlying genetic structure). However, a growing contingent of researchers (e.g., Hall, 2001; Helms, Jernigan, & Mascher, 2005; La Roche, 2005) is extending REM's view. We assert that race and ethnicity may only be distally related to psychological attributes (e.g., intelligence, personality characteristics) if even related at all. Instead, more proximal—and often cultural—variables (e.g., self-orientation, ethnic identity, acculturation) yield greater correlations with psychological attributes. Thus, the efficacy of cultural adaptations increases when they are designed according to participants' cultural (e.g., self-orientation, acculturation, and ethnic identity) characteristics rather than race or ethnicity.

Research does show that when more modifications to interventions are included that match clients' cultural characteristics, they become more effective (Smith, Domenech Rodriguez, & Bernal, 2010). Furthermore, Helms et al. (2005) explain that when ethnicity and/or race are employed as the sole independent variables, by default other factors within a cultural group are assumed to be homogeneous, overlooking intragroup variation and assuming that all individuals within one racial or ethnic group benefit more from an intervention designed for that group. However, research on ethnic identity (see Helms & Cook, 1999, for a review) and acculturation (see Chun, Balls Organista, & Marin, 2003, for a review) are two significant and promising exceptions to the outcome literature in which cultural variables complement the meaning of race and ethnicity. Furthermore, Helms and Cook's (1999) research underscores the fact that cognitive match may at times be more relevant than ethnic match. We[2] (La Roche & Christopher, 2008, 2009; La Roche & Lustig, 2010, 2012) have argued that adapting interventions to our clients' cultural variables such as acculturation, ethnic identity, or self-orientation may not only be more realistic (it is impossible to always match clients and therapists on all racial and ethnic variables) but also more therapeutic. Although current guidelines have advanced significantly since universalist assumptions reigned (Cardemil, 2010), I believe these guidelines could be further refined. My suggestions are framed with this goal in mind.

First, we argue that a clear operationalization of culture allows researchers to determine when and how to adapt an intervention to individuals of a specific cultural group (La Roche & Christopher, 2008, 2009; La Roche & Lustig, 2010, 2012). As noted by Cardemil (2010), traditionally, an intervention is culturally adapted if members of an ethnic or racial group do not benefit as much as other groups do. In contrast to this approach, we have proposed a three-step methodological process (consistent with CMT) that uses an enhanced operationalization of culture to evaluate the need for, design, and evaluation of cultural adaptations of interventions (La Roche & Lustig, 2010, 2012).

1. *Psychotherapeutic interventions are not value free, and research is needed to examine the degree to which they are influenced by specific cultural values.* Numerous authors have pointed out that interventions reflect specific cultural values (e.g., Cushman, 1995; Gergen, 1991; La Roche & Christopher, 2009). Unfortunately, most psychotherapeutic models seem to conceptualize their interventions within a historical and geographical vacuum, assuming that their ideas are value free and effective for most people (La Roche & Christopher, 2008). I initially took this universalist assumption when I treated Megumi with a standard relaxation intervention. A lack of awareness and implicit endorsement of universal values may hinder researchers'/clinicians' ability to determine when cultural adaptations are necessary. Therefore, we suggest that the first step in constructing a cultural adaptation involves an examination of the cultural assumptions of an intervention (e.g., individualism, materialism, heterosexism). Focus groups with different cultural groups may assist researchers in detecting these differences. Additionally, content analyses are also useful to assess cultural values in different literatures (La Roche et al., 2010).

   I should underscore here that in the past research has been used to confirm social assumptions. For example, nineteenth century researchers examined physical differences among racial groups in an effort to document Black intellectual inferiority and thus justify and perpetuate racial inequities. Physical measurements of the brain were used to rank racial groups along a continuum of worth. Brain size differences were taken as indicative of the innate cognitive inferiority of the Black race and the superiority of the White race (Eberhardt, 2005)—a "scientific fact" then used to continue discriminating and mistreating African Americans. Cultural psychotherapy also aims to identify these social biases as means to prevent them from being replicated in our studies and interventions.

2. *Culturally diverse groups have differing constellations of cultural characteristics that need to be assessed, not assumed.* Each group or individual has specific cultural characteristics (that may vary from their racial and ethnic groups) that should be measured and examined when assessing the usefulness of different psychotherapies. Unfortunately, clinicians and researchers often assume the presence of specific characteristics because of phenotypic characteristics (e.g., skin and hair color) or ethnicity.

3. *A larger difference between the identified cultural assumptions of an intervention and the cultural characteristics of a target group suggest a greater need for a cultural adaptation.* For example, after treating clients such as Megumi, I noticed that the individualistic nature of the guided imagery exercise (e.g., imagine you are on a beach alone) did not coincide with the relational values of my Japanese client and many of my Latino clients, which led me to design an allocentric guided imagery exercise. Having a measurement of the difference between the cultural characteristics of an intervention and the cultural characteristics of a group/individual emphasized the need to adapt this intervention. Furthermore, the development of the intervention (or adaptation) should respond to the differences identified in Steps 1 and 2. The difference between an intervention and participants' characteristics allows researchers to use these cultural differences as a guide to adapt an intervention.

This three-step process also helps researchers identify the common underlying factors of a mental health disorder and its differing cultural idioms (Kleinman, 1988). This enhanced understanding allows researchers to preserve the unique treatment factors of an intervention and adapt the cultural factors, thereby ensuring that a cultural adaptation is not a novel treatment (Castro, Barrera, & Martinez, 2004). Furthermore, it allows researchers to assess the levels of fidelity of an intervention. I will now describe our efforts to develop the culturally competent relaxation intervention (CCRI) as an example of cultural psychotherapy.

AN EXAMPLE OF A CULTURAL PSYCHOTHERAPY RESEARCH PROJECT: CULTURALLY COMPETENT RELAXATION INTERVENTION

My work with Megumi and other clients led us to design the cullurally competent relaxation intervention (CCRI), which is consistent with the CMT. A first step to develop an intervention that is consistent with the CMT is to clearly define the cultural variables influencing an intervention. For this reason, I start by defining the self-orientation before illustrating cultural psychotherapy research methods through the CCRI. The self-orientation is a central cultural concept that has been the focus of a proliferation of research in the last few decades (e.g., La Roche & Turner, 1997; Markus & Kitayama, 1991; Oyserman, Coon, & Kemmelmeir, 2002; Shweder & Bourne, 1984; Triandis, 1994). I then follow with a brief review of the relaxation literature which is the type of clinical strategy adapted in the CCRI.

Self-Orientation

Triandis (1994) defines self-orientation as the way people understand themselves and the world and underscores two orthogonal self-orientations: individualism/idiocentrism and collectivism/allocentrism. Individualism refers to societies and cultures in which goals that pertain to the person predominate over collective goals. Collectivism describes societies and cultures in which the goals of the group are either equal to or predominate over personal goals. Idiocentrism and allocentrism describe the levels of individualism and collectivism (respectively) that characterize the person (Triandis, 1994). Individuals with high levels of idiocentrism define themselves in isolation from others (e.g., "I am a smart and funny person") and emphasize personal over group goals (e.g., "I need to go to college so I can make money for myself"), whereas individuals with high levels of allocentrism tend to define themselves in relation to others (e.g., "I am Maria's son and Jose's brother") and prioritize group over individual goals (e.g., "I need to make money to help my family"). See Table 6.1 for a description of some of the differences between allocentrism and idiocentrism. Idiocentrism and allocentrism are somewhat stable and consistent traits across time and contexts and are often independent of each other (Oyserman et al., 2002).

Self-orientation is an important cultural concept and is used to assess CMT. Megumi's objections to standard guided imagery related to a lack of fit between her cultural understanding of herself as relational (allocentric) and the individualistic (idiocentric) assumptions embedded within the traditional relaxation exercises. Numerous studies have suggested that most ethnic minority groups living in the United States are predominantly collectivistic in orientation (Oyserman et al., 2002; Triandis, 1994). For example, Asian Americans

TABLE 6.1 Characteristics of Allocentrism and Idiocentrism		
	Idiocentrism	**Allocentrism**
Self	• People understand themselves in isolation from others. • People emphasize unique attributes and differences.	• People understand themselves in relation to others. • People emphasize similarities.
Composition of the self	• The self is composed of self-attributes (e.g., intelligent, energetic).	• The self is part of a web of relationships (e.g., "I am part of my family").
Goals	• People prioritize their own goals.	• People prioritize group goals.
Boundaries	• The self is separate and has impermeable boundaries.	• The self is interconnected with others and has permeable boundaries.
Sense of agency	• Self-efficacy and an inner sense of agency are emphasized.	• Relational and collective agency is emphasized.
Group prevalence	• Most frequent among Americans of Northern European descent (e.g., Norwegians, British).	• Most frequent among ethnic minorities (e.g., Latinos, Asians) and Southern Europeans (e.g., Greeks, Italians).

and Latino Americans living in the United States often report higher levels of collectivism than Whites, who frequently report higher levels of individualism (Oyserman et al., 2002; Triandis, 1994). Despite general tendencies for certain groups to be of a particular orientation, some individuals who belong to a group that is more collectivist in nature (e.g., Latino) may themselves be predominantly idiocentric. Similarly, there are people from predominantly individualistic groups (e.g., Americans) who are more allocentric than idiocentric. From this point on, I will use the terms idiocentrism and allocentrism rather than collectivism and individualism, because the discussion that follows refers largely to individuals.

In the next section, I describe relaxation interventions and explain how we assessed levels of allocentrism and idiocentrism in this literature.

Relaxation Strategies

Relaxation strategies are widely recognized as an effective tool in treating anxiety disorders. The main goal of relaxation strategies is to evoke the relaxation response. Herbert Benson (1975) was the first to scientifically describe this phenomenon in his classic book, *The Relaxation Response.* The relaxation response is described as an inner process through which individuals learn to control and reduce their anxiety, although they may never be completely free of it. Many techniques, ranging from prayers and mantras to progressive muscle relaxation (PMR), can be used to evoke the relaxation response (Benson & Klipper, 2000). More recent findings suggest that the relaxation response also affects gene expression as it deactivates gene pathways that prompt cell death or trigger gene inflammation (Benson, 2001).

Three of the main relaxation strategies are (1) diaphragmatic breathing, (2) PMR, and (3) guided imagery. Diaphragmatic breathing decreases the frequency and intensity of hyperventilation, a common symptom of anxiety, by regulating oxygen and carbon dioxide levels in the body. PMR helps individuals learn the physical sensations associated with relaxation by recognizing the differences between tension and relaxation (Jacobsen, 1978). Guided imagery uses specific images guided by one's own imagination to influence psychological and physiological states.

Guided imagery is one of the more powerful processes associated with relaxation and the most likely of the three mentioned here to be influenced by cultural processes. The effectiveness of guided imagery depends on the ability of an image to evoke a relaxation response as determined by an individual's history with the image(s) selected. Thus, therapists need to identify "relaxing images" before a guided imagery experience is initiated (Wolpe, 1973). An individual's cultural upbringing is important to consider in this process because each culture tends to promote values that can aid or impede the effectiveness of an image (Triandis, 1994). Therefore, individuals may be more familiar and comfortable with images specific to their cultural upbringing (Kagitcibasi, 1994). Consistent with CMT, allocentric individuals may benefit more from allocentric-guided imagery.

While it seems logical that tailoring imagery to a person's level of allocentrism or idiocentrism may aid the effectiveness of the intervention, to the best of my knowledge the guided imagery literature seemed to be highly influenced by individualistic and idiocentric assumptions. In working with Megumi, I could not recall any relational guided imagery scripts (an imagery that included others). All of the scripts that I came across were purely individualistic. This led me to wonder if the guided imagery literature is highly influenced by individualistic assumptions. We (La Roche et al., 2010) decided to examine this question by assessing the levels of idiocentrism and allocentrism in all guided imagery scripts published in journals by the American Psychological Association and the American Psychiatric Association from 1989 to 2008. The following key words were used to search for articles that used relaxation: relaxation, guided imagery, imagery, visualization, and mindfulness. A total of 378 articles were identified. When a script was not included in an article, it was requested from the author, and a total of 393 guided imagery scripts were obtained. The final sample consisted of 123 scripts; those that were not included did not instruct participants to imagine something specific (e.g., they would ask participants to repeat a positive phrase or use a mantra).

These 123 guided imagery scripts were analyzed using content analysis techniques (La Roche et al., 2010). Six orthogonal categories of allocentrism and idiocentrism were grouped in three dimensions: (1) connection with others/self-separation, (2) presence/absence of others, and (3) relational/internal agency. The first category of each dimension is indicative of allocentrism and the second of idiocentrism. On the mean score, a maximum score of four could be obtained and a minimum of zero. All categories were significantly ($p > 0.01$) more frequent on all three idiocentric categories than the allocentric ones. For that reason, I use a "times more frequent" percentage in Table 6.2 to illustrate the proportion of times the idiocentric categories are more prevalent than the allocentric ones. For example, in the first comparison (i.e., connection with others vs. self-separation), the 52.5 times more frequent proportion indicates that the idiocentric (e.g., self-separation) category ($M = 2.1$) is 52.5 times more frequent than the allocentric one ($M = 0.04$) (e.g., connection with others). These findings clearly suggest that the guided imagery literature is highly influenced by individualistic assumptions and suggests to some degree that the psychotherapeutic literature in general could be more individualistic than relational.

The development of our culturally competent relaxation intervention (CCRI) is a response to the prevalence of idiocentric assumptions in the psychotherapuetic literature. Individuals who are high on allocentrism may not be benefiting sufficiently from idiocentric strategies.

TABLE 6.2 Frequencies of Allocentric and Idiocentric Categories on Guided Imagery Scripts

Allocentric	Mean	Idiocentric	Mean	Times More Frequent
Connection with others	0.04	Self-separation	2.1	52.5
Presence of others	0.78	Absence of others	1.9	2.4
Relational agency	0.98	Internal agency	1.47	1.5

A DESCRIPTION OF THE CULTURALLY COMPETENT RELAXATION INTERVENTION

The essential feature of the CCRI study is that it incorporates an allocentric imagery exercise (AIE) such as "imagine yourself with significant good people," while traditional relaxation interventions employ idiocentric imagery exercises (IIE) such as "imagine you are alone on a beautiful beach" (La Roche, D'Angelo, et al., 2006). Just as I did with Megumi, in the CCRI we used relational rather than idiocentric imagery. The CCRI is consistent with an allocentric self-orientation, as it has participants meet in a group setting (La Roche, Mitchell, & Gualdron, 2006). In the first part of the group session, participants socialize in an informal manner and review psychoeducational information (e.g., identifying anxiety triggers, sleep, and exercise). The main part of the session entails the implementation of an allocentric relaxation exercise that is taught during the last 30 minutes. The same format and topics are addressed in all groups.

Consistent with the CMT, we wondered if, in fact, Megumi and a growing number of diverse clients could empirically benefit from allocentric-guided imagery. More specifically, we explored if people with higher levels of allocentrism benefited more from allocentric relaxation interventions than idiocentric ones and if people with higher levels of idiocentrism benefited more from idiocentric relaxation interventions than allocentric ones. Unfortunately, the full scope of this proposal was shortened by limitations set by the Institutional Review Board (IRB) that reviewed the proposal. The IRB's main criticism was the need for more preliminary data before conducting a randomized controlled trial study, as this was a novel idea at the time and the literature did not support the tenets of our research. As a result, we proposed instead a correlational study that yielded much of the data reported in this chapter (La Roche, D'Angelo, et al., 2006). For this reason, we were unable to test the hypothesis that idiocentric-leaning individuals benefit more from idiocentric relaxation interventions than allocentric individuals. Five years later, the significant findings on the preliminary correlational study finally convinced the IRB to allow a randomized controlled trial. This study is ongoing and results are as yet not available.

For several years we worked on the correlational study refining a CCRI that aimed to provide a relaxation intervention that is consistent with an allocentric worldview (La Roche, D'Angelo, et al., 2006; La Roche et al., 2011). The CCRI is being implemented in a predominately (85%) Latino community health center called the Martha Eliot Health Center (MEHC), in which most are immigrants of Dominican descent who live in poverty. The MEHC is affiliated with the Children's Hospital Boston and the Harvard Medical School. I have worked at the MEHC for the last 16 years as a clinical psychologist and as the director of mental health training.

Perhaps because the majority of the clients at the clinic are Latino, it has been challenging to recruit participants from different ethnic groups (e.g., African Americans, Asians). However, my hope still remains that other researchers who work with diverse communities will adapt and test these ideas with individuals of different ethnicities, socioeconomic statuses, and cultural variables. Only as other ethnic groups are assessed will we be able to test the idea that cultural variables are more effective in predicting treatment outcomes than race or ethnicity.

In this study, we hypothesized that as Latinos were more allocentric, they would not only adhere more frequently to treatment recommendations (i.e., they would more frequently practice AIEs) that are consistent with their self-orientation, but also benefit more from the intervention (e.g., higher reductions of anxiety symptoms). More specifically, we developed two hypotheses: (1) A positive relationship would exist between levels of allocentrism and the frequency participants practiced the AIE (index of treatment adherence) and (2) A positive correlation would exist between the frequency with which participants practiced the AIE and their reductions in anxiety levels. Consistent with hypothesis one, a significant relationship ($r = .36, p = .04$) was found between levels of allocentrism and times participants practiced the AIE (La Roche, D'Angelo, et al., 2006). Consistent with hypothesis two, a positive correlation was found between frequency of practicing AIE and reduction of anxiety symptoms ($ß = -.36, p = .001$) (La Roche, D'Angelo, et al., 2006).

In addition, we found that individuals who were more idiocentric dropped out of the allocentric intervention more frequently. Furthermore, one year after the preliminary intervention ended it was found that decreases in anxiety levels (pre-posttest differences) were related with decreased urgent care visits (La Roche, Batista, Brahms, & D'Angelo, under submission). Similarly, decreased anxiety levels were related to lower levels of medication use (La Roche, Batista, Brahms, & D'Angelo, under submission). These findings are similar to our previous asthma psychoeducational studies (La Roche, Mitchell, & Gualdron, 2006), in which participants in the culturally adapted intervention visited the ER 50% less often than those in the nonadapted intervention, while the nonintervention group had a 25% increase in ER visits. This evidence suggests that enhancing the cultural match of psychotherapeutic interventions with clients' cultural characteristics not only increases clients' well-being (e.g., reducing anxiety levels) but also decreases health costs (e.g., reducing the number of emergency department or urgent care visits and medications).

SOME IDEAS FOR FUTURE STUDIES

As we have developed the CCRI, many ideas for future studies have emerged. Here are a few.

1. There are many cultural variables (e.g., spiritualism, familism), and we have only started to systematically study the self-orientation. It is important that future studies examine the influence of additional cultural variables (e.g., discrimination, gender roles) and their interactions on treatment outcomes.

2. The use of social networking strategies via technology (e.g., Internet, virtual networks, Facebook, Twitter, video games, and chat rooms) has grown exponentially in our society, and it is important that psychotherapeutic strategies start benefiting from these advances. CMT could be extended to "match" these technological avenues. For example, strategies that employ clients' preferred technological identities (e.g., avatars) need to be designed.

3. The generalizabity of our studies is limited by the fact that the majority of the sample is Latino/a. Our hope is that future studies (by our team or others) use the

adapted CCRI with a more diverse sample that includes multiple ethnic groups (e.g., African Americans, Asians, and Whites). Additionally, a more diverse age range (e.g., children) and groups from different economic levels, religious backgrounds, educational levels, gender orientations, and countries are necessary to learn more about the potential benefits of the CCRI.

4. Studies that incorporate neuroscience methods have much potential and need to be introduced to assess the CCRI and other culturally adapted interventions. For example, instead of using an anxiety questionnaire, fMRI strategies could examine changes in brain patterns after each type of imagery is used. Studies that explore which explicit or implicit systems are triggered by idiocentric or allocentric images or both would also be useful. Furthermore, as research shows that the relaxation response can change gene expression, it would be interesting to explore any differences according to type (e.g., AIE or IIE) of relaxation.

5. In our review of the psychotherapeutic literature, we used content analysis procedures to exclusively examine the levels of allocentric/idiocentric orientations on the guided imagery literature. Future studies could examine other types of interventions (such as ESTs) that may unknowingly reflect individualistic/relational biases. Similarly, it would be useful to quantify the levels of additional cultural (e.g., spiritualism/materialism, androcentrism) variables.

6. It is important to frame the cultural competence literature within the current health care debate and emphasize that culturally competent interventions are beneficial in reducing not only human suffering but also medical costs (e.g., reduction in emergency department visits, medication use). In addition, it would also have been useful to assess other outcome variables. For example, how did these interventions affect participants' empowerment feelings, just as Megumi's improvement also transformed her firm (e.g., she started attracting a more diverse clientele for her firm).

7. It would have been useful to measure self-orientation on several occasions as means to assess if it changed throughout the CCRI.

8. It is important to further refine our measures, including that of self-orientation. In fact, this project is currently ongoing and is briefly described in the next section.

Assessment of Self-Orientation

A specific example of a research project that stemmed from the CCRI is our current work on refining the assessment of self-orientation (La Roche, Poplock, Batista, Lustig, & Brahms, under submission). Throughout our studies, we have consistently used the IndCol (Singelis, Triandis, Bhawuk, & Gelfand, 1996) as a self-construal measure. The IndCol uses a Likert-type scale for item response and includes two main scales, each with 16 items. One scale measures allocentrism/collectivism and the other scale measures idiocentrism/individualism. Higher scores on each scale indicate stronger self-orientation for that particular dimension. To assess cross-cultural validity, each item was reviewed and approved by experts in 45 different cultures. The IndCol has demonstrated strong reliability and validity with Latino/a samples (Oyserman et al., 2002). La Roche and Turner (1997) back translated this scale into Spanish using Brislin's (1990) back-translation technique. It could be argued that the IndCol is an etic measure. An etic measure refers to scales that have been developed in one or a set of cultures and are assumed to be useful independently of context (Jahoda, 1992; La Roche & Christopher, 2008). In contrast to *etic,* the term *emic* is used for scales, ideas, or interventions that are derived from a specific group and are useful solely for that group (Jahoda, 1992).

In exploring our clients' and participants' narratives, we started to design and assess additional measurement strategies to examine self-orientation in a more effective and experiential way than those used by traditional psychometric instruments. Although the IndCol has moderately adequate psychometric properties and has been used in thousands of studies (Oyserman et al., 2002), its usefulness is increasingly being questioned (Heine, Lehman, Peng, & Greenholtz, 2002; Kitayama, 2002). For example, some researchers (e.g., Greenfield, 1997; Oyserman et al., 2002) have argued that certain cultures may have more or less familiarity with completing Likert-type scales, which could limit the IndCol's ability to make effective cross-cultural comparisons. Furthermore, Kitayama (2002) and Heine et al. (2002) have questioned the relevance and validity of attitudinal scales such as the IndCol in measuring cultural variations. They explain that people from different cultures often adopt different standards when evaluating themselves on subjective Likert-type scales; therefore, the reference group to which they compare themselves varies from culture to culture, diminishing the comparability and validity of the IndCol (e.g., Heine et al., 2002; Kitayama, 2002).

To avoid these methodological pitfalls, it is important to develop alternative strategies that are based on the client's narrative, particularly measures that are time-efficient and not limited by Likert-type scale assumptions, such as qualitative measures. Furthermore, the development of additional quantitative and qualitative measures would allow researchers to use multimethod strategies to more accurately detect the proportion of variance due to the unique properties of a measure (Triandis, 1994).

As a result of the IndCol's limitations, we started work on a cultural adaptation of a sociocentric egocentric interview that we call the sociocentric egocentric questionnaire (SEQ). Two anthropologists working at the University of Chicago first developed this interview system (Shweder & Bourne, 1984). The goal of our adaptation of the SEQ was to employ clients' descriptions of others as means to measure the frequency with which they use idiocentric/individualistic or allocentric/relational narratives as identified through qualitative measures such as content analysis procedures (La Roche et al., under submission). Preliminary data suggest that the adaptation of the SEQ has good indicators of reliability and validity, and it is highly correlated with the IndCol.

A PERSONAL NOTE ABOUT THESE RESEARCH PROJECTS

Throughout these pages I have underscored the development of our work as a logical and sequential process. Nevertheless, this process has been highly influenced by personal experiences that I need to include here. One of the most difficult aspects of starting the CCRI was deciding what was going to be studied and omitted from our research agenda. Several factors were relevant in making this decision. First, our awareness that I was stereotyping not only Megumi but other clients led our research team to explore strategies to avoid further guessing and stereotyping. We knew we needed to develop culturally competent interventions that benefited from clients' cultural characteristics, not our assumptions. Much of our work on the CCRI is a result of our clinical experience with clients such as Megumi or Rosa (see Chapter 7), who kept bringing up the relational and contextual components of psychotherapy and reminding us of the immense diversity among our clients irrespective of ethnic background.

In addition, my experiences of discrimination as a Latino male living in the United States were also an important motivator to develop the CCRI. Unfortunately, it has not been unusual for me to feel oppressed and constrained by ethnic assumptions. I am often expected to be late, lazy, and flirtatious, while some of my own perceived self-attributes (e.g., sensitive, hardworking, and faithful) are clouded by these stereotypes. Given these experiences, it may not come as a surprise that I ended up repeatedly questioning the validity and usefulness of racial and ethnic labels.

I must also mention that the CCRI research projects have been ongoing for more than a decade. The pace of these projects is fueled by the financial support (or lack thereof) I have received. Although I have been fortunate to receive some awards (e.g., Milton Research Award, Pilot Research Award, Bridge Award) from the Harvard Medical School, these have been insufficient to keep up with all the research requirements and the many ideas that are continuously emerging from our work. Much of our research has been supported by the tireless efforts of a wonderful but shifting handful of student volunteers.

I have often felt the frustration that many in the field can understand. Despite our tremendous efforts to apply for funding from larger sources such as the National Institutes of Health, only once out of three attempts did our submission actually receive a score; meaning that it obtained a score above the mean that allowed it to be thoroughly reviewed. Unfortunately, it was not funded. Similarly, I unsuccessfully applied for additional grants from the Harvard Medical School. Perhaps I underscore these failures in securing funding as means to not only justify some of the deficiencies of my research projects (insufficient statistical power and methodological rigor), but also to suggest how my research agenda is not valued by the traditional funding institutions. The lack of institutional support ultimately affects the dissemination of our ideas. Without significant funding, our ability to conduct more rigorous studies that get published in top tier journals diminishes. Clearly, if funding were available it would be ideal to start testing additional assumptions of the three-phased cultural psychotherapeutic model described in the early chapters of this book.

Currently, most funded studies are mapping the influence of genes on human behavior, and neuroscience is developing a deeper understanding of the brain. The current culture of institutions (e.g., NIH) is to prioritize the development of some areas (e.g., genetics, neuroscience) while others are less valued. My research agenda does not respond to current biomedical research priorities. It is thus not surprising that it has not received much financial support. Nevertheless, despite our funding limitations or because of them—not having to comply with administrative and some methodological requirements—we may have been allowed to think outside the box.

Conclusion

Throughout this chapter, I have described some of our efforts to assess and develop psychotherapeutic strategies to help different cultural groups through the description of Megumi's case and the development of a culturally competent relaxation intervention (CCRI). To conclude, I summarize some of cultural psychotherapy's main research assumptions.

1. Ethnicity and/or race do not define psychological attributes; there is much intragroup variation. As evidenced by the findings on the CCRI, Latinos/as differed in their levels of allocentrism, which influenced the levels of benefit they obtained from the CCRI. Thus, cultural characteristics need to be examined, not assumed, in individuals of any and all ethnic/racial groups.

2. Culture is crucial to all aspects of research—from the design and translation of instruments to the conceptual models that guide hypothesis development. Furthermore, psychotherapy research requires a conceptual framework that incorporates culture in a multifaceted manner. Culture is more than a moderating or an independent variable. Cultural psychotherapy argues that psychotherapy research can no longer treat culture solely as an independent variable (e.g., as REMs do) or as a source of extraneous "noise" (e.g., as universalist approaches do) that must be controlled for. Cultural psychotherapy emphasizes all these elements and even argues that the "noise" is a central aspect of a cultural/contextual message.

3. It is beneficial to employ multiple research methods (e.g., quantitative, qualitative, clinical) in a coordinated manner to measure different cultural and outcome variables. In the development of the CCRI, we used clinical (my clinical work with Megumi allowed us to generate the main hypotheses of the CCRI example), qualitative (e.g., the content analyses of the guided imagery literature), and quantitative (e.g., RCT). The use of other research strategies (e.g., virtual techniques, neuroscience, fMRI, gene mapping) could also be beneficial.

4. A strategy to validate psychotherapeutic strategies with different groups has been proposed in which the level of cultural match of an intervention and the characteristics of the participant inform what modifications are needed.

5. Cultural psychotherapy assumes that psychotherapeutic interventions are reflective of dominant cultural assumptions (e.g., individualism) that if not checked may lead us to measure differences as deficits. Furthermore, culturally diverse clients may not benefit as much from these interventions (just as Megumi did not benefit as much from the individualistic intervention).

6. It is crucial to listen to clients' narratives rather than to assume socially constructed categories that may further oppress and marginalize them.

7. It is important to be aware of the influence of our personal biases (e.g., my dislike of the concepts of race and ethnicity because of my own experiences of discrimination) and/

or how these biases can reflect dominant cultural ideas. Furthermore, it is important to note how different contexts may facilitate or hinder the development of a given project. For example, more financial support from NIH or the medical school would have allowed us to test these ideas in different ethnic groups; on the other hand, it could have also steered us in a different direction if through revision processes of the grant they required us to look at more traditional variables, taking us away from the original aims of the research. Cultural psychotherapy attempts to be cognizant of individualistic, relational, and contextual variables that continuously shape the questions and results of each research project.

8. Cultural meanings vary. Cultural psychotherapy argues that cultural meanings are fluid and flexible. Thus, it is not enough to measure them at baseline; it is important to examine how cultural meanings change at different times of the research project and to examine how and why they changed.

9. People, relationships, and contexts are inseparable from one another. A basic tenet of cultural psychotherapy is that culture embeds individuals' experiences within their cultural contexts, making individuals' meanings inseparable from their cultures and highlighting the need to assess one's context (e.g., measuring SES, neighborhood violence, health access, or perceived community discrimination).

10. It is important to help change the individual, but also his or her relationships and contexts. An additional advantage of incorporating the cultural context into outcome studies is that it allows research to move beyond the traditional conceptualization of therapeutic change as a process that occurs not only within individuals but also in contexts (Megumi's firm started working with more diverse clients). It is recommended that future studies also include relational and contextual outcomes.

Notes

1. Microaggression is a theory of specific interaction between those of different cultures that focuses on interactions experienced as nonphysical aggression. It involves demeaning implications and other subtle insults. Microaggressions have been defined as brief, commonplace verbal, behavioral, or environmental indignities, whether intentional or unintentional, that communicate hostile, derogatory, or negative attitudes toward people of color (Sue, 2010).

2. It is important to note that CCRI has had many contributors, and for that reason I employ the plurals, "our," "we," or "us" rather than "I" or "me." The contributors to this research project include many wonderful collaborators: Leyla Gualdron, PhD; Erin Brahms, MA; Kara Lustig, MA; Janet Helms, PhD; Michael Christopher, PhD; Castellano Turner, PhD; David Shriberg, PhD; Cynthia Batista, PhD; Jessica Leavell, PhD; Stephanie Poplock, PhD; Aprile Maxie, PhD; Eugene D'Angelo, PhD; John Tawa, MA; Jill Bloom, PhD; Alesha Harris; Kim Santora; and Amy Orecchia, to name just a few. I would not have been able to develop these ideas without them as well as countless others.

References

Alegria, M., Chatterji, P., Wells, K., Cao, Z., Chen, C., Takeuchi, D., et al. (2008). Disparity in depression treatment among racial and ethnic minority populations in the United States. *Psychiatric Services, 59*(11), 1264–1272.

Barlow, D. (2004). Psychological treatments. *American Psychologist, 59*(9), 869–878.

Benson, H. (1975). *The relaxation response.* New York: HarperCollins.

Benson, H. (2001). Anxiety is a good indicator for somatic symptom reduction through a behavioral medicine intervention in a mind /body medicine clinic. *Psychotherapy and Psychosomatics, 70,* 50–57.

Benson, H., & Klipper, M. (2000). *The relaxation response.* New York: HarperCollins.

Bernal, G., Jiménez-Chafey, M., & Domenech Rodrıguez, M. (2009). Cultural adaptation of treatments: A resource for considering culture in evidence-based practice. *Professional Psychology: Research and Practice, 40,* 361–368.

Blatt, S. J., & Felsen, I. (1993). Different kinds of folks may need different kinds of strokes: The effects of clients' characteristics on therapeutic process and outcome. *Psychotherapy Research, 3,* 245–259.

Brislin, R. (1990). *Applied cross-cultural psychology.* Newbury Park, CA: Sage.

Cardemil, E. V. (2010). Cultural adaptations to empirically supported treatments: A research agenda. *The Scientific Review of Mental Health Practice, 7*(2), 8–21.

Castro, F. G., Barrera, M., & Martinez, C. R. (2004). The cultural adaptation of prevention interventions: Resolving tensions between fidelity and fit. *Prevention Science, 5,* 41–45.

Chambless, D. L., Baker, M. J., Baucom, D. H., Beutler, L. E., Calhoun, K. S., Crits-Christoph, P., & Daiuto, A. (1998). An update on empirically validated therapies II. *The Clinical Psychologist, 51,* 3–16.

Chun, K., Balls Organista, P., & Marin, G. (2003). *Advances in theory, measurement and applied research.* Washington, DC: American Psychological Press.

Cook, B., McGuire, T., & Miranda, J. (2007). Measuring trends in mental health care disparities, 2000–2004. *Psychiatric Services, 58,* 1533–1540.

Cushman, P. (1995). *Constructing the self, constructing America: A cultural history of psychotherapy.* New York: Addison-Wesley.

Doyle, A. B. (1998). Are empirically validated treatments valid for culturally diverse populations? In K. S. Dobson & C. D. Kenneth (Eds.), *Empirically supported therapies: Best practice in professional psychology* (pp. 93–107). Thousand Oaks, CA: Sage.

Eberhardt, J. (2005). Imaging race. *American Psychologist, 60*(2), 181–190.

Gergen, K. (1991). *The saturated self: Dilemmas of identity in contemporary life.* New York: Basic Books.

Gonzalez, H. M., Vega, W. A., Williams, D. R., Tarraf, W., West, B. T., & Neighbors, H. W. (2010). Depression care in the United States: Too little too few. *Archives of General Psychiatry, 67,* 37–46.

Greenfield, P. M. (1997). Culture as process: Empirical methods for cultural psychology. In J. W. Berry, Y. H. Poortinga, & J. Pandey (Eds.), *Handbook of cross-cultural psychology* (Vol. 1). Boston: Allyn & Bacon.

Hall, G. C. (2001). Psychotherapy research with ethnic minorities' empirical, ethical, and conceptual issues. *Journal of Consulting and Clinical Psychology, 69,* 502–510.

Heine, S. J., Lehman, D. R., Peng, K., & Greenholtz, J. (2002). What's wrong with cross-cultural comparisons of subjective Likert scales? The reference-group problem. *Journal of Personality and Social Psychology, 82,* 903–918.

Helms, J., & Cook, D. (1999). *Using race and culture in counseling and psychotherapy*. Needham, MA: Allyn & Bacon.

Helms, J., Jernigan, M., & Mascher, J. (2005). The meaning of race in psychology and how to change it: A methodological perspective. *American Psychologist, 60,* 43–50.

Huey, S., & Polo, A. (2008). Evidence-based psychosocial treatments for ethnic minority youth. *Journal of Clinical Child & Adolescent Psychology, 37,* 263–301.

Jacobsen, E. (1978). *You must relax*. New York: McGraw-Hill.

Jahoda, G. (1992). *Crossroads between culture and mind: Continuities and change in theories of human nature*. Cambridge, MA: Harvard University Press.

Kagitcibasi, C. (1994). A critical appraisal of individualism and collectivism: Toward a new formulation. In U. Kim, H. Triandis, C. Kagitcibasi, S. Chin Choi, & G. Yoon (Eds.), *Individualism and collectivism: Theory, method and applications* (pp. 52–65). Newbury Park, CA: Sage.

Kitayama, S. (2002). Culture and basic psychological processes—toward a system view of culture: Comment on Oyserman et al. (2002). *Psychological Bulletin, 128*(1), 89–96.

Kleinman, A. (1988). *The illness narratives: Suffering, healing and the human condition*. New York: Basic Books.

La Roche, M. (2005). The psychotherapeutic process and the cultural context: Towards a cultural psychotherapy. *Journal of Behavioral Integration, 15,* 169–175.

La Roche, M., Batista, C., & D'Angelo, E. (2010). A content analysis of guided imagery scripts: A strategy for the development of cultural adaptations. *Journal of Clinical Psychology, 67*(1), 45–57.

La Roche, M., Batista, C., & D'Angelo, E. (2011). A culturally competent relaxation intervention for Latinos/as: Assessing a culturally specific match model. *American Journal of Orthopsychiatry, 81*(4), 535–542.

La Roche, M., Batista, C., Brahms, E., & D'Angelo, E. (under submission). Reducing urgent care visits amongst Latinos with a Culturally Competent Relaxation Intervention: An exploratory study.

La Roche, M., & Christopher, M. S. (2008). Culture and empirically supported treatments: On the road to a collision? *Culture and Psychology, 14,* 333–356.

La Roche, M., & Christopher, M. S. (2009). Changing paradigms: A cultural perspective of empirically supported treatments and evidence based practice. *Professional Psychology Research & Practice, 40,* 396–402.

La Roche, M., D'Angelo, E., Gualdron, L., & Leavell, J. (2006). Culturally sensitive guided imagery for allocentric Latinos: A pilot study. *Psychotherapy: Theory, Research, Practice, Training, 43,* 555–560.

La Roche, M., & Lustig, K. (2010). Cultural adaptations: Unpacking the meaning of culture. *The Scientific Review of Mental Health Practice, 7*(2), 26–30.

La Roche, M., & Lustig, K. (2012). Being mindful about the assessment of culture: A cultural analysis of culturally adapted ABBT approaches. *Cognitive and Behavioral Practice*.

La Roche, M., Mitchell, K., & Gualdron, L. (2006). A culturally competent asthma management intervention: A randomized controlled pilot study. *Annals of Asthma and Immunology, 96,* 85–91.

La Roche, M., Poplock, S., Batista, C., Lustig, K., & Brahms, E. (under submission). Assessing the validity of an adaptation of the sociocentric egocentric questionnaire.

La Roche, M., & Turner, C. (1997). Self-orientation and depression levels among Dominicans in the United States. *Hispanic Journal of Behavioral Sciences, 19,* 479–488.

Leavell, J. (2004). *Assessing individualistic and materialistic influences in the practice of guided imagery treatment by health psychologists*. Unpublished dissertation, Bouve Health College of Sciences Graduate School, Northeastern University.

Markus, H. R., & Kitayama, S. (1991). Culture and the self: Implications for cognition, emotion and motivation. *Psychological Review, 98,* 224–253.

Oyserman, D., Coon, H., & Kemmelmeier, M. (2002). Rethinking individualism and collectivism: Evaluation of theoretical assumptions and meta-analyses. *Psychological Bulletin, 128,* 3–72.

Rosselló, J., & Bernal, G. (1999). The efficacy of cognitive-behavioral and interpersonal treatments for depression in Puerto Rican adolescents. *Journal of Consulting and Clinical Psychology, 67,* 734–745.

Rosselló, J., Bernal, G., & Rivera-Medina, C. (2008). Individual and group CBT and IPT for Puerto Rican adolescents with depressive symptoms. *Cultural Diversity and Ethnic Minority Psychology, 14,* 234–245.

Shweder, R. A., & Bourne, E. J. (1984). Does the concept of the person vary cross-culturally? In R. A. Shweder & R. A. LeVine (Eds.), *Culture theory: Essays on mind, self, and emotion* (pp. 158–199). New York: Cambridge University Press.

Singelis, T., Triandis, H., Bhawuk, D. M., & Gelfand, M. (1996). Horizontal and vertical dimensions of individualism and collectivism: A theoretical and measurement refinement. *Cross-Cultural Research, 29,* 240–276.

Smith, T., Domenech Rodriguez, M., & Bernal, G. (2010). Culture. *Journal of Clinical Psychology in Session, 67*(2), 166–175.

Sue, D. (2010). *Microaggressions and marginality: Manifestation, dynamics and impact.* Hoboken, NJ; John Wiley.

Sue, S. (1998). In search of cultural competency in psychotherapy and counseling. *American Psychologist, 53,* 440–448.

Tharp, R. G. (1991). Cultural diversity and the treatment of children. *Journal of Consulting and Clinical Psychology, 59,* 799–812.

Triandis, H. C. (1994). *Individualism and collectivism.* Boulder, CO: Westview.

U.S. Department of Health and Human Services. (2001). *Mental health: Culture, race and ethnicity— supplement to mental health: A report of the Surgeon General.* Rockville, MD: National Institutes of Health, National Institute of Mental Health.

U.S. Department of Health and Human Services, Substance Abuse and Mental Health Services Administration. (1999). *Mental health: A report of the Surgeon General.* Rockville, MD: National Institute of Mental Health, National Institutes of Health.

Wolpe, J. (1973). *The practice of behavioral therapy* (2nd ed.). New York: Pergamon.

A Clinical Illustration of the Three-Phased Cultural Psychotherapeutic Model

A failure to develop a balanced perspective between person and system focus can result in false attribution of the problem.

—Sue & Sue, *Counseling the Culturally Diverse,* 2008

Liberation is a praxis: the action and reflection of (people) upon their world in order to transform it.

—Paulo Freire, *Pedagogy of the Oppressed,* 1972

The aims of this chapter are to illustrate the three phases of the cultural psychotherapy model, highlight strategies to address cultural differences (Chapter 4), and discuss psychotherapeutic cultural formulations (Chapter 5) through one integrated clinical case. In previous chapters, I have described each phase in detail without much consideration given to the other phases and various aspects of treatment. Unfortunately, as a result of this fragmentation, some pieces of clinical information were not viewed in relationship to others. In contrast, the goal of this chapter is to present a comprehensive view of the cultural psychotherapeutic model. Clearly, there is no single case where all clinical recommendations are applicable; however, through the case in this chapter the reader should be able to see how recommendations are applied across phases in an integrated way.[1]

The case described in this chapter is that of a Dominican woman I call Rosa. I have written elsewhere about her (La Roche, 2002) and had the privilege of having one of my most significant intellectual influences, Arthur Kleinman, review the article at the *Harvard Review of Psychiatry.* I have also presented this case at numerous seminars and conferences. At each presentation, I have received a wide range of feedback, and this chapter includes some of this feedback as it pertains to the basic ideas of cultural psychotherapy.

This chapter is divided in four parts: (1) Phase I: *Addressing basic needs and symptom reduction,* (2) Phase II: *Understanding clients' experiences,* (3) Phase III: *Fostering empowerment,* and (4) conclusions. In the first three sections, I highlight interventions that address cultural differences (Chapter 4) and the psychotherapeutic cultural formulation (Chapter 5). I also present various individualistic, relational, and contextual ideas on how to make sense of Rosa's issues. In the conclusion, I underscore the assumptions of the three-phased model.

PHASE I: ADDRESSING BASIC NEEDS AND SYMPTOM REDUCTION

I started treating Rosa during my first week at my new job (now over 16 years ago!) at a community outpatient health center located in a poor and dangerous neighborhood in Boston. When I first met Rosa, she was a 53-year-old mother of four, and grandmother of eight. Rosa was born in a rural area of the Dominican Republic and had never been married. The father of her children had abandoned her for another woman some 10 years earlier. Rosa was the eldest child in a large family and was taken out of school by her parents in the third grade to help take care of her growing number of siblings--a total of 13.

The day I met Rosa was her first encounter with the mental health system. She was brought in to the clinic by her two daughters. Rosa reported coming to psychotherapy because, as she said, *"I'm giving my family a hard time; I'm not helping them anymore. I feel like a* trapo viejo *[old rag]. . . . I'm useless to my family."*

I was immediately struck by her chief complaint. Her presenting problem was embedded in her relationships, not only residing within her (La Roche, 2002; Lewis-Fernandez & Diaz, 2002; Oyserman, Coon, & Kemmelmeier, 2002). This suggested a relational self-orientation rather than an individualistic one (clinical recommendation 1.1: *Chief complaints need to be understood in a culturally sensitive manner*).

Rosa proceeded to describe symptoms of major depression with psychotic features that included anergia, anhedonia, depressed affect and mood, tearfulness, and feelings of guilt. Moreover, when she was severely depressed, she experienced auditory hallucinations. She heard voices telling her she was so useless that she deserved to die. She had in fact attempted to burn her hair on several occasions and could not assure me that she would not try it again. I immediately started thinking about the need to hospitalize her (clinical recommendation 1.3: *Safety and basic needs are always a priority*), but when I suggested this possibility she looked directly into my eyes and said convincingly, *"If you put me in a mental hospital, I will kill myself."*

When I present this case, I usually ask the audience at this point if I should hospitalize Rosa. I have repeatedly heard eminent clinicians respond that she has schizophrenia and/or a borderline personality disorder, she is clearly unable to contract for safety, and she should be hospitalized. However, in a handful of settings, I have heard clinicians wonder about Rosa's family or community resources as avenues for help. This is in fact what I ended up exploring. Her two daughters had brought Rosa to therapy, so I thought it made sense to assess their perspective.

I explained to both of her daughters that I was about to hospitalize Rosa because she could not contract for safety; however, I told them, she had threatened to kill herself if I hospitalized her. I asked them if they thought their mother would in fact hurt herself.

"She never bluffs. She will do whatever she says," said one of Rosa's daughters and quickly added, *"In the past, when she has threatened to burn her hair she has done so."* However, the other daughter said, *"She will be OK at home. I really don't think she will hurt herself."*

I had a hard time agreeing with them. How could Rosa be safe at home when she could not contract for safety? If necessary—I thought—I would have to be firm about hospitalizing her or developing a safety plan (clinical recommendation 1.4: *Establish a culturally sensitive therapeutic relationship: It is acceptable initially to take an expert stance*). I asked Rosa's daughters, *"What had changed that would keep her from burning her hair from now on?"* Her daughters seemed to understand my concern, and we worked on creating an elaborate safety plan, in which hospitalization would not be required. We were able to design a plan with the following three elements. First, Rosa would never be alone. They identified this as a significant trigger for her risky behavior, so they would take turns being with her. Second, they would immediately bring her to the clinic or call 911 if they noticed any risky behavior. Third, we agreed that Rosa would come to psychotherapy twice a week (clinical recommendation 1.2: *The goals and structure of psychotherapy are established as soon as possible*), and we would ensure her safety by exploring and defusing the triggers (e.g., put-down comments) for her risky behavior as well as by developing strategies to help Rosa help her family again. We agreed to assess the effectiveness of our plan by meeting every two weeks to make sure Rosa was doing well.

It is important to have a mutually agreed upon set of psychotherapeutic goals by the end of the first session (Kleinman, 1988; Sue & Sue, 2008). Treatment compliance is often enhanced if these goals are framed according to the client's cultural meanings. Thus, I asked Rosa, *"Why don't we meet every Tuesday and Thursday at 2:00 to find ways to help you help your family?"* In contrast, with a client who was more individualistic, I would have said, *"Why don't we meet every Tuesday and Thursday at 2:00 to find ways to decrease your depressive symptoms?"* A culturally consistent understanding of the chief complaint is crucial if therapeutic alliances are to be formed and goals are to be pursued.

Rosa agreed to comply with our safety and treatment plan, and she promised not harm herself as long as she was not hospitalized. Furthermore, Rosa agreed to immediately inform her daughters if she was feeling unsafe. Although her daughters believed that her word could be trusted, they agreed to take turns bringing her to therapy and for psychopharmacological treatment (which had been set up that day). It is important to state that there was a long history of mental health issues in her family and that psychopharmacological treatment was extremely beneficial for Rosa, particularly in decreasing her auditory hallucinations (e.g., "you don't deserve to live"). However, this biological dimension often emphasized in traditional formulations has more psychopharmacological than psychological implications. For this reason, I am not at this time emphasizing this crucially important dimension of treatment.

In addition to safety issues, during the first few sessions we worked on many case management issues (clinical recommendation 1.3: *Safety and basic needs are always a priority*). Many underserved clients experience significant socioeconomic difficulties (e.g., housing and welfare issues). Thus, for psychotherapy to be effective, Rosa had some basic needs that needed attention. With the assistance of a case manager, we looked for welfare assistance (food stamps), affordable housing, appropriate insurance coverage, and help to "legalize" her immigration status since she was undocumented. As Rosa and I started working together on these issues, she started to share personal experiences. Furthermore, as we got to know each other we would increasingly laugh about silly things. I enjoy making silly jokes and she seemed to like these jokes. Gradually, her symptoms started to abate.

Six weeks after I met Rosa, however, she again reported feeling extremely depressed and feared she would not be able to control her impulses to harm herself. As per the initial safety plan, her family brought her in for an emergency appointment. She had been crying and had seriously considered setting fire to her hair. She said she was in so much pain that she *"deserved to burn in the flames of hell."* She lamented feeling like an *"old rag"* after being *"stepped on"* by a welfare worker. According to Rosa, this person had suggested that Rosa return to Santo Domingo because she was a burden on Americans who work hard to earn a living. Rosa described intense feelings of wanting to hurt herself following that comment. Her pain was so magnified that she could not bear it anymore and felt that to escape it she needed to hurt herself. Worried again about the need to hospitalize her, I explored Rosa's feelings and thoughts.

"It sounds very painful to feel like an old rag that gets stepped on" (clinical recommendation 1.6: *Learn and use clients' language*).

"Yes, it really is painful! It hurts, I feel useless, like I can't do anything or help with anything. It is being nothing . . . and not being able to do nothing about it. . . . I do not want to be a burden to anyone. I want to help. . . . I have always helped my family."

"Rosa, I can see how important it is to help your family. You have helped your family all your life," I said.

"Yes, I have always helped them. Since I was a girl. . . . I took care of my brothers and sisters and now I can't do anything to help. I am useless! I can't even cook or take care of my grandchildren. Now I am a burden to my family and this country."

"I can understand how painful the comments of that insensitive welfare officer were. He treated you very unprofessionally (clinical recommendation 1.4: *Establish a culturally sensitive therapeutic relationship: Maintain solidarity with clients' struggles*) *and I can see why that comment made you feel like an old rag. We can put in a complaint to the welfare office if you like,"* I said, reflecting and remembering Judith Herman's (1992) point that maintaining a bystander position can be equated with siding with injustice. I then added, *"Rosa, you have been working hard all your life and now you feel you can't. What the welfare officer said hurt you because he rubbed that in your face. That is not appropriate professional behavior and we can do something about it."*

After a brief discussion, Rosa decided not to file a complaint and said, *"I feel I can't do anything! I am useless! I am an old rag that should be thrown away . . . or burnt. . . . I am an old rag that deserves to burn in the flames of hell."*

"You feel like an old rag and you think you should be thrown away because right now you can't do much to help your family," I reflected.

We talked further about the meanings of her narratives (e.g., *"old rag," "burning in the flames of hell"*). After a while, the emotional intensity of her comments subsided, and she was clearly and convincingly able to contract for safety (clinical recommendation 1.3: *Safety and basic needs are always a priority*). I was certain that it was important for Rosa to feel productive, so we looked for a safe activity that would allow her to feel useful to her family. Her daughters did not feel comfortable allowing her to cook (too many times she had left the oven on) or take care of their children. However, they remembered that Rosa was very good at knitting. She had first started when she was 10 years old as a means to support her father's kiosko.[2] Rosa excitedly realized that she could start knitting again and soon her family was asking her to make sweaters for different family members.

Although I continued to be concerned about her high relapse risk and was not yet certain if I should hospitalize her, I decided to go in a very different direction and asked, *"Rosa, tell me about times that you feel well."* After a pause, timidly, almost hesitantly, she said, *"I feel good when we are laughing together about silly things."* She described a few incidents in which we had laughed. So I asked her to imagine that we were joking and laughing whenever she felt like an old rag, and she agreed to do so. This experience led me to think that many people whose upbringing is rooted in allocentric/collective values are more soothed by relational imagery than by the standard individualistic imagery common in the psychotherapeutic literature. Thanks to Rosa and other clients (e.g., Megumi), I decided to research this hypothesis (see Chapter 6), and now there is preliminary evidence that supports this idea (La Roche, Batista, & D'Angelo, 2011; La Roche, D'Angelo, Gualdron, & Leavell, 2006). Clearly, we can learn much by actively listening to our clients.

During Rosa's next sessions, we monitored how she employed this visualization technique and discussed her knitting projects. During many check-ins, which occur at the beginning of each session, she reported effectively using the technique. She would describe an incident in which she started to feel like an old rag, and then how she used visualization to assuage the feeling. What I was employing with Rosa was an adaptation of a standard cognitive behavioral intervention (clinical recommendation 1.9: *Use evidenced-based psychotherapies*), in which I encouraged her to monitor her thoughts, behaviors, and feelings to identify potential depressive triggers (Beck, Rush, Shaw, & Emery, 1979) as means to prevent her from *"burning in the flames of hell."*

Several weeks later, Rosa again reported feeling extremely depressed and feared that she would not be able to control her impulses to harm herself. She came to the clinic for an emergency appointment. Unfortunately, I was out sick that day. Despite my absence, Rosa sat in the waiting room for almost 3 hours. She said that as she sat there, she had imagined that we were about to start joking and that this image gradually relieved her stress/depression level.

I realized at this point that she was relying too much, almost solely, on the support provided by the psychotherapeutic relationship (by me), and what she needed now was to solidify and extend her social network outside of psychotherapy. Accordingly, Rosa and I explored various community resources. She reported benefiting from prayer and enjoying attending church, so I suggested that she participate in a local prayer group (clinical recommendation 1.8: *Use indigenous healing practices to address symptoms*). She reluctantly joined the prayer group at a Catholic church nearby her home. Her first comments about the group were not promising. Rosa reported being uncomfortable with many of the group members who *"have too many personal problems."* I was very firm in encouraging her to give the group a try (clinical recommendation 1.4: *Establish a culturally sensitive therapeutic relationship: It is acceptable initially to take an expert stance*), explaining that it often takes a few weeks or even months to start feeling part of any group. After just a few weeks, she became more comfortable and was able to engage in the group. This prayer group seemed to function as a support group in which participants shared their lives and sought solutions to different problems. There, she discovered that whenever she felt overwhelmed, she could share these thoughts with others as well as pray as a way to soothe herself. She explained that God was giving her the strength to cope with adversity (clinical recommendation 1.7: *Understand clients' formulations of problems in a culturally sensitive manner*). As she prayed, she felt more capable of dealing with various issues.

Rosa's depressive symptoms decreased as she described her feelings of frustration, anger, and hopelessness and as the antidepressants she was taking began to have an effect. After four months in treatment, we decreased the frequency of therapy to once a week. Furthermore, after she finished knitting each sweater, she seemed to feel more confident in her ability to regulate her emotions. Her identification of depressive triggers coupled with having an emergency plan—going to an outside prayer/support group, and engaging in positive activities such as knitting—all had the effect of enhancing her ability to regulate her affect (clinical recommendation 1.14: *Enhance affect regulation and psychological flexibility*). As Rosa became more aware of her feelings, cognitions, relationships, and context, she was better able to respond, rather than to automatically react to discomforting situations. Once clients' basic needs and chief complaints are assessed and addressed in a culturally sensitive manner and their safety is assured, they are often ready to start narrating their stories in more detail.

PHASE II: UNDERSTANDING CLIENTS' EXPERIENCES

A main therapeutic goal during the second phase of the cultural psychotherapeutic model is to explore, acknowledge, and understand the different dimensions of a client's experiences, including his or her experiences of injustice (e.g., trauma, poverty, and discrimination). In this process, the psychotherapeutic relationship becomes a central tool for the support, exploration, and transformation of clients' lives. During the second phase, as clients feel increasingly safe and stable, they can relate their experiences of injustice in more detail. However, therapists need to continuously monitor clients' symptoms.

In Rosa's case, even after almost a year of treatment since an episode of self-harm (clinical condition 2a: *No recent psychological crises*), I continued to assess her safety by noting symptoms she either reported or exhibited as she narrated her story. If she became too distressed or depressed, we would discuss postponing a description of her experiences until she regulated her symptoms. However, rather than stopping these narrations, she would often decide to pray. She explained that *"God would give her the strength to carry on."* Praying was an effective strategy for her to regulate her affect when symptoms escalated, to push through discussing difficult issues.

At this point, Rosa's symptoms had significantly abated and her ability to regulate her affect had increased. During this time, she was increasingly eager to describe her life in the Dominican Republic, which is consistent with clinical recommendation 2.2 (i.e., *Start by describing clients' lives, not just their problems*).

"*My first memories,*" Rosa would say, "*are filled with people. We were always surrounded by many people. It was not only my family but also our neighbors who lived in our home, although they were not blood family we called each other* primos *[cousins] as we also lived in their homes. Together (more than 30 people), we would celebrate holidays, loudly, almost laughing, particularly Christmas and Easter . . .*"

In sharp contrast, her life in the Boston area was lonely and isolated; almost no one visited or called her. Furthermore, not all had been fine during her childhood. In fact, she had experienced much suffering. Rosa started talking about being neglected and being physically abused by her father. When Rosa would forget one of her chores, her father would whip her with a leather belt and call her "*useless*" and "*lazy,*" among many other insults. During these outbursts, her father would also repeatedly scream that because of her laziness she would "*burn in the flames of hell.*" Rosa's duty was to make sure that her siblings were clean and fed.

In therapy, Rosa realized that her feelings of being an ethnic minority (e.g., Black, Dominican) and being poor in the United States triggered emotions similar to those she had following her father's abuse and that the voices she heard were a reflection of these experiences. She explained that when she felt victimized by government officials (i.e., the welfare worker), she felt helpless and useless (clinical recommendation 2.3: *Examine the complex and changing nature of meanings*). She described feeling worthless, like an "*old rag*" because of her skin color, insufficient economic resources, lack of English fluency, and being a woman in a predominantly white, male-dominated, English-speaking community (clinical recommendation 2.4: *Address the cultural influences of explicit and implicit systems*). Although she had experienced much discrimination in the Dominican Republic (as she was dark skinned and poor), discrimination was even more pronounced in the United States. As we explored the multiple layers of these experiences, we continued to work on case management issues.

On one occasion, Rosa asked me to write an important letter in support of her application for low-income housing. Although she repeatedly reminded me about the letter, I did not write it. I explained to Rosa that I had been extremely busy during the last weeks. She immediately sobbed, "*It seems that most things are more important than me!*" She added that she felt "*unimportant, useless, and stepped on like an old rag.*" I then realized that I had fulfilled her expectation of being disappointed (clinical recommendation 2.8: *Understand that ruptures are inevitable*). I had neglected her request/needs and considered mine more important than hers just as her father had repeatedly done. This experience seemed to trigger many implicit memories (clinical recommendation 2.3: *Examine the complex and changing nature of meanings*), so we began to explore her expectation that people would inevitably overlook her as I had. It is likely that this expectation started during her early childhood as her family struggled to get by. Throughout her life, she had to take care of her siblings, her children, and her "husband"; but who took care of her? Who had ever taken her into account? Westen and Gabbard (2002a, 2002b) explain that many implicit relational meanings are evoked only as therapists become more important to their clients, just as she had become more sensitive to my omission (i.e., not writing the letter).

In addition, my comments had rested on my authority as the "doctor," an authority that is construed and supported by the dominant sociocultural group. Even though I am Latino, for Rosa I represented the authoritative White American sociocultural environment that consistently dismissed her needs (e.g., being a burden to Americans that work hard). Thus, in keeping with the cultural psychotherapeutic formulation, there were three stories occurring and overlapping simultaneously in Rosa's life: (1) her expectations of not being acknowledged, as her needs had not been recognized by her parents, siblings, and "husband" (individual level); (2) the here and now (or real) relationship in which I had not written her letter (relational level); and (3) the societal perspective in which I represented the American White establishment that had oppressed and marginalized her (contextual level). Although I have differentiated these three sets of explanations for heuristic purposes, in reality they were mixed up and interacting with each other. However, consistent with the cultural psychotherapeutic formulation, each of these three levels could also be construed as a distinct explanation with many different subsystems (e.g., biological, spiritual). An important psychotherapeutic challenge is to explore and validate different meanings that are beneficial for each client at the right phase of treatment.

Clinicians often do not like to be challenged and may react critically or judgmentally when this occurs. For example, I felt like saying to Rosa, *"Why can't you give me a break?"* Obviously, such a reaction would have been detrimental to the therapeutic relationship. When we treat individuals of different cultural backgrounds, we need to remain even more sensitive to our own frustrations and cultural biases to prevent them from hindering treatment (La Roche, 1999, 2002; Sue & Sue, 2008). However, these complex meanings and disappointments are also a unique opportunity to intervene in multiple domains. In attempting to use this disappointment in an effective therapeutic manner, I decided to start by validating her feelings in the here and now. I had not written her letter and I apologized for that delay, to which she said, *"Didn't I tell you this letter was important for me? I need this letter to apply for housing . . ."* To which I responded, *"Yes you did tell me and I am really sorry. I wish I could have written it sooner . . ."*

Thus, I validated her anger and frustration that had been so often dismissed by her parents, siblings, family, and American culture. I acknowledged my mistake, which allowed her to revise her implicit relational assumptions and develop new meanings. These new meanings were supported by the fact that she did get what she requested. I wrote the letter that same day. In later sessions, we explored alternative ways in which she could have confronted me as well as the welfare officer who had insulted her. The aim was to increase her ability to respond, rather than to react, to situations in which she was not being acknowledged. An enhanced ability to respond flexibly (clinical recommendation 1.14: *Enhance affect regulation and psychological flexibility*) to injustices would ultimately help her to avoid *"burning in the flames of hell."*

Questioning the therapist provides a unique opportunity to challenge the power dynamics scripted within the psychotherapeutic relationship. The psychotherapeutic session often reflects the power arrangements of the broader cultural context. Thus, I attempted to increase her power by validating her and acknowledging that I should have given more importance to her letter (clinical condition 2d: *The ability to confront their therapists*). As I validated her feelings, she described additional situations in which she felt *"useless,"* *"unimportant,"* and *"stepped on."* Furthermore, she began to describe these experiences in a more detailed manner (clinical recommendation 2.6: *Explore and expand meanings*). During the next few sessions, we continued to explore our interaction, which triggered more memories in which her father and mother would forget her needs and prioritize those of her brothers. It seemed in her family, the needs of females were less relevant than those of the males; just as my needs, a male, had been more important than hers, a female. Thus, Rosa began to notice how many of her assumptions were based on *machismo*[3] values. In examining these values, Rosa could distinguish between what was culturally scripted and what was not. She began to question gender roles. I never encouraged Rosa to change her cultural values. I just helped her notice them and explore their consequences in her life. Each client decides which values to endorse or not.

As Rosa became less distressed, the therapeutic relationship became more egalitarian. During this period, I too became more open and shared some of my feelings about the therapeutic relationship. Such openness can encourage clients to further explore the therapeutic relationship. Such exchanges can enrich and energize the therapeutic process. I also realized that as treatment proceeded, Rosa and I were feeling closer (clinical recommendation 2.9: *Make contact*). We may have started with a greater distance between us (see Figure 7.1), but we gradually became closer (see Figure 7.2). Thus, not only were Rosa's interactions changing, but mine had changed with her. My client interactions increasingly reflected some of my singular personal characteristics rather than solely conducting technical therapeutic interventions.

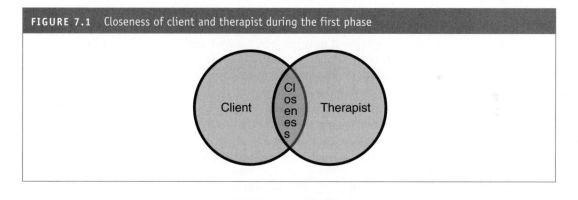

FIGURE 7.1   Closeness of client and therapist during the first phase

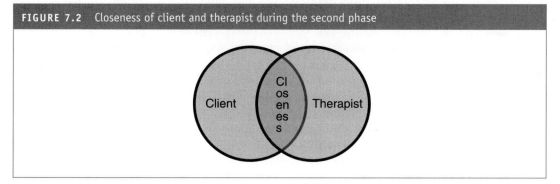

FIGURE 7.2   Closeness of client and therapist during the second phase

As the therapeutic relationship grew closer, Rosa's depressive symptoms decreased through our tears, laughter, and disagreements. Gradually, Rosa reclaimed her history and felt a renewed sense of hope and empowerment (clinical recommendation 2.10: *Use clients' renewed sense of vitality*). She strengthened her desire to pursue her goals and develop her own voice. She had reached a point in the therapeutic process termed "empowerment," which constitutes the third phase of the cultural psychotherapy model.

PHASE III: FOSTERING EMPOWERMENT

The empowerment phase involves an awakening of social consciousness—a realistic awareness of one's sociocultural environment and experience—which leads to a desire to transform and improve oneself and one's context. Individuals become empowered as they understand themselves and identify community stressors and resources. As clients confront the injustices of the socioeconomic environment (e.g., discrimination, sexism, economic inequalities, materialism), they realize they can refuse to conform to a marginalizing and oppressive status quo. The empowerment phase is by nature paradoxical; the injustices that have hindered clients' development and growth fuel their quests to overcome difficulties and seek new challenges. Their struggles have a new meaning, and clients are motivated by a desire to prevent others from suffering similar misfortunes and deprivations (Bulhan, 1985; Herman, 1992; Ivey, 1999). However, embedded in this motivation, clients need to be cognizant of the socioeconomic, historical, and cultural forces driving and defining the society around them (La Roche, 2002; La Roche & Christopher, 2010).

As Rosa began to comprehend how her parents had valued her male siblings over her and how American culture devalues women and ethnic minorities, she felt helpless and angry. However, an increased understanding of these explicit and implicit messages, coupled with the validation of Rosa's experiences in different contexts (e.g., at church, welfare office), allowed her to realize that she was not "bad" for being who she is and that she does not deserve "*to burn in the flames of hell*" because of the way she looks or talks. Rosa soon grasped the idea that it is American culture that has a problem, not her. In her experience, American culture judges people according to superficial characteristics (e.g., skin color, money) that end up marginalizing many (clinical recommendation 3.1: *Link contextual influences to clients' lives*). This enhanced contextual understanding of explicit and implicit messages allowed her to better understand some of her feelings (Ivey, 1999). In this way, Rosa arrived at a desire to help others avoid similar experiences of discrimination (clinical recommendation 3.5: *Awaken to social justice*).

Furthermore, by more accurately understanding society's complexities, Rosa was better equipped to develop specific behavioral responses to each situation. Rosa understood that each social context had a different set of expectations and rules. For example, if she went to the welfare office or the homeland security office she would not be treated as well as when she attended church. Consequently, some responses are more appropriate for some situations. So I encouraged her to develop and practice alternative responses outside of therapy for each of these different contexts.

The reaffirmation of multiple experiences within different contexts is not only empowering but also facilitates a more integrated self (White & Epston, 1990). As Rosa progressed through the therapeutic process, she learned that she did not need to construct a single story within which to live (clinical recommendation 3.6: *Embrace multiple stories*). Rather, she could experience multiple, often contradictory stories within different contexts. Through in-depth exploration and understanding of her stories, Rosa discovered that she could change the meaning of the personal injustices by making them the basis for social action (Bulhan, 1985; Herman, 1992; White & Epston, 1990). She was not condemned to be the victim of an oppressive cultural context; she was much more than these cultural stereotypes.

Rosa became more confident in questioning others and in pursuing her own goals. She was also more active in directing the psychotherapeutic relationship, as she would set the agenda for each session (clinical recommendation 3.2: *Clients lead the way*). At the beginning of the session, Rosa would list the topics she wanted to cover. Now, she could easily confront me when necessary. As Rosa seemed more empowered, psychotherapy seemed more open-ended and less frequent. During this period, Rosa was scheduling sessions only about once every six weeks.

After two years in psychotherapy, Rosa reported tearfully that a small town in the Dominican Republic had been devastated by a hurricane. I asked her what we could do to help (clinical recommendation 3.7: *Talking is not enough: Action is necessary*). She immediately said she wanted to organize her prayer group and send money to the people of that town. Her prayer group received this idea with enthusiasm. In fact, they not only organized their families and their church, but they also took up a collection within each group member's neighborhood. This intensive activity throughout the community produced numerous donations of food and clothing.

A few weeks later, Rosa proudly showed me photographs of herself and her prayer group in front of hundreds of boxes of food and clothing that had been shipped to the Dominican Republic. She reported feeling proud of her accomplishment. By helping others, she no longer felt like an old rag; her improvements had had an effect on a little town in the Dominican Republic (clinical recommendation 3.9: *Understand that what is local is global*). Perceiving that I was impressed by her achievements, she jokingly said, *"and you wanted to hospitalize me,"* to which we both erupted in whole-hearted laughter. We certainly had come a long way and learned much from each other. At this point, I realized how close I felt to her, as she probably felt toward me (clinical recommendation 2.9: *Make contact*). I realized that we had also incorporated the cultural context into treatment (see Figure 7.3). We had discussed not only many of its contextual problems (e.g., racism, gender inequality, socioeconomic injustice), but also some of its strengths (e.g., spirituality, community).

As the psychotherapeutic relationship is embedded within the broader context, it can have an effect on the context itself (clinical recommendation 4.9: *Cultural contexts affect the therapeutic relationship,* and 4.10: *Dialogues about cultural differences can impact the cultural context*).

Rosa is now in her 70s and has survived breast cancer. During chemotherapy, her prayer group was wholly supportive of her and her family. Rosa remained in therapy for a couple of more years (for a total of 10 years) and terminated treatment on several occasions (clinical recommendation 3.10: *Coping with termination issues*). However, she resumed treatment as new crises arose (e.g., one of her grandsons was suicidal). During her last years of psychotherapy, I saw her an average of two or three times a year with the exception of her eighth year of treatment, after her sister died, in which I saw her weekly

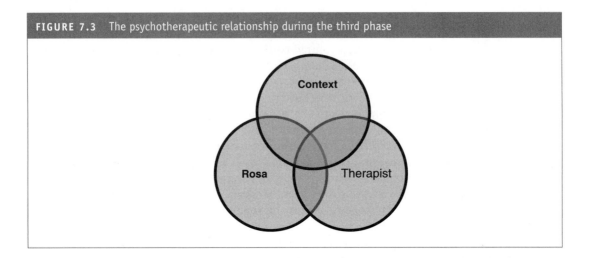

FIGURE 7.3   The psychotherapeutic relationship during the third phase

for several months. During this crisis, hospitalization once again seemed like an imminent possibility. At this point, she reported having no faith in God or anyone. After a few months of treatment, she reported feeling well and ready to help her family again. One prominent issue that was frequently explored in treatment was her desire to help others, particularly her family. She decided that this was a core implicit system (now also explicit) issue that she would like to conserve. Nevertheless, she discovered that she had redefined her meaning of family: Family was not just her bloodline—it was the world.

Conclusions

This case illustration attempts to further illuminate a cultural psychotherapeutic model that can allow clinicians to assess and intervene in a culturally appropriate manner using a three-phase sequence of clinical considerations. More specifically, clients' ability to transform themselves and their contexts depends first upon creating a safe and stable environment in which their chief complaints and symptoms are addressed in a culturally consistent manner. In Rosa's case, her allocentric orientation was understood and respected throughout the psychotherapeutic process while the symptoms that threatened her safety were relieved.

During the second phase, it is important to articulate, explore, and integrate clients' understandings within the psychotherapeutic relationship. As Rosa described experiences of discrimination and poverty, she understood how these evoked past experiences of trauma and cultural marginalization. Her feelings of *"being stepped on"* or being an *"old rag"* were integrated into a new understanding of how her personal history of trauma, her experiences of poverty and discrimination were interwoven as well as my contribution to this dynamic (e.g., forgetting to write her letter, power differential within the session).

Furthermore, having been the eldest of 13 siblings, and female, she had been responsible for raising them. Much of her identity and self-worth stemmed from this duty. In contrast, not being able to fulfill her duties made her feel useless and therefore worthless—thus, the importance of encouraging her to be helpful and productive (e.g., knitting, gathering donations).

During the third phase, clients become increasingly aware of how their strengths and relationships are embedded within historical and sociocultural contexts. Cultural psychotherapy argues that as the influence of the broader socioeconomic and cultural context is recognized and effectively utilized in psychotherapy, clients become increasingly empowered to change themselves and their contexts. Although an acknowledgment of the influence of the cultural context is always present, it becomes more important during the last phase. Had culturally sensitive strategies not been employed to treat Rosa's problems, she might well have dropped out of treatment or had several hospitalizations and relapses. Such hospitalizations could have been not only traumatic but also expensive and ineffective. Just one hospitalization could have been more expensive than her entire episode of psychotherapy. Furthermore, Rosa might have experienced these hospitalizations as revictimizations by a system that treated her cultural differences as deficits. While it took Rosa almost two years to reach the empowerment phase, it is important to note that most clients do not ever reach this stage. I must admit that when I first met Rosa I never imagined that she would end up accomplishing and teaching me so much.

Although I emphasize differences between each of the three phases of cultural psychotherapy, they are complementary and build on each other. Even during the first phase, I fostered Rosa's empowerment as I encouraged her to weave. Furthermore, even in the third phase as she was helping victims in Santo Domingo, I was assessing her symptoms to make sure she would not relapse. The fact that she briefly relapsed after eight years of treatment (when her sister died) underscores the need to continuously emphasize safety and that the sequence of phases is not linear but spiral.

However, most striking were the changes that unfolded within the psychotherapeutic relationship. During the first phase, I was directive and structured: I constantly ensured that Rosa was stable by assessing her symptoms and rehearsing safety plans. In the second phase, the psychotherapeutic relationship became more emotional and egalitarian. During this phase, she started confronting me (e.g., when I was unable to write her letter). Furthermore, what happened during the session significantly informed and guided the psychotherapeutic process. In interacting with her, I had learned more about her implicit systems (e.g., her expectation of not being acknowledged). This knowledge came partly from what she said but to an even larger degree from our interactions. In the final and third phase, the psychotherapeutic relationship became more authentic (e.g., she was able to know who I was, not so much colored by her past relationships but in the here and now of our exchanges). She increasingly took charge of the therapeutic relationship. In complete contrast to the first phase when I directed the sessions, during the third phase I often followed Rosa's agenda. As the phases progressed, I learned increasingly more about her explicit and implicit relational systems and made contact with her as we explored explicit and implicit social messages. What started in the first session as our laughter about silly things had by the third phase developed to the point that a simple joke (e.g., and you thought I should be hospitalized!) conveyed a greater sense of connection and understanding than what could be said after a long explanation.

Cultural psychotherapy emphasizes the need to promote individual change and relational change as well as contextual change. In Rosa's case, she learned to regulate her affect and became more psychologically flexible. She understood and changed her expectation that people would not acknowledge her (as her parents prioritized the needs of her brothers). And finally, Rosa was able to change not only her immediate social context as she helped her family (knitting, sweaters), but also her larger social context as she helped a devastated town in the Dominican Republic as well as leading her church and prayer group to become an active force in her community. Cultural psychotherapy's understanding of clients within relationships and contexts allows treatment to have an impact on our clients' lives, relationships, and context.

Notes

1. As noted earlier, the clinical recommendations discussed in this chapter are assigned two numbers. The first number corresponds to the chapter in which the clinical recommendation is described, and the second is the number of the recommendation in that chapter. For example, 2.6 would indicate the sixth recommendation in Chapter 2, or the second phase. If a letter appears, it refers to a prerequisite of a phase. For example, 3a would refer to the first condition of the third phase in Chapter 3. The purpose of this system is to allow readers to find more information on a clinical recommendation if they need it.

2. A little, portable street store that sold miscellaneous goods, including her handmade clothes.

3. *Machismo* is a traditional cultural value common among Latino/as in which men are assumed to be strong, in control, and providers for the family (Marin & VanOss-Marin, 1991). Women in turn are expected to be submissive and respectful toward men.

References

Beck, A., Rush, J., Shaw, B., & Emery, G. (1979). *Cognitive therapy of depression.* New York: Guilford.

Bulhan, H. A. (1985). *Frantz Fanon and the psychology of the oppressed.* New York: Plenum.

Freire, P. (1972). *Pedagogy of the oppressed.* New York: Herder & Herder.

Herman, J. L. (1992). *Trauma and recovery: The aftermath of violence—from domestic abuse to political terror.* New York: Basic Books.

Ivey, A. (1999). Psychotherapy as liberation: Toward specific skills and strategies in multicultural counseling and therapy. In J. Ponterotto, J. M. Casas, L. A. Suzuki, & C. M. Alexander (Eds.), *Handbook of multicultural counseling.* Thousand Oaks, CA: Sage.

Kleinman, A. (1988). *Rethinking psychiatry: From cultural category to personal experience*. New York: Free Press.

La Roche, M. (1999). Culture, transference, and countertransference among Latinos. *Psychotherapy, 36,* 389–397.

La Roche, M. (2002). Psychotherapeutic considerations in treating Latinos. *Harvard Review of Psychiatry, 10,* 115–122.

La Roche, M., Batista, C., & D'Angelo, E. (2011). A culturally competent relaxation intervention for Latinos/as: Assessing a culturally specific match model. *American Journal of Orthopsychiatry, 81*(4), 535–542.

La Roche, M., & Christopher, M. S. (2010). Cultural diversity. In J. C. Thomas & M. Hersen (Eds.), *Handbook of clinical psychology competencies* (pp. 95–122). New York: Springer.

La Roche, M., D'Angelo, E., Gualdron, L., & Leavell, J. (2006). Culturally sensitive guided imagery for allocentric Latinos: A pilot study. *Psychotherapy: Theory, Research, Practice, Training, 43,* 555–560.

La Roche, M., & Turner, C. (1997). Self-orientation and depression level among Dominicans in the United States. *Hispanic Journal of Behavioral Sciences, 19,* 479–488.

Lewis-Fernandez, R., & Diaz, N. (2002). The cultural formulation: A method for assessing cultural factors affecting the clinical encounter. *Psychiatric Quarterly, 73,* 271–295.

Marin, G., & VanOss-Marin, B. (1991). *Research with Hispanic populations*. Thousand Oaks, CA: Sage.

Oyserman, D., Coon, H., & Kemmelmeier, M. (2002). Rethinking individualism and collectivism: Evaluation of theoretical assumptions and meta-analyses. *Psychological Bulletin, 128,* 3–72.

Sue, W. S., & Sue, D. (2008). *Counseling the culturally diverse: Theory and practice* (5th ed.). Hoboken, NJ: John Wiley.

Westen, D., & Gabbard, G. (2002a). Development in cognitive neuroscience: I. Conflict, compromise, and connectionism. *Journal of the American Psychoanalytic Association, 50*(1), 53–98.

Westen, D., & Gabbard, G. (2002b). Development in cognitive neuroscience: II. Implications for theories of transference. *Journal of the American Psychoanalytic Association, 50*(1), 99–134.

White, M. J., & Epston, D. (1990). *Narrative means to therapeutic ends*. New York: Norton.

Beyond Cultural Psychotherapy

Cultural Thinking

"Liberty, Sancho, my friend, is one of the most precious gifts that Heaven has bestowed on mankind."

—Miguel Cervantes, *Don Quixote,* 1605

Besides, narrative acts of self-making are usually guided by unspoken, implicit cultural models of what selfhood should be, might be—and, of course, shouldn't be.

—Jerome Bruner, *Making Stories: Law, Literature, Life,* 2002

The name of this book is *Cultural Psychotherapy,* and throughout its pages I have focused on the practice of psychotherapy. However, these ideas are a result of a set of ontological, epistemological, and ethical assumptions that could broadly be called "cultural thinking" and have significant practical implications that go beyond the praxis of psychotherapy. In the introduction of this book, I explained that many of cultural psychotherapy's ideas could be traced back to anthropology, Wundt's *Volkerpsychologie,* or quantum physics. Furthermore, multiple variations of these ideas have appeared in different disciplines (e.g., history, philosophy, and physics). In this final chapter, I first summarize some of the core philosophical concepts of cultural thinking and then suggest some of its applications. I think that cultural thinking is rich in possibilities. In this chapter, I mention a handful of these applications. The chapter concludes with some core ideas about cultural thinking and cultural psychotherapy.

CORE CONCEPTS

A Cultural Ontological Framework

The ontological framework of cultural thinking is based on the idea that what we "know" is a result of the qualities of the object (what is being observed); the properties of the observer (or subject), which includes the interaction between the observer and observed; and the influence of the cultural context (La Roche, 2005). We are embedded in socioeconomic, cultural, and political systems that influence the way we understand others and ourselves. Cultural psychotherapy emphasizes the need to include the observed (object), the observer (subject), and the context to adequately describe the psychotherapeutic process. Knowledge is inseparable from our clients, therapeutic relationships, and context. As different types of influences (i.e., individual, relational, contextual) are examined, we are more thorough in our clinical work and consequently we can refine our psychotherapeutic interventions more effectively. This ontological position is applicable not just to the psychotherapeutic process, but to any type of knowledge (e.g., historical, anthropological, etc.).

Cultural thinking can help us move beyond the dichotomous categories fostered by the dominant objective approach that represent the object separated from the subject and context (e.g., nature vs. nurture, black vs. white, male vs. female, mind vs. body, internal vs. external, explicit vs. implicit, material vs. spiritual, individualistic vs. relational). Unfortunately, this type of decontextualized thinking tends to overlook many shades and colors, simplifying our understanding of reality. As means to make knowledge objective (measured similarly by others), many of its particularities are stripped out and only certain prominent features are identified by these categories. For example, in treating diverse clients, many of us could agree on their skin color, immigration status, or place of birth but have a much harder time categorizing their spirituality or understanding of themselves. People's spirituality, sense of self, and sense of other vary from culture to culture, and the categories we use to understand them in one context may not be applicable in another. Cultural thinking aims to widen our range of observations by broadening our categories or developing new ones that capture these cultural complexities and variations. Broader categories allow us to understand our experiences in more complex and diverse manners, enabling us to perceive the many different shades within our lives.

The cultural categories (Bruner, 2002; Kleinman, 1988) we use not only allow us to organize and give meaning to our reality; they also influence the way we interact. Unfortunately, some of these decontextualized (assumed to be universal) cultural binary—or simplistic—categories separate and divide us (e.g., White vs. Black, poor vs. rich, immigrant vs. nonimmigrant, educated vs. noneducated). They make it more difficult to recognize and connect with the "Other" and lead us to emphasize a fragmented, disconnected, and individualistic view of ourselves. The "Others," particularly if they are from a different group that is easily recognizable, are construed as more distant and different, which makes it more difficult to connect or interact. Furthermore, these differences are often construed as deficits or even as threats during extreme crisis.

Cultural Epistemology

Cultural thinking includes a research and epistemological model that attempts to examine the object's qualities as well as the influence of the observers/researchers/therapists and context in which the exchanges between researchers/clinicians and participants/clients take place. These research ideas were explored more fully in Chapter 6. The basic research implication of these epistemological ideas is the importance of using multimethod strategies that include objective, qualitative, contextual, emic, and etic approaches that assess individual, researcher, and contextual influences.

Cultural Ethics

Cultural thinking includes an ethical approach. Each psychotherapeutic intervention is far from being ethically neutral and each clinical decision is based on a set of assumptions of what is good, which in turn promotes a particular moral stance. It is important to be aware and further explore these moral stances. Cultural psychology emphasizes the need to consider "goodness" beyond the individual (i.e., client), the immediate social context (e.g., family), or the therapeutic relationship. In sessions of cultural psychotherapy, the possibility of acting and changing communities can be explored. Often it is not enough to ameliorate clients' symptoms if these are just going to be retriggered by an unjust context. Therefore, it is necessary to foster skills that allow clients—individuals, couples, or groups—to transform injustices (as defined by themselves).

An ethical assumption of this book is that diversity is often useful. One of the main reasons for this affirmation is that as we acknowledge differences, we understand ourselves and others more thoroughly (see Chapter 4). As a result of these enhanced understandings, we are able to question, broaden, clarify, enrich, and even rediscover our views. Diversity can widen our views and possibilities. For example, diversity in the broadest sense extends to the fact that we can select from endless products (e.g., clothes, music, and spices) that come from all over the globe, and similarly, we can expand this diversity of choice to other areas of our lives such as when to marry, whether or not to have children, the gender of our partner, or whether to adhere to traditional or religious values or practices. Nevertheless, the possibility that in some situations diversity is harmful cannot be discarded.

Another important ethical assumption underlying cultural psychotherapy is that each person makes his or her own decision about what is important for him or her. Therapists should not impose their agendas, values, or assumptions. We need to respect people's views even—and particularly—when we do not agree with them. One of our main goals as clinicians is to broaden these views (including our own) as far as clients want or are able to, and as far as it is helpful for them and others. Many of our moral decisions are influenced by the biases underlying our implicit systems or implicit messages, and these need to be clarified. Cultural psychotherapy aims to explore these biases so that we have more information about our possibilities. Although some actions are never acceptable (e.g., violence, murder, child molestation), all possibilities can be discussed and explored within a session.

A Cultural Praxis

Cultural thinking includes a praxis, which is more than a systematic set of psychotherapeutic interventions. The bulk of this book illustrates through multiple clinical examples the psychotherapeutic implications of cultural thinking. Ultimately, this set of psychotherapeutic strategies aims to reduce the conflict between what is categorized as cultural as opposed to clinical. Both good clinical and good cultural work are necessary to achieve an optimal therapeutic outcome. Nevertheless, the applications of cultural thinking go beyond the psychotherapeutic process. I will briefly describe some of its different applications in different fields.

APPLICATIONS OF CULTURAL THINKING

Culture and Law

Cultural assumptions about what is good or bad frequently and inadvertently shape our laws. "Common sense" or "self-evident truths" are highly influenced by our cultural beliefs. Although there are countless illustrations of how cultural beliefs have influenced American law, I focus on a few brief examples in the history of immigration law in the United States. These examples provide an interesting backdrop from which to analyze our country's views on race and ethnicity. For example, in 1882 Congress passed the Chinese Exclusion Act (National Archives and Records Administration, 1989). This law was passed when White European workers felt that Chinese immigrants threatened their jobs. The act suspended the immigration of all Chinese laborers for 10 years and forbade any court to admit Chinese people for citizenship. Congress soon began expanding the list of "undesirable classes," hoping to upgrade the quality of immigrants and limiting the overall number of immigrants of darker skin and/or of non-Protestant faiths. During this time, immigration law reflected the dominant definition of who was desirable and welcomed to the United States—White, Anglo-Saxon, Protestant.

After World War I, Congress enacted the Emergency Quota Act (US Immigration Legislation Online, n.d.), which limited the number of immigrants allowed to enter the United States to 3% of the nationality already residing in the country. More recently, laws have been passed that denied benefits (e.g., health, education, preferential home loans) to undocumented or permanent residents (e.g., holding a green card but not citizens) living in the United States. Such laws began taking form when people of color from developing nations started immigrating to the United States in large numbers.

Another example of the intersection of law and culture is seen in the disproportionate number of ethnic minorities who are incarcerated. For example, in 2010 there were 6.4 times more African American males, and 2.6 times more Hispanic males in state, federal, and local jails than Whites. Furthermore, out of an estimated 1,446,000 prisoners in 2010, ethnic minorities made up 69% of the state and federal population (Guerino, Harrison, & Sabol, 2011). This disparity is alarming and speaks to the influence of our cultural stereotypes and unequal distribution of economic resources. When I think of these statistics, I often remember two 17-year-olds I treated at the same time who were stopped by police on the same weekend. The first, I will call James. James is White, blond, tall, well educated, and from an affluent family. I will call the second adolescent Ron. Ron is African American, Muslim, and from a lower socioeconomic status. James and his friends were driving while using heroin. A White policeman stopped and lectured them about the risks of driving while intoxicated. They were sent home with only a warning. Ron and his friends were not that fortunate. One Latino and one White policeman stopped them. The first pointed a gun at them, while the second searched and found a small amount of marijuana. Ron and his friends were incarcerated and were in court a few days later. Ron missed classes and did poorly on the SAT that week. As a result, his college choices were more restricted. James went on to an Ivy League college.

In these and many other cases, justice does not seem to be color-blind. Being of color or an ethnic minority increases the likelihood of being treated and sentenced more severely by the American justice system (Kansal, 2005). Explicit and implicit messages about racial and ethnic background not only inform our personal decisions and acts but also affect us institutionally. Although much has been done, much more cultural thinking is needed to identify and develop strategies to prevent the perpetuation of injustices.

Educational Work

Many diverse students are not faring well in the American school system. A disproportionate number of African Americans are still diagnosed with mental retardation, while more Latinos are referred to special education classes than their White counterparts (Hursh, 2007; Skiba et al., 2008; Sullivan & Artiles, 2011). Similarly, it is a commonly held belief that girls do not do as well in math or science as boys (Kafir, 2007; Salahu-Din, 2008). However, recent studies suggest similarities in achievement between genders (Hyde, Lindberg, Linn, Ellis, & Williams, 2008; Scafidi & Bui, 2010). Nonetheless, perceptions held hostage by cultural stereotypes may impede girls from reaching their potential in these fields (Leaper, Farkus, Brown, & Spears, 2012). Similarly, negative cultural expectations (e.g., explicit and implicit messages) seem to hinder many ethnic minorities (except some Asian American groups who are benefiting from positive social messages) from excelling in school. Students' cultural differences (including gender) are being construed as deficits, which leads to stigmatization in educational settings. For example, many Latino children are taught by their families to first seek help within the home and only after exhausting family resources are they encouraged to "bother teachers with their questions." Unfortunately, many times teachers believe that this lack of questioning reflects a lack of interest, which often leads them to invest less energy in these children (La Roche & Shriberg, 2003). Pedagogical research needs to keep exploring ways in which cultural differences can be construed as assets that enrich the classroom.

Computer Technology

Recent advances in software technology have dramatically changed the cultural landscape. Most families have several computers at home, and many have computers at work and/or at school. In addition, a growing number of people have cell phones (e.g., smart phones) that function as portable computers.[1] Computers have become an inescapable reality. These days we spend a significant amount of time in front of our computer screens (Lenhart, Purcell, Smith, & Zickuhr, 2010). Computers have changed the way we work and learn as well as the way we socialize. Sites such as Facebook have penetrated the social scene by reorganizing and redefining social practice, including the formation and maintenance of social relations. We easily and instantly connect with people from all around the globe; we not only e-mail, tweet, or text people dozens of times a day, but also hear them or see them through "Skype" and other such services (Lenhart et al., 2010). Furthermore, through computers we virtually connect with others. We are entering an age where relationships that sometimes turn into marriage start online through Internet dating sites. People are increasingly seeking social support through technology. Nevertheless, computers and the Internet are also creating different challenges.

Consider the example of Ho, a 29-year-old, married, employed Chinese software engineer who first came to therapy because of marital problems. Ho spent many of his nights "Skyping" with Maya, his "dear" friend from India. When he spoke of Maya, he did it so passionately that his wife believed he was having an affair with her. In fact, on one occasion, she caught him "Skyping" almost naked with Maya. Nevertheless, he had never met Maya. Was Ho's wife right in considering his relationship with Maya an affair? I have also heard via therapy sessions with various clients how virtual friendships can develop where people consider each other "best friends" and become a significant source of social support and/or disappointment. Clearly, the Internet is transforming our understandings of relationships in the social world.

In addition, this enhanced connectivity has blurred national frontiers and time. Not only have space and time become less restrictive, but the boundaries between what is real and fantasy have also diminished. People can create their own identities, avatars, and selves in different virtual worlds. This is especially relevant for adolescents, who are exploring their identity. Profile creation allows for self-experimentation, an activity facilitating identity exploration (Mori, 2009). People sink themselves into these worlds where they can create their own lives. Through these portals, they become millionaires, playboys/playgirls, or social activists. These transformations pose significant conceptual challenges to traditional understandings of culture, context, identity, and reality. Geertz (1973) defined culture as a *"historically transmitted pattern of meanings embodied in symbol"* (see Chapter 4 for a discussion of this term). Nevertheless, it seems that we can no longer talk about historically transmitted patterns of meanings, since many of these have very little or no history. Nor can we talk about embodied symbols as many of these are now enveloped within technological hardware and/or software. The idea that our cultural identity stems mostly from our country, history, or race is challenged as we are bombarded in the here and now by virtual information that goes beyond our cultural, national, or even continental borders. Furthermore, these influences are very quick. We can almost immediately retrieve or "Google" any type of information and know (and even see, through YouTube.com) what has happened thousands of miles away. As time and space fade on the Internet, virtual worlds become a cultural context unto themselves that has an increasingly powerful influence in our lives.

Unfortunately, these technological transformations have often been neglected in our conceptualizations of culture and have only recently started to influence the development of virtual psychotherapeutic strategies. For example, current digital learning technologies and wireless devices have enormous potential to increase mental health access. These technologies create opportunities for client support and consumer education that overcome many barriers (e.g., lack of time, distance) in access to care. This may be particularly important to reduce health disparities in a number of areas, including nutrition, education, weight management, chronic disease management, and mental health (e.g., anxiety, PTSD) (Cousineau et al., 2010; Franko et al., 2008). It is likely that many psychotherapy clients (and therapists) use these technologies through the use of mobile phones, PDAs, and laptops. Such communication tools and "apps" are now a common part of daily life and may increasingly percolate into therapeutic discourse (Cousineau et al., 2010; Franko et al., 2008). It may be that as psychotherapy includes and benefits from these advances, it will become more consistent with its clients' cultural characteristics.

The power of these technologies is also sparking political empowerment in many communities, countries, and even regions. For example, the Arab Spring of 2011, and the fall of several long-term dictatorships (e.g., Egypt, Libya) in the Arab world are said to have started on the Internet. The chance to connect and change environments through technology needs to be underscored and deserves significantly more study than it has thus far received. This paucity of psychological research and development is regrettable because technological changes pose immense possibilities that could enrich our conceptualizations, assessments, and treatment interventions across many areas of study (e.g., political, economic, etc.).[2]

Nevertheless, the Internet is also creating new problems. Many crimes are now perpetrated through the Internet (e.g., identity theft). Cyber bullying, for example, is becoming more prevalent. In many industrialized countries such as Japan, the United States, and many European countries, a new psychological disorder known as "Internet addiction" is spreading rapidly. As the Internet now dominates the way adolescents communicate and socialize, it introduces an addictive potential for a significant portion of youth. At its extreme, persistent Internet use can lead to isolation and neglect of social, school, or recreational activities (Kormas, Critselis, Janikian, Kafetzis, & Tsitsika, 2011; Norasakkunkit & Uchida, 2011; Tsitsika et al., 2011). As the cultural context changes, new psychological disorders emerge (Hacking, 2002).

Economic Work

Global markets are increasingly interconnected, and the world has become a global community in which commodities transfer from one country to another. Coffee is imported from Africa and Brazil, while computers are designed in India and sold in the United States and Europe. What happens in one market has significant effects in others. The influences of these interconnections need to be understood in more detail along with the many challenges that emerge because of globalization. For example, the volatility and credibility of markets can be shaped by cultural biases, and it is not rare for financial decisions to be influenced by cultural assumptions that end up reducing returns. As Nobel Laureate Daniel Kahneman (2011) notes, many of our economic decisions are irrational because they are solely based on "System 1" judgments that are automatic, quick, and unconscious. If they go unchecked by System 2, which is rational, slow, and conscious, they often lead to catastrophic consequences. System 1 is defined very similarly to how implicit systems are defined in this book (see the introduction), while System 2 resembles explicit systems. Drew Westen (2007), in his eloquent book *The Political Brain,* describes very similar processes in the way we elect our leaders. Explicit and implicit systems have an influence that extends beyond the socioemotional to the political and economic realms of our lives.

Another cultural challenge that many countries face is seeking ways to benefit from open markets while maintaining their own cultures. Markets require and foster a homogenizing force that employs a common language and currency, so that transactions can run smoothly. This poses a challenge for those in different countries who want to preserve their cultural identities (e.g., religion, traditional lifestyles). Cultural thinking may help us further elucidate such challenges posed by globalization.

Peace Work

As the world becomes more interconnected and global, we live with a growing number of people of different backgrounds, who endorse different values and assumptions. The risk of misunderstandings and conflicts grows as people of different cultures increasingly interact. Although many cultural differences are subtle, some can divide us. Furthermore, during conflict ridden periods some cultural differences are emphasized and construed as insurmountable, irreconcilable threats that endanger a society's identity or way of life, rather than opportunities for growth. A clear example is how Nazi Germany's propaganda portrayed Jews as a threat to their society and economic development. A dehumanizing construction of Jews as "Others" was used to justify their segregation and extermination.

In extreme cases cultural constructions exacerbate racial tension and ethnic conflict, leading to war and even genocide. The genocide and atrocities committed in Bosnia, Kosovo, Rwanda, Burundi, and more recently in Sudan's Darfur region are extreme examples of how polarized identities are constructed and manipulated to antagonize and destroy. Although it is clear that economic and political forces play a pivotal role in influencing these tragedies, they are also influenced by the cultural constructions of the "Other" as evil and dangerous (Jowitt, 2001). During these conflicts, individuals experience explicit and implicit messages (e.g., social stereotypes) rather than themselves or people. Often, a collective mentality takes over in which the "Others" are construed as the enemies rather than as neighbors, friends, or even people. Identities are barricaded against each other and flexibility, individuality, and complexity are discouraged (Jowitt, 2001). In these cases, people surrender their humanity and compassion to an abstract and rigid ideology that does not allow them to engage with the "Other."

It is crucial that we continue to explore these psychological and social processes. Once we are able to recognize that there are structural, cultural, psychological, political, and economic conditions that bring about conflict, we might be able to develop an effective "world watch" to warn us of situations that are degenerating into serious conflict (Chirot, 2001). We may be able to intervene before it is too late. The development of strategies that allow us to create cultural dialogue is essential, not only for individual and community growth or international and economic development but very likely for the very survival of humanity. Furthermore, a broader understanding of these processes will allow us to grapple with the legacies of mass violence (Kirmayer, Lemelson, & Barad, 2007) and develop more effective interventions for recovery and reconciliation (Hinton & O'Neill, 2009).

Much research has been conducted, and theories or interventions have been posited in the areas of law, education, computer technology, economics, peace work, and other areas. However, much needs to be done to integrate cultural thinking and cultural psychotherapy into these arenas. As we do, we not only start elucidating these processes further; we may also start understanding our sociocultural context more clearly.

Conclusion

Cultural thinking is a reflection of a particular time and context and as such it is evolving just as our ideas, feelings, and lives are changing. The cultural context exerts a powerful influence in shaping our understandings and lives. Our socioeconomic context is endlessly conveying explicit and implicit messages about what is good, wrong, or expected. If we are not aware of these powerful contextual influences, they will end up narrowing our lives, views, and possibilities. We will follow what culture has prescribed for us rather than choosing what we want or decide is best for us. Cultural thinking and cultural psychotherapy aim to help us become more aware of cultural prescriptions and to question them. Some examples of questions that often arise in cultural psychotherapy include the following: Do I really need to earn as much money as I can? Is marriage what I really want? Why can't I spend more time with my children or friends? Why do I have to write this book? Do I have to follow these gender role assumptions? Why are men not supposed to cry? Why can't I aim to live a life in harmony in nature? Do I have to be heterosexual? Why can't I date someone from a different race or religion? Why do I have to endorse individualistic values? Why can't I live in accordance with the word of God? The aim of this questioning is to increase awareness of how culture influences and shapes us and then for each of us to make decisions based on this enhanced understanding.

Cultural thinking and cultural psychotherapy underscore the bidirectional influence of the context and person/group. Clearly, culture influences who we are but we too—to some degree—influence our context. We are not a passive result of sociopolitical and economic forces. We too can be agents of our own destiny. The promise of change and improvement are highlighted throughout all the chapters of this book. Nevertheless, the risks should not be overlooked. If we do not take all of these processes (e.g., individual, relational, contextual) into account, we can miss opportunities to enrich our lives and context. Cultural thinking reminds us that we are not isolated, fragmented individuals. Instead, we live in a particular community with a history and we can assume responsibilities toward our contexts (e.g., neighborhoods, schools, country, and world). We can impact our context as we are changed by situations and social systems. Cultural psychotherapy and cultural thinking in general are a systematic effort to influence our understandings, relationships, and contexts in ways that are consistent with our goals and life.

Notes

1. In this chapter, I speak of cell phones, computers, and other advanced communicational devices as computers, rather than specifying each.

2. In the introduction, I proposed some ideas on how to use the Internet, Google Earth, and other applications within the psychotherapeutic process; nevertheless, these ideas are works in progress and will be developed more fully in the future. In addition, there is a fast-growing literature that uses virtual images for systematic desensitization and biofeedback to treat posttraumatic stress disorder, panic disorder, and many other disorders. For a review, see Clough and Casey (2011).

References

Bruner, J. (2002). *Making stories: Law, literature, life.* Cambridge, MA: Harvard University Press.

Chirot, D. (2001). Introduction. In D. Chirot & M. Seligman (Eds.), *Ethnopolitical warfare: Causes, consequences, and possible solutions.* Washington, DC: American Psychological Association.

Clough, B. A., & Casey, L. M. (2011). Technological adjuncts to enhance current psychotherapy practices: A review. *Clinical Psychology Review, 31*(3), 279–292.

Cousineau, T. M., Franko, D. L., Trant, M., Rancourt, D., Ainscough, J., Chaudhuri, A., & Brevard, J. (2010). Teaching adolescents about changing bodies: Randomized controlled trial of an Internet puberty education and body dissatisfaction prevention program. *Body Image, 7*(4), 296–300.

Franko, D. L., Cousineau, T. M., Trant, M., Green, T. C., Rancourt, D., Thompson, D., et al. (2008). Motivation, self-efficacy, physical activity, and nutrition in college students: Randomized controlled trial of an Internet-based education program. *Preventive Medicine, 47*(4), 369–377.

Geertz, C. (1973). *Interpretation of cultures.* New York: Basic Books.

Guerino, P., Harrison, P. M., & Sabol, W. J. (2011). *Prisoners in 2010* (NCJ236096; rev. 02/09/12). Washington, DC: U.S. Department of Justice, Office of Justice Statistics.

Hacking, I. (2002). *Historical ontology.* Cambridge, MA: Harvard University Press.

Hinton, A. L., & O'Neill, K. L. (2009). *Genocide: Truth, memory, and representation.* Durham, NC: Duke University Press.

Hursh, D. (2007). Exacerbating inequality: The failed promise of the No Child Left Behind Act. *Race, Ethnicity and Education, 10*(3), 295–308.

Hyde, J. S., Lindberg, S. M., Linn, M. C., Ellis, A. B., & Williams, C. C. (2008, July 25). Gender similarities characterize math performance. *Science, 321*(5888), 494–495.

Jowitt, K. (2001). Ethnicity: Nice, nasty, and nihilistic. In D. Chirot & M. Seligman (Eds.), *Ethnopolitical warfare: Causes, consequences, and possible solutions.* Washington, DC: American Psychological Association.

Kafir, K. (2007). *Taking the boy crisis in education seriously: How school choice can boost achievement among boys and girls.* Washington, DC: Independent Women's Forum.

Kahneman, D. (2011). *Thinking, fast and slow.* New York: Farrar, Straus and Giroux.

Kansal, T. (2005). *Racial disparity in sentencing: A review of the literature.* Washington, DC: The Sentencing Project.

Kirmayer, L. J., Lemelson, R., & Barad, M. (Eds.). (2007). *Understanding trauma: Integrating biological, clinical, and cultural perspectives.* New York: Cambridge University Press.

Kleinman, A. (1988). *The illness narratives: Suffering, healing, and the human condition.* New York: Basic Books.

Kormas, G., Critselis, E., Janikian, M., Kafetzis, D., & Tsitsika, A. (2011). Risk factors and psychosocial characteristics of problematic and potential problematic Internet use among adolescents: A cross-sectional study. *BMC Public Health, 11,* 595.

La Roche, M. (2005). The psychotherapeutic process and the cultural context: Towards a cultural psychotherapy. *Journal of Behavioral Integration, 15,* 169–175.

La Roche, M., & Shriberg, D. (2003). High stakes exams and Latino students: Toward a culturally sensitive education for Latino children in the United States. *Journal of Educational & Psychological Consultation, 15*(2), 205–223.

Leaper, C., Farkus, T., Brown, C. S. & Spears, C. (2012). Adolescent girls' experiences and gender-related beliefs in relation to their motivation in math/science and English. *Journal of Youth and Adolescence, 41*(3), 268–282.

Lenhart, A., Purcell, K., Smith, A., & Zickuhr, K. (2010). *Social media and young adults.* Retrieved April 17, 2012, from PewInternet.org/Reports/2010/Social-Media-and-Young-Adults.aspx.

Mori, M. (2009). Teens and social networking services: An overview. In C. Romm-Livermore & K. Setzekorn (Eds.), *Social networking communities and e-dating services: Concepts and implications* (pp. 160–187). Hershey, PA: Information Science Reference/IGI Global.

National Archives and Records Administration. (1989). *Teaching with documents: Using primary sources from the National Archives.* Washington, DC: Author. Retrieved April 26, 2012, from http://www.ourdocuments.gov/doc.php?flash = true&doc = 47.

Norasakkunkit, V., & Uchida, Y. (2011). Psychological consequences of postindustrial anomie on self and motivation among Japanese youth. *Journal of Social Issues, 67*(4), 774–786.

Salahu-Din, D. (2008). *The nation's report card: Writing 2007.* Washington, DC: U.S. Department of Education.

Scafidi, T., & Bui, K. (2010). Gender similarities in math performance from middle school through high school. *Journal of Instructional Psychology, 37,* 252–255.

Skiba, R. J., Simmons, A. B., Ritter, S., Gibb, A. C., Rausch, M. K., Cuadrado, J., & Chung, C.-G. (2008). Achieving equity in special education: History, status, and current challenges. *Exceptional Children, 74,* 264–288.

Sullivan, L., & Artiles, A. (2011). Theorizing racial inequity in special education: Applying structural inequity theory to disproportionality. *Urban Education, 46,* 1526–1552.

Tsitsika, A., Critselis, E., Louizou, A., Janikian, M., Freskou, A., Marangou, E., et al. (2011). Determinants of Internet addiction among adolescents: A case-control study. *The Scientific World Journal, 19*(11), 866–874.

US Immigration Legislation Online. (n.d.). *1921 emergency quota law.* Retrieved April 26, 2012, from http://library.uwb.edu/guides/usimmigration/1921_emergency_quota_law.html.

Westen, D. (2007). *The political brain: The role of emotion in deciding the fate of the nation.* New York: Public Affair Books.

About the Author

Martin J. La Roche, PhD, is a Latino American psychologist who received his PhD in clinical psychology from the University of Massachusetts Boston. For the last 16 years, he has been Director of Psychology Training at the Martha Eliot Health Center (the second-oldest health center in the country), where he treats members of a culturally diverse, inner-city community and trains doctoral-level psychology students. In addition, Dr. La Roche is an Assistant Professor in Psychology at the Harvard Medical School Children's Hospital Boston. He has authored numerous articles and chapters on specific ways to provide ethnic minorities with culturally competent psychotherapeutic services and has been the principal investigator on research projects designed to refine these strategies. Dr. La Roche has received several research/academic awards, such as the Bollinger Award at UMass Boston, and several from the Harvard Medical School, such as the Milton Fund Research Award, the Pilot Research Award, and the Bridge Award. Dr. La Roche has also been a private practitioner in the Cambridge, Massachusetts, area for the last 15 years. Finally, Dr. La Roche served for 7 years as the Co-chair of the Committee on Ethnic Minority Affairs at the Massachusetts Psychological Association and was a board member, where he also advocated for the well-being of diverse groups.

Index

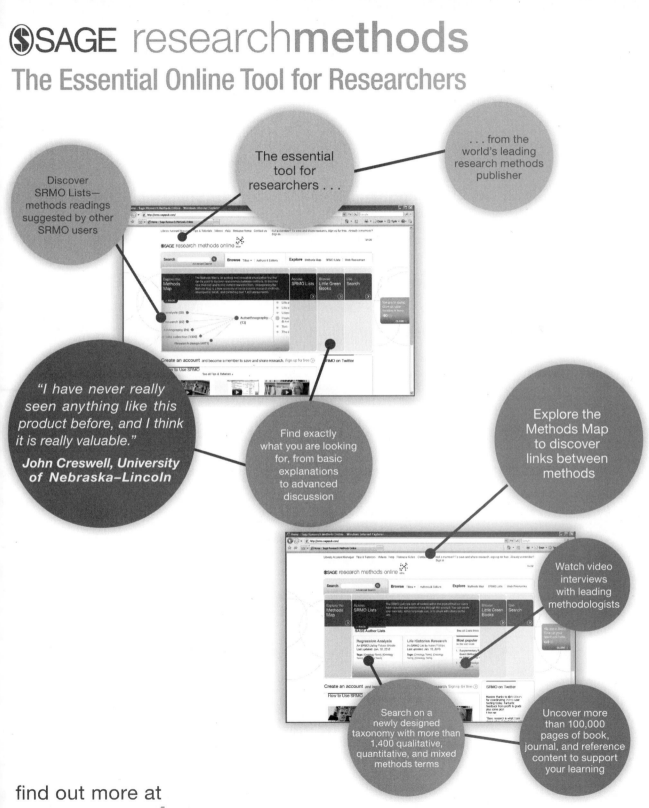